1995

AN ETHIC
OF CITIZENSHIP
FOR PUBLIC
ADMINISTRATION

TERRY L. COOPER
University of Southern California

PRENTICE HALL, Englewood Cliffs, New Jersey 07632

Library of Congress Cataloging-in-Publication Data

Cooper, Terry L.,
    An ethic of citizenship for public administration / Terry L.
Cooper.
      p.   cm.
    ISBN 0-13-290248-6
    1. Civil service ethics--United States. 2. Government executives-
-Professional ethics--United States. 3. Citizenship--United States.
4. Political participation--United States.   I. Title.
JK468.E7C65 1991
172'.1'0973--dc20
                                                        90-7224
                                                           CIP

Editorial/production supervision
  and interior design: *Mary Kathryn Leclercq*
Cover design: *Ben Santora*
Manufacturing buyer: *Maryanne Gloriande*
Prepress buyer: *Debbie Kesar*

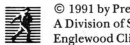 © 1991 by Prentice-Hall, Inc.
A Division of Simon & Schuster
Englewood Cliffs, New Jersey 07632

Printed in the United States of America
10 9 8 7 6 5 4 3 2 1

ISBN   0-13-290248-6

Prentice-Hall International (UK) Limited, *London*
Prentice-Hall of Australia Pty. Limited, *Sydney*
Prentice-Hall Canada Inc., *Toronto*
Prentice-Hall Hispanoamericana, S.A., *Mexico*
Prentice-Hall of India Private Limited, *New Delhi*
Prentice-Hall of Japan, Inc., *Tokyo*
Simon & Schuster Asia Pte. Ltd., *Singapore*
Editora Prentice-Hall do Brasil, Ltda., *Rio de Janeiro.*

This book is dedicated to Saul D. Alinsky, who helped me begin a long quest for the meaning of active citizenship in the United States by pointing me to the American revolutionary tradition in my early adult years; to those countless citizens in the East Harlem area of New York and the Pico-Union community of Los Angeles who advanced my citizenship education during my eight years as a community organizer; and to the many public administrators with whom I have worked who are struggling to understand how best to make their contribution to democracy in America.

CONTENTS

PREFACE

> The question for us is, how shall our series of governments within governments be so administered that it shall always be to the interest of the public officer to serve, not his superior alone, but the community also, with the best efforts of his talents and the soberest service of his conscience?[1]

This seldom quoted question from the closing paragraphs of Wilson's famous essay, penned in 1887, might well be adopted as an agenda for public administration ethics during the coming decades. These words suggest the need for organizational structures, training strategies, personnel policies, and management techniques that will direct and motivate public administrators toward serving the interests of a democratic political community as well as those of their employing organizations.

However, Wilson's questions should also direct our thinking to a more fundamental level. Resolution of the problems posed here requires us first to reflect upon the ethical identity of the public administrator. Who is this person called *public administrator*? What is his or her source of legitimacy? Of obligation? What are the internal goods and virtues of the practice of public administration?

---

[1]Woodrow Wilson, "The study of administration," *Political Science Quarterly*, 2 (1887), 197-222. See p. 221 for this quotation.

This book will attempt to respond to these questions by developing an argument for the citizenship role as an appropriate normative foundation for the public administrative role in modern American society. Understanding the public administrative role means thinking of ourselves not only as free-floating individuals, employees of some public organization, or as participants in various interest groups, but also as members of a political order, as *citizens* in a democratic society. That is the public role which needs to be dusted off, renovated, cultivated, and adopted as a *normative foundation* for the practice of public administration: the role of the administrator as citizen. It is the citizenship role which links us, along with our individual private lives and professional interests, to the polity in which we find ourselves.

Citizenship presents us with duties and obligations beyond our families, associations, and places of employment which cannot be neglected if these more intimate and voluntary relationships are finally to be possible. Saul Alinsky insisted that

> People cannot be free unless they are willing to sacrifice some of their interests to guarantee the freedom of others. The price of democracy is the ongoing pursuit of the common good by *all* of the people. One hundred and thirty-five years ago Tocqueville gravely warned that unless individual citizens were regularly involved in the action of governing themselves, self-government would pass from the scene. Citizen participation is the animating spirit and force in a society predicated on voluntarism.[2]

This book presents an argument along these lines. I do not suggest here that citizens must totally abandon self-interest, but that they must understand the concept of self-interest in ways that include the interests of others. I argue that the public administrator's most fundamental obligation is to encourage citizens in their active pursuit of the common good in this way.

The focus of my efforts in the pages to follow is on the problematic nature of citizenship and its relationship to public administration in one particular democratic society—that of the United States. I have attempted to discern and analyze the roots of citizenship in the American context from both the legal and ethical perspectives, and then draw out the implications of that analysis for administrative ethics. My intent has been to develop these findings into a role prescription for public administrators which one might call the *citizen-administrator*.

This book is not a *how to* handbook for administrative decision making, nor is it an elaborate code of administrative conduct with specific *do's and don'ts*. Rather, it attempts to provide what I believe public administrative ethics needs most at this point in its evolution—a broad fundamental perspective which establishes a legitimate place in the American polity for the

---

[2]Saul D. Alinsky, *Rules for Radicals: A Pragmatic Primer for Realistic Radicals* (New York: Vintage Books, 1971), p. xxv.

public administrator, upon which specific codes and norms of conduct may be coherently developed by a community of practitioners, scholars, and citizens. In this sense it reflects an attempt to develop the democratic *ethos* of public administration within which the cultivation of ethical decision making skills and the preparation of professional codes of ethics may be addressed.[3]

ACKNOWLEDGMENTS

Chapters one, three, five, and six contain materials previously published in scholarly journals, and collections of essays. I deeply appreciate the willingness of these journals and publishers to grant me permission to use the following selections in this book:

> "Public Administration in an Age of Scarcity: A Normative Essay on Ethics for Public Administrators," in *Politics and Administration: Woodrow Wilson and Public Administration,* eds. Jack Rabin and James Bowman (New York: Marcel Dekker, 1984) 297–314. Used with permission by Marcel Dekker, Inc.
>
> "Citizen Participation," in *Organization Theory and Management,* ed. Thomas D. Lynch (New York: Marcel Dekker, 1983) 13–45. Used with permission by Marcel Dekker, Inc.
>
> "Citizenship and Professionalism in Public Administration," *Public Administration Review,* 44 (march 1984) 143–149. Used by permission from *Public Administration Review* © 1984 by The American Society for Public Administration, 1120 G Street, N.W., Suite 500, Washington, D.C. All rights reserved.
>
> "Hierarchy, Virtue and the Practice of Public Administration," *Public Administration Review,* 47 (July/August 1987) 320–328. Used by permission from *Public Administration Review,* © 1987 by The American Society for Public Administration, 1120 G Street, N.W., Suite 500, Washington, D.C. All rights reserved.
>
> "The Public Private Continuum: Interdependence in a Democratic Society," *Public Budgeting and Finance,* 5 (Autumn 1985) 99–122. Used by permission from *Public Budgeting and Finance.*

My initial insights into the relationship between citizenship and public administration were stimulated by public administrators who participated in workshops on administrative ethics which I conducted under the auspices of the Environmental Management Institute of the School of Public Administration at the University of Southern California during the late 1970s. Some described their most troubling ethical dilemmas as conflicts between their obligations as citizens and their obligations as public administrators. This unique role tension between being citizens and, simultaneously, em-

---

[3]Mark Lilla rightly criticized the focus of most treatments of administrative ethics in the late 1970s and early 1980s as too narrowly emphasizing ethical decision making skills in relation to ethical dilemmas while neglecting the more basic normative framework growing out of the democratic ethos. See Mark T. Lilla, "Ethos, 'Ethics,' and Public Service," *The Public Interest,* 63 (Spring 1981), 3–17.

ployees of the citizenry emerged in my thinking as a significant problem to be addressed.

The National Association of Schools of Public Affairs and Administration offered me an opportunity to begin working out the implications of this problematic *role identity* by inviting me to address their San Antonio, Texas, 1980 conference on the normative bases for teaching public administrative ethics. Comments and criticisms following my presentation helped me to discern at an early stage the most serious problems to be addressed in developing a theoretical treatment of citizenship and public administration.

My fellow faculty members and students at USC, colleagues around the nation, and the many practitioners of public administration to whom I have exposed my partially formed ideas have helped me recognize the weaknesses in my conceptualization and the gaps in my logic, and have generously offered their wisdom and knowledge.

During the course of working out the ideas in this book my two deans at the USC School of Public Administration, Robert Biller and Ross Clayton, have both offered their support and encouragement through years when tangible products were limited.

The Huntington Library in San Marino, California has provided me with a delightful place to work, a marvelously rich collection of resources, and the kind assistance of its readers' services staff for five years during work on the manuscript.

The Charles F. Kettering Foundation offered me a contract to do bibliographical research on citizenship which advanced my work significantly at a crucial stage in its development.

I would like to thank H. George Frederickson, University of Kansas and Dalmas H. Nelson, University of Utah for reviewing the manuscript and making helpful suggestions.

And throughout it all my wife, Megan, and my daughter, Chelsea, have tolerated my cantankerousness and loved me anyway.

As one must always honestly say at the end of such expressions of appreciation, all these contributions to my work are reflected in whatever is found in this book to be of value to the administration of the public's business; the deficiencies are my own.

Terry L. Cooper

1
INTRODUCTION: CITIZENSHIP AS A SOURCE OF OBLIGATION

THE PROBLEMATIC NATURE OF CITIZENSHIP IN THE UNITED STATES

Any undertaking to establish citizenship as a source of ethical norms for public administration should acknowledge forthrightly that citizenship has not been a powerful concept for conveying public obligation in the United States. Explicitly and legally, citizenship has been related more to rights than responsibilities. The United States Constitution for example, guarantees certain civil rights and liberties, but nowhere does it enumerate the obligations of citizenship. Citizens have the *right* to vote, but the duty to do so is not mentioned. The *freedom* to assemble is guaranteed, but no responsibility to engage in public discussion is stated. A citizen's property is *protected* by "due process of law" and "just compensation," but nothing is said about one's *obligations* to use that property in a manner which is considerate of other members of the citizenry. In fact, jury duty appears to be the only legal obligation peculiar to citizenship; all other obligations under the law, including general obedience to the laws of the land, military service, and taxpaying are imposed on legal residents of the United States as well as citizens.

Furthermore, citizenship does not require an oath to uphold the Constitution except in certain special circumstances such as naturalization, election to public office, and induction into the armed services. Those of us who

1

were born into the citizenry are seldom confronted in any direct and power-ful way with what we ought to do in our citizenship role. The perfunctory reminders to "do our civic duty" on election day are about the extent of it.

Also, citizenship as a public role has been attenuated by the essentially negative view of democratic government which characterized the authors of the Constitution, as well as by the representative republican form of govern-ment we have adopted. Citizens, from these prospectives, are those who elect others to engage in the business of governing in the public interest, and who otherwise are assured of protection from undue interference in their lives by either the state, or their fellow citizens.

Wilson, one of the pioneers of modern American public administra-tion, stood squarely in this tradition. Deeply concerned for social order and efficient administration in the face of corrupt municipal machines, Wilson was inclined to buffer the governing process from popular interests and emotions through the election of representative political actors.[1] He did not want the people to be "meddlesome" by becoming directly involved in government.[2] And of course, similar preferences for a limited role of the citizenry and a reliance upon representation have been articulated at length by scholars such as Schumpeter, Berelson, and Lipset, to name only a few leading examples.[3]

The citizenship role under these conditions easily becomes a largely passive and intermittent one which is secondary to other roles involving the active and continuous pursuit of private interests. *Interest group theory*, of the kind articulated by Bentley and Truman, provided a convenient rationale for this more intense commitment to organizational roles, which express one's individual preferences and demands. Why worry about the larger general welfare if one can believe that the interaction of organized private interests will lead to the best approximation of the interests of all? Pushed to an extreme, the avaricious quest for self-interest will be transformed into democratic government by the "invisible hand" of the political market. Under the sway of this kind of thinking, citizenship tends to be reduced to the ceremonial and symbolic. The ritualistic visit to the voting booth, like the annual attendance at church or synagogue, becomes a way of maintaining a semblance of a role, but without much of its substance.

Another dimension of the problem with citizenship that must be faced squarely was identified by Michael Walzer. He expressed doubt concerning the moral priority of citizenship. Walzer argued that the "state has simply outgrown the human reach and understanding of its citizens." He continued:

> It is not necessarily monstrous, divided, or subjugated, but its citizens are alienated and powerless. They experience a kind of moral uneasiness; their citizenship is a source of anxiety as well as of security and pride—[4]

It is this problem of citizenship in a large scale, increasingly complex nation state which John Dewey analyzed in 1927.[5] With the rise of modern, industrial, technological, urban society, the interdependencies that emerge on a national scale are beyond the comprehension of most citizens. We know that great forces are impacting our lives, both positively and negatively, but we are unable to discern what they are, where they originate and who controls them. We see the public interest threatened; we sense the general welfare being eroded; but we feel impotent to act. There is some irrepressible, but amorphous feeling of responsibility to intervene in the flow of events; however, the knowledge of where, when or how eludes us.

Thus passivity overtakes us, and according to Walzer, "if the citizen is a passive figure, there is no political community."[6] However, as he rightly asserts, there *is* a political community; *some* citizens are actively engaged in influencing public policy. It is just that *most* citizens live like aliens within it, and finding themselves alienated from the political process, they easily take refuge in pluralism. Citizenship is just one minor role among many other roles for the pluralists. The inability to make citizenship a significant one leads to a fragmented commitment to a number of others. By turning to our private interests, we feel less frustrated with the failure of our public role.

Lawrence Scaff summarized the situation pointedly when he suggested that "The central actor and strongest constituent of democratic politics, the citizen, appears to have been displaced by the more compelling realities of mass society, pluralist competition and bureaucratic elites."[7] Thus, the reconstruction and amplification of the citizenship role is a challenging task to undertake in the face of such forces. However, it is an important one to engage because it is essential to the rediscovery and maintenance of popular government in the United States.

PROMISING DEVELOPMENTS

Although the picture of the citizenship role which emerges here is bleak indeed, I am assuming that the gap between the world as it is and the world as we would like it to be is fraught with opportunity for change. Scholarly interest in the restoration of citizenship and its relationship to the practice of public administration has suggested that change may, indeed, be in the wind. When I first addressed the peculiar problem of the dual roles of the public administrator as both citizen and employee of the citizenry in *The Responsible Administrator*[8] I used the term "citizen administrator" to suggest the normative implications of that unique, complex role. My treatment of the subject was cursory since my focus was a descriptive rather than normative treatment of administrative ethics. At that time citizenship was not on the scholarly agenda of the field; it was not being discussed either in professional conferences or in publications on administrative ethics.

However, an invitation by The National Association of Schools of Public Affairs and Administration (NASPAA) to do a presentation on normative foundations for administrative ethics in the 1980s provided me with an opportunity to explore the topic further.[9] Although there was reluctance among some of those present to see much promise in citizenship as a normative basis for public administration ethics, a number of others seemed intrigued with the idea.

In 1982, George Frederickson published an article entitled "The Recovery of Civism in Public Administration" in which he argued for the reintegration of civic values into the field and explored the implications of such a move for organization theory.[10] Then in 1983 Frederickson organized the first conference to deal primarily with citizenship and public administration. At that three day conclave of scholars and practitioners, citizenship received extensive treatment in relationship to almost every aspect of public administration including democratic theory, ethics, public service delivery, personnel administration, and microcomputer usage.

The most significant initial consequence of the conference was the realization among those present that they were not alone in seeing citizenship as a subject needing urgent development in relationship to a wide array of administrative functions, problems, and issues. However, the longer term outcome was that George Frederickson and Ralph Chandler edited the conference papers for a special issue of *Public Administration Review* with Chandler adding some useful integrative conceptual material of his own.[11] This special issue provided the first comprehensive treatment of citizenship and public administration in print.

As a result of these occurrences, changes have been obvious; citizenship has since been given serious scholarly attention. Numerous journal articles, conference papers, and doctoral dissertations have dealt with citizenship and public administration, and citizenship has been recognized as a legitimate topic for research and education, although it is still considered to need theoretical development and translation into training strategies.[12] There is enough work to occupy the best efforts of a generation of scholars, practitioners, and citizens. However, even our best efforts need to proceed on the basis of clearly understood assumptions. In a political community with the scale and complexity of the United States, citizenship will never have the intensity and immediacy of the Athenian forum or the New England town meeting. However, the assumptions which undergird this book are:

1. Citizenship has the potential to play a more powerful role in orienting American society toward the common good than is currently the case.
2. The maximization of that potential is essential for the cultivation and maintenance of a democratic political community with its core values of political participation, political equality and justice. Public policies and governmental practices must then be consistent with those values.
3. The democratic legitimacy of public administration grows out of the fiduciary nature of the public administrative role. The public administrator is most fundamentally a citizen who acts on behalf of the citizenry in carrying out certain public functions. Therefore, the technical expertise of the administra-

tor, important as it may be, must be subordinated to the obligations of fiduciary citizenship.

The reader should reflect upon the validity and viability of these assumptions regularly throughout the book. The chapters to follow are an exposition of the meaning and congruence of these assumptions, which are steeped in the American political tradition.

DEFINITIONS OF CITIZENSHIP

Since the terms *citizen* and *citizenship* are employed in a variety of ways with a range of meanings, from precise and limited, to vague or broad, it is essential to establish some definitional boundaries. We might begin with a very broad definition of citizenship and citizen such as the following:

> *Citizenship* is the status and role which defines the authority and obligations of individual members of a community. This status and role may be *formally* codified in terms of qualifications, rights and obligations by constitutions, charters and laws, or *informally* determined by values, tradition and consensus. A citizen is one who qualifies for the status of citizen as prescribed formally, or informally, by a particular community, and is encumbered by laws and norms with the obligations assigned to this role by that community.

This definition is so broad in scope that it requires more detailed distinctions within its boundaries if it is to be useful for our purposes. Richard Flathman and T. J. Lowi provide two dimensions of citizenship which establish more specific definitional reference points. Each of these dimensions can be viewed in terms of its polar extremes, and/or in terms of continua between those poles.

The first of these dimensions has to do with the distribution of authority. Flathman deals with this in terms of *high* and *low* views of citizenship.[13] High definitions of citizenship are those which assume wide distribution of authority and describe citizens as peers who share equally in the exercise of authority. Low citizenship assumes a hierarchical distribution of authority, with only a limited claim provided for the individual citizen. Flathman associates the high view with Aristotle and Rousseau, together with current authors such as Walzer, Ahrendt, Thompson, and Barber who argue from a similar perspective. The low view is identified with Hobbes and those such as Michael Oakeshott who currently share his basic position on authority. Flathman also associates the twentieth century *democratic elitists* with this perspective.[14]

Lowi deals with the extent to which the citizenship role is defined by law, on the one hand, or by less formal influences such as values, norms, traditions, culture, and religion on the other.[15] The terms which he uses to identify the poles of this dimension are *legal citizenship* and *ethical citizenship*. Legal citizenship is prescribed and defined in terms of qualifications, rights, and obligations by constitutions and statutes. It is related to particular governmental jurisdictions. Citizenship in this sense is a purely political status or role.

Ethical citizenship involves a much broader definition of the role which includes the social and economic aspects of life, as well as the political.[16] Citizenship, from this perspective, has to do with membership in a community. These communities include, but are not limited to, political communities. Ethical citizenship is a role in neighborhoods and voluntary associations, as well as governmental jurisdictions such as cities and nations. The qualifications, rights, and obligations of citizenship understood in this way, are defined and prescribed by the values, norms, traditions, and culture of any given community, or by consensus among members of the community in specific instances.

Table One depicts the results of relating the four poles of the two dimensions of citizenship to each other. Four types of citizenship can then be identified: *high legal, low legal, high ethical*, and *low ethical*. This simple typology provides us with a useful conceptual chart for clarifying how citizenship is used by various authors and what is implied by their particular usage. Flathman, for example, deals primarily with the legal dimension of citizenship. His concern is with the problems of adopting either a high legal or a low legal view of citizenship. He leans toward the high perspective with a shared exercise of political authority and insists that the citizenship role be narrowly confined to the political realm.

However, the ethical dimension of citizenship becomes the fundamental focus for other scholarly treatments of the concepts as well. For example, William Mosher's preface and opening chapter in *Introduction to Responsible Citizenship* assumes a high ethical understanding of citizenship. In the preface, Mosher explains that the citizenship course at the Maxwell School during the 1930s and 1940s, from which his book evolved, began by defining citizenship "largely with respect to politics and government." However, "in the course of time," according to Mosher, "the citizen was considered to be man in society."[17] In his introductory chapter, Mosher identifies two characteristics of a good citizen which fit this high ethical perspective of citizenship: (1) "Sensitiveness to the Social Rights and Needs of Others" and (2) "Capacity of Independent Thinking and Critical Evaluation." In a summary statement, he argues that "Acceptance of the predominance of human values in all situations and under all circumstances is a primary characteristic of the thoughtful citizen."[18]

And of course, in the literature there are treatments of citizenship which focus on the interaction or blending of types. These more complex variations on the four simple types in Table One indicate of course, that in reality there are continua among the types with a range of gradations.

TABLE 1
Definition of Citizenship

	LEGAL	ETHICAL
High	• Membership in a governmental jurisdiction • Membership status, rights, and obligations legally defined • Obligations limited to governmental arena • Authority shared among members by law • Extensive participation provided by law	• Membership in any community, including, but not limited to governmental jurisdictions • Membership status, rights, and obligations defined by values norms, tradition, and culture • Obligations include political, social, and economic arenas • Authority shared among members by custom, tradition, and consensus • Extensive participation provided by custom, tradition, and consensus
Low	• Membership in a governmental jurisdiction • Membership status, rights, and obligations legally defined • Obligations limited to governmental arena • Authority hierarchically distributed by law • Minimal participation provided by law	• Membership in any community, including, but not limited to, governmental jurisdictions • Membership status, rights, and obligations defined by values, norms, traditions, and culture • Obligations include political, social, and economic arenas • Authority hierarchically distributed by custom, tradition, and consensus • Minimal participation provided by custom, tradition, and consensus

Although the full development of these continua is not of prime importance for our purposes here, a few illustrative examples may be helpful in suggesting some of the permutations that are possible.

One such perspective is Norton Long's discussion on the relationship between legal constitutions and ethical constitutions.[19] Building upon the Aristotelian assumption that a consensus about the nature of the good life is more fundamental than the legal structures of a polity, Long argues that the legal constitution of the United States must be "interpreted by the ethical constitution that informs it." Effective citizenship, by his line of argument, is the result of this process of interaction between the ethical and legal dimensions of citizenship.

Paul Sniderman's research on citizens and the attitudes they hold toward government led him to some conclusions about the nature of citizenship in democratic society which are a complex blending of types. He assigns primary importance to factors which I have identified with Lowi's ethical dimension, but his exclusive concern is with the governmental arena. He does not view citizenship in the broad fashion associated with the ethical types in Table One but neither are the legal definitions of citizenship the exclusive considerations in his study.

In treating this hybrid type, which suggests a continuum between the legal and ethical types, Sniderman argues that the existence of a civil temper, coupled with certain attitudes and values concerning the nature of political authority and allegiance owed to government, are the critical factors in the working out of the citizenship role in the United States. He is concerned with the citizenship role established by laws, but he views these "ethical" components of the role, rather than any legal provisos, as critical in shaping the forms of citizenship in this country.

The two major role types which emerged from Sniderman's field research are the supportive citizen and the committed citizen.[20] The latter tends to be passive, acquiescent, and compliant in the face of hierarchical governmental authority, while the former is far more likely to resist, criticize, question, and insist on sharing the authority of government. In this way, Sniderman's work also suggests the continuum which exists between the high and low types of citizenship in Table One.

Robert Salisbury views citizenship in the broadest sense, consistent with the ethical types in Table One, but does not ignore the legal bases of citizenship.[21] Salisbury's view is similar to Long's in that he views both the ethical and legal components as essential, but he gives greater weight to the former. Salisbury argues that citizenship in any community requires at least a minimum degree of formal rules, laws or agreements to establish peer status among the members. In communities such as the United States Congress, there are also elaborate systems of rules for distributing specific responsibilities, granting conditional authority and establishing procedures. According to Salisbury, these formal, legal definitions are never sufficient, even when fully elaborated. They merely provide a foundation or framework for "the moral community" with its informal norms and values such as "civic commitment" and "loyalty."

Salisbury's emphasis on equality of status among citizens, and the necessity for active citizenship identify him with the high view. These commitments, coupled with the significance which he attributes to the ethical dimensions, locate him somewhere in the high ethical category. However, Salisbury's view of the formal legal aspects of citizenship as the essential structures within which ethical citizenship emerges, once again, suggests a continuum between the legal and ethical types. Since he does not deal with the legal structures of citizenship in depth, it is not possible to determine on the basis of Salisbury's article, whether it is a continuum between high ethical and high legal, or high ethical and low legal.

This application of the conceptual matrix in Table One to the works of Flathman, Mosher, Long, Sniderman, and Salisbury has been presented to illustrate its usefulness in clarifying what particular authors intend by the term citizenship. However, beyond functioning as an analytical device for dealing with literature, this matrix should be of value in orienting one's own concerns and commitments. It should help one to specify the dimensions of citizenship one wants to address, the streams of literature which are most relevant and the critical issues which need to be engaged.

LEGAL AND ETHICAL CITIZENSHIP IN THE UNITED STATES

With these broad definitional types before us, I wish to indicate that the ultimate concern of this book is with the ethical dimensions of citizenship in the American political tradition, and that my own commitment lies somewhere in the high ethical category. However, my position also evidences the existence of a more complex continuum than is portrayed in Table One, and extends between the high ethical and low legal types of citizenship. In other words, I recognize that the legal constitutional definition of citizenship in the United States is one which distributes authority in a limited hierarchical fashion. That was the intent of the framers of the Constitution and their reasons for doing so are evident in the Federalist Papers.[22] Their preference for a limited exercise of authority by the citizenry resulted in the original structure of our representative government with its limited franchise, indirect election of the Senate and President, and the dependence of local governments upon the states.

However, some of these constitutional provisions have been subsequently amended and statutory action has created more extensive opportunities for citizens to participate more directly in government. Thus, our legal definitions of the status of citizens are not now as low as originally stated, but still fall into that category.

This relatively low legal framework for citizenship has provided us with a weak, formal tradition of citizenship in the United States, as suggested at the beginning of this chapter. The founders did not distribute authority in an egalitarian fashion, nor did they articulate the functions and obligations of citizenship in much detail. The emphasis of the Constitution is more on rights rather than obligations. While one might argue that obedience to the law is certainly an obligation, obligation is imposed upon everyone—citizens, resident aliens, and tourists alike. Obedience to the law is not distinctly associated with citizenship.

In spite of this weak, formal approach to citizenship there has been a rather lively informal American tradition of ethical citizenship. From the covenantal tradition of the early Puritan communities with their forms of participatory self-governance; the New England town meetings; the experience of forming voluntary associations, which captured the attention of Tocqueville; Anti-federalist thought; and the cooperative establishment of frontier settlements, there has emerged a set of values, customs, beliefs, principles, and theories which provide the substance for ethical citizenship.[23]

In the founding years it was informed by the participatory democratic thought of Jefferson and the egalitarian philosophy which he put forth in the Declaration of Independence. It has been further inspired and legitimized by certain reformist strains of the Judeo-Christian tradition such as the Social Gospel led by Walter Rauschenbusch.[24] This participatory dimension of ethical citizenship has found expression in the *abolitionist movement*, the *populist movement*, the *labor union movement*, the *feminist movement*, the *civil rights movement*, the *peace movement*, the *environmental movement*, the *neighborhood movement*, the *anti-nuclear movement* and the *anti-tax movement*, among many others.

All of these perspectives, ideas, experiences, and activities represent tributaries of a continuing stream in American history which has functioned as a counterpoint to the formal legal provisions of citizenship. They have tended to encourage more active participation in political, social and economic affairs. They have motivated citizens to assume greater obligations for collective life and they have provided experience in the sharing of responsibility. Without this multifaceted tradition of ethical citizenship the nation would have lacked political and social dynamism. It has been the source of motivation to collaborate, build, and maintain the common good.

The ethical dimensions of the citizenship tradition have also regularly given rise to changes in the legal definitions of citizenship. The franchise has been extended to nonwhites and women, slavery has been abolished, civil rights have been expanded, the right to equal employment opportunities has been established, the voting age has been lowered from twenty-one to eighteen years, and citizen participation in public policy-making has been mandated in numerous legislative acts. These changes based on law would never have taken place without the sense of obligation and right to active participation in governance which has been embodied in the tradition of ethical citizenship. It has been the driving force behind the democratization of the relatively elitist form of government provided in the Constitution and the elitist society of the founding era.

ETHICAL CITIZENSHIP, THE ADMINISTRATIVE STATE, AND PUBLIC ADMINISTRATION

On the other hand, I must acknowledge that while the participatory aspects of our tradition of ethical citizenship have elevated and expanded our legal definitions of citizenship, the results have not been so consistent in recent times. We now face a serious problem in maintaining the efficacious operation of the ethical citizenship tradition. The emergence and growth of the very interest groups which demand and generally receive greater participation in the political process has with increasing frequency lacked a broad sense of obligation for the common good. The *right* to participate in pursuit of self interest has tended to become severed from the *obligation* to participate in a search for larger public interests. The result of course, has been the tendency to fragment our political community and render considerations of the broader public good virtually impossible.

With the rise of the modern administrative state in the late nineteenth and early twentieth centuries the increasing emphasis on scientific approaches to government, as well as the professionalization of politics and public administration brought about some important changes. A growing focus on values such as efficiency and bureaucratic rationality developed. A trend emerged toward the standardization of public services, rules, regulations and administrative functions, largely under the aegis of the Progressive movement. The result was that the virtues and attendant obligations of the ethical citizenship tradition began to be displaced and attenuated. Deliberation among the citizenry began to be discouraged, both consciously and unconsciously; it seemed inefficient and unbusinesslike. Public participation was perceived and experienced by the emerging class of trained public administrators as unproductive interference with the orderly conduct of their professional roles and the most effective use of their expert knowledge and skill.[25] The costs to citizens in time, money, information, and stress (both emotional and physical) for participation tended to increase while professionals felt little or no obligation to reduce those costs.[26]

The central argument is that the emergence of the administrative state, with its professionalization of public functions, many of which had been managed and delivered by citizen volunteers and voluntary associations in the past, has made access increasingly difficult for associations of citizens with broad public purposes. Therefore, in order to penetrate professionalized government dominated by business, scientific, and professional values it has become more and more necessary to replace these more civic minded associations with sharply focused special interest, even single issue, organizations formed around the limited interests of a few. Thus, in an expanding economy, and with the blessing of pluralist theory, unfettered competition for power and resources has been pursued by interest groups and tolerated by the political community.

However, we have arrived at a point of economic constraint, population growth, and diversification when this quest for the satisfaction of particular interests must be balanced with the more cooperative and communal strains of our heritage of ethical citizenship in order to avoid destructive conflict, frustration producing impasses in the public policy process and intensely dysfunctional competition for scarce resources. Otherwise, services, resources and spaces which constitute the public realms of our society are likely to be neglected or appropriated for private use. Public decision making is likely to become even less civil and political leadership even more impotent. The exercise of citizenship as the public office of the individual must carry with it an obligation to consider individual and group interests in the context of larger social and community interests. The public administrator as fiduciary citizen in control of information, procedures, rules, personnel, and public budgets is in a key position, and can function as a powerful role model to either encourage or further discourage this exercise of citizenship responsibility.

Bellah, et al., follow a similar line of historical analysis and arrive at conclusions which are supportive of the central argument developed here concerning the problematic nature of the role of the public administrator. They recall Tocqueville's interest in those human groups which "filled the gulf between the individual and the state with active citizen participation." These include families, religious organizations, and the full array of voluntary associations. Furthermore, Bellah and his colleagues remind us of Tocqueville's worry that in modern society a kind of *democratic despotism* might emerge that could destroy mediating institutions through centralization, rational planning, and the assertion of the preeminence of professional expertise. They attribute at least the original impetus for this movement to the Progressives.

According to Bellah and company, what we now have is a "professionalism without content" that is "widespread among those in the higher echelons of American society" dominated by a "professional vision" which tends to assume the validity of a trade-off between utilitarian efficiency in work and individual expressive freedom within private lifestyle enclaves." What must be done in the face of this situation is to strengthen all those associations and movements through which citizens influence and moderate the power of their governments. *Vigorous citizenship,* they maintain, depends on "everything from families to political parties, on the one hand, and new organizations, movements, coalitions responsive to particular historical situations, on the other." They go on to assert that "The social movement has been of particular importance as a form of citizenship in the United States."[27]

According to Bellah and his colleagues, in order to accomplish this we must "succeed in transforming the spirit of centralized administration itself." This transformation, complex though it may be, should focus on *bringing a sense of citizenship into the operation of government itself.*" Their summary paragraph reads like a manifesto for the citizen administrator:

> In order to limit the danger of administrative despotism, we need to discuss the positive purposes and ends of government, the kind of government appropriate for the citizens we would like to be. Among other things, we need to reappropriate the ethical meaning of professionalism, seeing it in terms not only of technical skill but of the moral contributions that professionals make to a complex society. We undoubtedly have much to learn from the Progressives and the architects of the early New Deal, who still thought of professionalism partly in terms of the ethic of the calling. To change the conception of government from scientific management to center of ethical obligations and relationships is part of our task.[28]

Thus it is not the legal definition of citizenship that is of central concern here because it is not of primary consequence for conduct. It is important that we understand the legal framework and how it has evolved, both for perspective and in order to appreciate the extent to which the significant influence on conduct lies in ethical citizenship. However, it is the ethical dimension of citizenship which warrants our major attention at this time in public administration. It is the values, norms, and traditions which encourage the sharing of authority and active participation in collective life for the common good which are essential. They transcend sub-national governmental jurisdictions and extend across our political, social, and economic realms.

It is essential that public administrators identify with this perspective, both as a source of legitimacy for their own roles, and in order to encourage democratization through their professional activities. Public administrators, as key agents in the administrative state, play a critical role. They may actively and intentionally encourage democratic government, or they may subvert it consciously or unconsciously. Their professional identity and self-understanding will be *one* crucial element in moving them and American society in one direction or the other.

If citizenship is the appropriate normative basis for the public administrative role, it can be argued that it is the high ethical view of citizenship characterized above that should inform and shape the professional identity and role of public administrators. This is clearly a formidable task, and one should not be too idealistic about the possibilities of incurring an immediate impact. Intellectual modesty is required and patience is essential. The tides of the American political tradition change slowly, but ideas are potentially powerful. Reflection, conceptual experimentation and debate are the intellectual and civil processes that sift out those ideas which are meaningful to a society from those that are not. It is the scholars' lot to contribute to the process with humility and leave the rest to history.

OVERVIEW OF CHAPTERS

Chapter two develops the evolution of the legal definition of citizenship in the United States from the colonial era to the early twentieth century. This is organized into two major sections, each devoted to one of the fundamental problems associated with United States citizenship that required resolution by the Congress, the Federal Courts, or both. The first of these is the problem of dual citizenship—the question of whether state or national citizenship should have priority. The second is the relationship of the citizen to the governments of the United States as it was debated and finally defined legally with respect to naturalization, the conditions for gaining citizenship for those not born to it. Examination of these two fundamental issues illuminates the way in which the essential legal definition of citizenship evolved over a period of approximately one and a half centuries.

Chapter three turns to the ethical tradition of citizenship in the United States as the central focus of the book and the proposed normative point of reference for the public administrative role. As opposed to the rather low legal definitions of citizenship which emerged in chapter two, a more active participatory stream of high ethical norms and values concerning the rights and obligations of the citizenry is explored in this chapter. The chapter opens with an examination of some of the historic roots of ethical citizenship in the United States such as the Puritan covenantal tradition, Jeffersonian thought, and Antifederalist perspectives. It then argues that these various streams of ideas have interacted with frontier and community building experience in forming voluntary associations to produce a peculiarly American high ethical tradition of citizenship. This process has tended to democratize the legal tradition.

Chapter four focuses on the transformation of American public administration and the consequent "eclipse" of the ethical tradition during the American Progressive reform movement of the late nineteenth and early twentieth centuries. The implications for an ethic of citizenship of the emergence of public administration in its modern professionalized forms with its emphasis on "scientific values" as influenced by the Progressives are also reviewed. The perspective embodied in Mary Parker Follett's *The New State* is discussed as an example of the continued existence of the ethical tradition of citizenship still present during Progressivism's high noon.

Chapter five refocuses attention on the role of the American public administrator as *citizen administrator* by outlining a normative perspective for the *virtuous administrator*. The concept of *practice* is introduced as preferable to the more commonly used concept of *profession*. Civic virtue as "self-interest rightly understood" is offered as the central attribute of the citizen and as a necessity for community in order to sustain such a virtue. The obligations of the citizen administrator as fiduciary citizen also heightened the importance of three additional virtues: public-spiritedness, prudence, and substantive rationality.

Chapter six develops a perspective on the public realm in the United States appropriate for the citizen administrator. It is based on a complex continuum of relationships ranging from the most private to the most public. An argument is developed for the importance of maintaining the full spectrum of relationships and the citizen administrator's responsibility is defined.

Chapter seven offers some concluding thoughts concerning general courses of action to be considered in moving toward the citizen administrator perspective on the public administrative role.

REFERENCES

1. JOHN M. MULDER, *Woodrow Wilson: The Years of Preparation* (Princeton: Princeton University Press, 1978).
2. WOODROW WILSON, "The Study of Administration," *Political Science Quarterly*, 2 (1887), 499.
3. JOSEPH SCHUMPETER, *Capitalism, Socialism, and Democracy* 3rd ed. (New York: Harper, 1950); B.R. BERELSON, *Voting* (Chicago: University of Chicago Press, 1956); SEYMOUR MARTIN LIPSET, *Political Man* (New York: Doubleday, 1960).
4. MICHAEL WALZER, *Obligations: Essays on Disobedience, War, and Citizenship* (Cambridge: Harvard University Press, 1970), p. 204.
5. JOHN DEWEY, *The Public and Its Problems* (Chicago: Swallow Press 1927).
6. WALZER, *Obligations*, p. 210.
7. LAWRENCE A. SCHAFF, "Citizenship in America: Theories of the Founding," in *The Non-Lockean Roots of American Democratic Thought*, ed. J. Chaudhuri (Tucson: University of Arizona Press, 1977), p. 44.
8. TERRY L. COOPER, *The Responsible Administrator: An Approach to Ethics for the Administrative Role* (New York: Kennikat Press Corp., 1982). A second edition was published by Associated Faculty Press, Inc. in 1986, and a third edition is forthcoming from Jossey-Bass Publishers in 1990.
9. TERRY L. COOPER, "Citizenship in an Age of Scarcity: A Normative Essay on Ethics in Public Administration Education." This paper was later published in revised form under a slightly different title—"Public Administration in an Age of Scarcity: A Citizenship Role for Public Administisators," in *Politics and Administration: Woodrow Wilson and American Public Administration*, eds. Jack Rabin and James Bowman (New York: Marcel Dekker, Inc. 1984), pp. 297–314.
10. H. GEORGE FREDERICKSON, "The Recovery of Civism in Public Administration," *Public Administration Review*, 42 (1982), pp. 501–508.
11. *Public Administration Review*, special issue on "Citizenship and Public Administration," March 1984. *See* Chandler's article entitled "Conclusions: The Public Administrator as Representative Citizen: A New Role for the New Century," pp. 196–206.
12. Two excellent Ph.D. dissertations are presented: ROBERT CHARLES DUNEK, "The Citizen-

Administrator: A Role Integration Study of City Managers in Southern California" (Unpublished Ph.D. dissertation, University of Southern California, 1985); CAMILLA M. STIVERS, "Active Citizenship in the Administrative State" (Unpublished Ph.D. Dissertation, Virginia Polytechnic Institute and State University, 1988).

13. RICHARD FLATHMAN, "Citizenship and Authority: A Chastened View of Citizenship," *News for Teachers of Political Science*, 30 (1981), pp. 9–19.
14. Flathman cites Schumpeter, Berelson, and Lipset among others.
15. THEODORE J. LOWI, "The Two Cities of Norton Long" in *Cities Without Citizens*, ed. Benjamin R. Schuster (Philadelphia: Center for the Study of Federalism, 1981).
16. "Ethical" does not imply "good" or "moral." It simply refers to citizenship defined by ethical norms, values, and principles instead of laws.
17. WILLIAM E. MOSHER, ed., *Responsible Citizenship* (new York: Henry Holt and Company, 1941), p. iv.
18. *Ibid.*, pp. 4–7.
19. NORTON E. LONG, "Cities Without Citizens" in *Cities Without Citizens*, ed. Benjamin R. Schuster (Philadelphia: Center for the Study of Federalism, 1981), pp. 7–8.
20. PAUL SNIDERMAN, *A Question of Loyalty* (Berkeley: University of California Press, 1981), pp. 1–46.
21. ROBERT H. SALISBURY, "On Cities and Citizens" in *Cities Without Citizens*, ed. Benjamin R. Schuster (Philadelphia: Center for the Study of Federalism, 1981), pp. 22–29.
22. See No. 10 in particular.
23. ALEXIS DETOCQUEVILLE, *Democracy in America* (New York: New American Library, 1956).
24. WALTER RAUSCHENBUSCH, *A Theology for the Social Gospel* (New York: Abingdon Press, 1945).
25. *See* Robert Caro, *The Powerbroker: Robert Moses and the Fall of New York* (New York: Vintage Books, 1974), chapter 5 in particular, for an interesting, vivid account of this process as seen at the Bureau of Municipal Research in New York City in the first decades of the twentieth century.
26. For a discussion of participation costs and the role of the public administrator see Terry L. Cooper, "The Hidden Price Tag," *American Journal of Public Health*, 69 (1979), pp. 368–374.
27. ROBERT BELLAH and others, *Habits of the Heart: Individualism and Commitment in American Life* (Berkeley: University of California Press, 1985), p. 208–212.
28. *Ibid.*, p. 212.

2
THE EVOLUTION OF THE LEGAL DEFINITIONS OF CITIZENSHIP IN THE UNITED STATES

The title of this chapter is stated in the plural form because there has been no single fixed, comprehensive legal definition of United States citizenship. Since the birth of the nation there have been many legal instruments, including constitutional provisions, legislative acts, and court decisions which have given shape to the formal meaning of citizenship. These have evolved over time in a fragmented incremental fashion, giving rise to an expanding and more inclusive legal definition of the citizenry.

If one is to fully understand citizenship in the United States, it is essential to grapple with the complex and disjointed development of its legal aspects. It is *essential*, but not *adequate*; essential because the legalities of citizenship establish the conditions under which one may qualify to participate in governance, but not adequate because they tell us little about why or how one ought to participate in the official governing process and nothing about our obligation for the informal governance of day-to-day life. As indicated in the previous chapter and discussed more fully in the one to follow, an appreciation of the full significance of American citizenship requires a grasp of both the legal history and the streams of values and traditions that have informed that role. While the latter represents the emphasis of this book, it is important to review in at least a cursory fashion, how our official policies concerning membership in the political community have emerged during the last two hundred years or more. This chapter will attempt to provide that overview.

While a legal historian might find it necessary to identify and discuss a longer list of themes or issues with greater subtlety and more distinctions, it seems sufficient for the purposes of this book to address two major areas related to legal citizenship: the problem of dual citizenship, and the complex issues involved in naturalization. Each of these will be taken up in succession and developed chronologically with attention to points of overlap.

THE PROBLEM OF DUAL CITIZENSHIP: SUPREMACY OF STATE OR NATION?

Today, we typically think of citizenship as having to do with membership in a national political community. When questioned about their citizenship status, Americans automatically respond with their national citizenship. They identify themselves as citizens of the United States. However, it is important to begin this review of legal citizenship with a clear understanding that this was not the case, either in the period during or immediately following the war for independence from Great Britain. The more fundamental citizenship identity in those early decades of United States history was that of a particular state. One was a citizen of Virginia, or Connecticut, or New York, or one of the other thirteen original states. Prior to the Declaration of Independence most of the inhabitants of the colonies were legally British subjects first, and secondarily, citizens of a particular colony.[1]

Although there were British legal provisions for achieving citizenship in the colonies,[2] in practice citizenship was determined by each individual colony. The result was considerable variation in the characteristics of that status and no universal reciprocal arrangements for the recognition of citizenship. Kettner describes the situation at the time as "chaotic and disorganized," one in which "persons adopted by one colony remained aliens in the others."[3] To add to the confusion, certain cities such as New York also provided a legal citizenship status for those who could enjoy "the freedom of the city," including the suffrage, the right to hold office, and the privilege of carrying on a trade or profession.[4]

With the withdrawal of allegiance to the British crown a loose confederation of political communities emerged, describing themselves as United Colonies. These colonies declared they had a right to be "Free and Independent States."[5] Having rejected British subjectship, the primary legal role in the political community shifted from *subject* to that of *citizen* of one of the former colonies. One indication of the extent to which state citizenship carried the status of membership in a sovereign nation was the fact that, between the Declaration of Independence and the ratification of the Constitution, passports were issued by state governors or presidents for persons traveling abroad.[6]

One must be cautious however, about overemphasis on the autonomy and separateness of the thirteen states. The states had also experienced a significant community of interest among themselves. Their shared grievances against the crown, as well as their common economic interests and geographic setting, had created bonds among them over a long period of time. It was these common historical, economic, geographic, and political practices which had led these former colonies to revolution; it was these ties that made the risky undertaking possible and these same factors that cast their separate claims to state sovereignty in a softer light and created instability in the notion of state citizenship as primary.

This community of interest which transcended state boundaries was evident in the general acceptance of volitional allegiance as the basis for citizenship during the revolutionary era.[7] Although the authority to admit members to the political community was held by the separate states during the period immediately following the Declaration of Independence, the prevalent criterion for citizenship was support for the revolutionary cause. Beyond that commitment there was little concern for the individual qualifications of those who were former British subjects.[8]

One specific expression of this perspective was a resolution of the Continental Congress on June 6, 1776, a month before the adoption of the Declaration of Independence. In response to a report of the "Committee on Spies" the Congress resolved that "all persons abiding within any of the United Colonies and deriving protection from the laws of the same owe allegiance to the said laws, and are members of such colony."[9] The assertion by both Franklin and Kettner that in this act the Continental Congress "defined the citizenship of the colonies" is true only in a general sense. However, Kettner is probably closer to the truth in his further suggestion that such actions "revealed the assumption that 'national' goals and purposes ought to influence citizenship policies of the individual states."[10]

It seems clear that, while explicitly and formally advancing their sovereignty as independent states, historical experience on the American continent and common British roots made it impossible to define the political community in terms entirely restricted to state boundaries. Kettner observes that this was particularly evident with respect to naturalized citizens, persons not of British or American birth who became citizens of one of the thirteen states. Although legally they were citizens of Delaware, or Massachusetts, or New York, they "seemed to become members of a community that transcended state boundaries."[11]

This nascent national community evoked a need for closer ties than those which typically existed among sovereign states. They were not truly "foreign" to each other and the legal relationships among their members called for something more than provisions for dealing with aliens.[12] At a minimum it required some standard of reciprocity in citizenship status. The first attempt to establish such a standard was the inclusion of Article IV of the Articles of Confederation, which was adopted by the Continental Congress on November 13, 1777, and ratified on March 1, 1781, as part of the full document. The first paragraph of Article IV, in its final form, reads as follows:

> The better to secure and perpetuate mutual friendship and intercourse among the people of the different States in this Union, the free inhabitants of each of these States, paupers, vagabonds and fugitives from justice excepted, shall be entitled to all privileges and immunities of free citizens in the several States; and the people of each State shall have free ingress and regress to and from any other State, and shall enjoy therein all the privileges of trade and commerce, subject to the same duties, impositions and restrictions as the inhabitants thereof respectively, provided that such restrictions shall not extend so far as to prevent the removal of property imported into any State, to any other State of which the owner is an inhabitant; provided also that no imposition, duties or restriction shall be laid by any State on the property of the United States, or either of them.[13]

The inclusion of such a reciprocity clause is indicative of the unique character of the federation thus formed. Bancroft maintains that it was indeed this article which "gave reality to the union." Through this particular provision, problematic though it became, the free inhabitants of the states were declared to have a greater degree of political interdependence than was typical of alliances among sovereign nations.[14] However, Smith reminds us that "neither in Article IV nor in other provisions is there a recognition of national citizenship."[15] Nevertheless, this article represented the first step in that direction.

Although a logical and appropriate affirmation of their common heritage and experience, this article of reciprocity represented only a transitional link between that which had been and that which was yet to be, as was true of the entire document and the confederation it served. It attempted to maintain the sovereignty of the states on the one hand, while acknowledging a standard of intercitizenship on the other. There was obvious tension between these two concepts which was not mitigated by the loose and imprecise language of Article IV.

Most significant treatments of the problems of Article IV quote at length from James Madison's critique of its language in *The Federalist Papers*, No. 42.[16] Madison observed that the terms *free inhabitants, free citizens* and *the people* are used interchangeably in different parts of the Article and complained that "There is a confusion of language here which is remarkable."[17] Since the problems which had emerged during the eleven years since the adoption of the Articles of Confederation by the Continental Congress were the real source of Madison's consternation it appears likely that his criticism of the terminology has the benefit of hindsight not available in 1777. At that time the critical issue was not one of clarifying the relationship between state citizenship and some form of general citizenship in the new confederation, rather, it was one of distinguishing British subjects from citizens of the states seeking independence.

This problem had been addressed in the Congressional resolution of June 6, 1776, mentioned above. In this action the Congress gave notice that all those who continued to reside in one of the colonies would be presumed to have abandoned their subjectship to the British king and assumed the role of a member of that colony. The terms used in Article IV of the Articles of Confederation reflect that broad assumption. *Free inhabitants, free men* and the *the people* were used in a generally synonymous fashion without much precision because the political status of individuals inhabiting the thirteen newly declared states was, in fact, unclear and unresolved.[18]

The immediate and most pressing practical problem in 1777 was to establish a gross differentiation between those persons who were to be viewed as "enemy aliens" and those who should be presumed loyal and, therefore, bona fide members of the newly emerging political community by virtue of having remained a resident of one of the states in rebellion. This reciprocity article was not heavily debated, nor was the finest point put on its language, because the revolutionary situation eluded greater rigor in definition. It did provide an initial expression of what Kettner describes as "the almost instinctive" and "never fully articulated or theoretically explored" notion of a larger national community which transcended the boundaries of individual states.[19] For the time, it was sufficient to agree to a mutual recognition of the rights of those in each of the states who had signified allegiance to the revolutionary cause by remaining as inhabitants who benefited from the "protection" of the various states. Those who remained, but expressed or demonstrated loyalty to King George III, were considered citizens nevertheless, but disloyal citizens.[20]

Understandable as it may be that the language of Article IV was lacking in precision, problems in its implementation began to be apparent quite early. When Madison later complained in 1788 that the article granted free inhabitants of one state all the privileges of free citizens of another he was not indulging in theoretical legal speculation, but reacting to a record of confusion and inequity with which the states had been grappling for seven years, since the ratification of the Articles of Confederation in 1781.[21]

Recognizing that even if "inhabitant" and "citizen" are considered to be synonymous, Madison went on to observe that, in effect, such an interpretation of the article would still grant the power to each state to naturalize citizens of every other state. Aliens might take up citizenship in a state with minimal requirements and qualifications and then, by simply moving their place of residence, acquire citizenship in another state whose standards were more rigorous.[22] In a letter to Edmund Randolph on August 27, 1782, Madison acknowledged that this problem had been raised several times in the Congress and expressed his belief that the solution was the adoption of a uniform rule of naturalization.[23]

State courts had dutifully complied with the reciprocity provisions of the Articles of Confederation which implied some general citizenship status beyond the state level.[24] The authority of the Continental Congress to provide policies which directly affected the citizenship policies of the states had been established. Also, committees of the Congress began to deal with aliens in ways which suggested an assumption of authority to grant citizenship rights apart from membership in a particular state.

For example, on October 15, 1783, a Congressional commission was appointed to meet with the Indians in the northwest territories for the purpose of establishing boundaries. Included in the charge to the commission were instructions to meet with French inhabitants of that region in the name of the United States to indicate that all who "shall profess their allegiance to the United States . . . shall be protected in the full enjoyment of their liberty and their just and lawful property."[25]

This action resembled admission into national citizenship since the relationship involved allegiance to, and protection from, the collective entity known as the United States. Neither residence in, nor loyalty to, a particular state was involved. While treating this event as a grant of citizenship may be overstating its significance, it does indicate a certain inadequacy in the doctrine of the primacy of state citizenship. As the new confederation confronted its interests and needs as a collective body, central authority became increasingly necessary, the need to establish secure relationships with alien French inhabitants of the northwest territories being a case in point.

When the problem of citizenship status and other serious defects in the Articles of Confederation finally led to the convoking of the Philadelphia Convention of 1787, the framers of the new constitution addressed the problem of dual citizenship in only a cursory fashion.[26] The difference between the two major proposals sponsored by William Patterson and John Randolph is fine indeed, but nevertheless significant. It was a matter of whether the states were deemed incompetent to deal with naturalization, thus leading to the assignment of total authority in that area to the central government, or whether states were to continue to be involved in naturalization, but operate within the bounds of nationally established rules. Randolph's plan would have clearly tipped the balance toward the primacy of national citizenship, while Patterson's also would have eroded the priority of state citizenship, but less so.

The preponderance of opinion among the delegates seems to have been with maintaining the primacy of state citizenship and the derivative status of national citizenship. Their immediate concern with dual citizenship was to focus on solving the troublesome problems of uniformity among the states which had been experienced under the reciprocity provision of the Articles of Confederation.[27] The ambiguous nature of dual citizenship was not confronted head on or dealt with as an urgent problem demanding theoretical clarity. Resolution was left to the future.[28]

The Constitutional framers adopted two provisions. One was the comity clause, Article IV, Section 2, Clause 1 which was carried over from Article

IV of the Articles of Confederation in abbreviated form: "The Citizens of each State shall be entitled to all Privileges and Immunities of Citizens in the several States." The other provision was included in Article I, Section 8, which lists among the various powers of Congress: "To establish an uniform Rule of Naturalization. . . ." These two provisions were intended to preserve citizenship reciprocity among the states within a framework of national standards. It was clear that the uniform rule clause established a degree of authority for the Congress in citizenship policy. However, the extent of that authority remained ambiguous and was to be worked out through implementing legislation and court decisions.[29]

President George Washington, in his annual message on January 8, 1790, stated that "the terms on which foreigners may be admitted to the rights of citizens should be speedily ascertained by a uniform rule of naturalization."[30] The first piece of legislation intended to carry out this responsibility of Congress was the Naturalization Act of 1790.[31] The final bill that was enacted into law established a residency requirement of two years in the United States and one year in a given state. It provided citizenship status to those meeting that standard who applied to any common law court in the state where they had resided for one year. Applicants had to provide satisfactory evidence of good character, and take an oath administered by the court to uphold the Constitution of the United States.[32]

One provision of the Act of 1790 strengthened the concept of national citizenship. This was a stipulation that children who were born abroad of parents who were citizens were to be considered natural born citizens unless the father had never been a resident of the United States. This amounted to a recognition of citizenship in the United States not derived from citizenship in one of the states, but from blood relationship to a citizen.

Another provision tended to affirm the priority of state citizenship by specifying that any citizens proscribed by a state could not be readmitted to citizenship by any other state. Only the legislature of the proscribing state could do so. The implication here of course, was that citizenship was derived from and controlled by state power. The net effect of the first naturalization act under the new Constitution was to reaffirm the priority of the states in granting citizenship, and at the same time firmly establish a role for the Congress in regulating that process.

In 1794, the House of Representatives initiated the work of revising the Naturalization Act of 1790, leading to the Naturalization Act of 1795.[33] It included three elements which are directly relevant to the question of dual citizenship status.[34] The first of these was the new requirement for a *declaration of intention* which was to be sworn to in *either* a state *or* a federal court. This provision brought a federal branch of government into the administration of the naturalization process for the first time; a significant step beyond the rule-setting role previously exercised by the Congress.

A second element of the Act of 1795 was *the extension of naturalization to alien residents of the territories southwest and northwest of the Ohio River.* This could be done through the territorial courts in the same manner as specified for state courts and was, therefore, a substantial departure from the notion that state citizenship was primary. Roche concluded that "The citizens thus created were free of any state allegiance and could only be described as 'citizens of the United States.' An inconsistency had been created: People could be citizens of the United States without being citizens of a state."[35]

The *choice of certain language* was a third important aspect of the Act. During the Senate debate, it was moved that the following clause be added to the first section: "That no alien shall hereafter become a citizen of the United States, or any of them, except in the manner prescribed by this act." The amendment was accepted, but with a significant change. The words "any of" were inserted after "citizen of," thus deleting any reference to national citizenship. Also, "and not otherwise" was added at the end of the clause. Prior to final passage of the bill the prior language was restored, thus acknowledging both citizenship in the states and in the United States. Presumably this was done to make the wording consistent with the provision for admitting alien residents of the territories to citizenship.[36]

The inclusion of specific dual references to citizenship "of the United States, or any of them," together with the initial willingness to exclude any acknowledgment of national citizenship was an indicator of the continued strong assumptions concerning the primacy of state citizenship. However, the stipulation that aliens could be admitted to citizenship according to the conditions of this act "and not otherwise" implied a rejection of the states' independent power to naturalize. This was a clear denial of the *doctrine of concurrent jurisdiction* over naturalization.[37] The Congress once again staunchly reaffirmed the priority of state citizenship on the one hand while on the other, allowed federal and territorial courts to be involved in administering the process, providing citizenship for territorial residents, and claiming exclusive federal jurisdiction over naturalization.

Three years later, the Naturalization Act of 1798 was approved.[38] Two of its provisions are pertinent to the relationship between state and national citizenship. First was the effort in the amending process in the Senate once again to strike recognition of national citizenship. The House version of the bill provided "That no alien shall be admitted to become a citizen of the United States, or of any state, unless in the manner prescribed in this act." A motion to insert "any of the United States" in place of "the United States, or of any state" lost by an eight to thirteen vote. A significant minority held fast to the view that "only state citizenship had any real existence under the Constitution."[39]

The Act required for the first time that a report of all declarations of citizenship intent and all admissions to citizenship be made by the courts to the Secretary of State of the United States.[40] This provision gave the federal government a greater measure of administrative control over naturalization.[41]

The Naturalization Act of 1802 was pushed through the Congress by the Jefferson administration and became law on April 14, 1802. In it the essential features of the Act of 1795 were reinstated and provided the legislative standards for naturalization during the one hundred years that followed.[42]

With the adoption of the Naturalization Act of 1802, the question of dual citizenship remained unaddressed in any direct or systematic fashion. Kettner comments about this point in the legal history of the United States:

> It was readily apparent that American citizenship encompassed membership, rights, and obligations in both a local and a national community; yet the implications and ramifications of this dual status were never rigorously analyzed. The preliminary assumption seems to have been that the individual citizen, native or adopted, could bear his double membership in state and nation without inconsistency or conflict.[43]

But such was not the case; the tension between the two categories of citizenship manifested in the legislation of the 1790s only increased. The task of clarifying the relationship between state and national citizenship, and resolving the mounting tension between them, passed largely into the arena of the courts for the next fifty years. The plethora of cases in both state and federal courts which dealt with this issue would require a complex legal analysis if reviewed fully. However, for purposes of this chapter several key cases will be summarized.[44]

Two years after the Naturalization Act of 1790 was passed, the question of concurrent power of naturalization was addressed in Collet v. Collet.[45] The Act had left the administration of naturalization to the state courts, but the question confronted by the United States Circuit Court of the Pennsylvania District was whether both states and the federal government exercised this power concurrently. Some states continued granting citizenship at the state level with requirements which were different from those established for citizenship in the United States as provided by the Act.[46]

The decision of the court was "that the States, individually, still enjoy a concurrent authority upon this subject," but that authority may not be exercised "so as to contravene the rule established by the authority of the Union." The court ruled that the states may not exclude citizens naturalized by the United States, but that it is within their powers to grant state citizenship with less stringent qualifications than those established by Congress. This decision left the two types of citizenship intact without resolving the priority of their relationship.

The issue of concurrent naturalization came before the United States Supreme Court again twenty-five years later in 1817 in Chirac v. Chirac.[47] The Naturalization Act of 1795 had provided that any free white alien who wanted to become "a citizen of the United States, or of any of them" might do so by complying with its requirement "and not otherwise."[48] Although this claim to exclusive authority over admission requirements was generally accepted, some states continued naturalizing under their own laws.[49] In delivering the opinion of the court, Chief Justice John Marshall declared at the outset "That the power of naturalization is exclusively in Congress does not seem to be, and certainly ought not to be controverted." This unequivocal judgment by the high court firmly established the exclusive jurisdiction of the federal government over the rules for granting citizenship. It was acknowledged and affirmed by both state and federal courts in subsequent decisions.[50]

Chirac v. Chirac officially defined the locus of authority for regulating naturalization, but the priority relationship between state and federal citizenship was yet unresolved. The establishment of the primacy of national citizenship continued to evolve over the ensuing half century. Roche maintains that one of the critical factors in this process was the enormous territorial acquisition involved in the Louisiana Purchase.[51]

The Louisiana Purchase in 1803 raised several difficult constitutional questions, not the least of which was the status of the territorial inhabitants.[52] Article 3 of the "Treaty Between the United States of America and the French Republic" represented an unprecedented approach to the granting of citizenship:

> The inhabitants of the ceded territory shall be incorporated in the Union of the United States, and admitted as soon as possible, according to the principles of the Federal Constitution, to the enjoyment of all the rights, advantages, and immunities of citizens of the United States; and, in the meantime, they shall be maintained and protected in the free enjoyment of their liberty, property, and the religion which they profess.[53]

During the Congressional debates on the Treaty, the constitutional authority of the president and the senate to grant citizenship en masse and unilaterally through the treaty-making process was called into question.[54] The supporters of the treaty ultimately prevailed, and the United States took possession of the Louisiana territory on December 20, 1803.[55]

The unusual nature of this approach to naturalization is worthy of emphasis. In the case of native-born citizens, the right to citizenship was grounded either in *jus sanguinis*, one's parentage, or in *jus soli*, one's place of birth, or a combination of these two legal principles.[56] Naturalization on the other hand, was generally assumed to require an act of allegiance on the part of a particular individual. In the case of the Louisiana Purchase, none of these three conditions was satisfied. Residents of the Louisiana territory became citizens not by an act of their own volition, either individually or collectively, but by an act of the president and congress of the United States. They were *adopted* into citizenship.

The challenge to the validity of the naturalization process incorporated in the treaty reemerged in the courts and was resolved definitively in 1828 by the United States Supreme Court in American Insurance Company

v. Vales of Cotton, Canter, Claimant.[57] Chief Justice Marshall declared such treaties to be "the law of the land" with the effect of admitting territorial inhabitants "to the enjoyment of the privileges, rights, and immunities of the citizens of the United States." However, they do not "participate in political power; they do not share in the government" until the territories become states.[58]

Thus in this one decision the United States Supreme Court contributed to the establishment of two principles which are generally accepted today. The authority of the federal government over the granting of citizenship was confirmed, and the existence of a general national citizenship not derived from citizenship in a state was upheld.

The Court also affirmed a principle which was generally accepted until the victory of the women's suffrage movement—that political participation was not necessarily a privilege of citizenship. One might have citizenship without possessing the right to vote or hold elective office.

The status of dual citizenship was far from settled. Contention over the relationship of state and national citizenship continued for another forty years. It surfaced in the 1830s in the nullification crisis over a loyalty oath adopted by the South Carolina legislature which would require all state officers to swear primary allegiance to the state.[59] Dual citizenship status was also one of the strands in the recurring debates on expatriation.[60] It was dealt with again in the context of the Native Americanism movement.[61] And of course, it emerged in an abrasive and highly visible fashion in the Dred Scott case of the 1850s.

Dred Scott v. John F. A. Sanford, argued before the United States Supreme Court on February 11, 1856, concerned Dred Scott, a slave in Missouri, who claimed his freedom on the grounds that he had been taken by his master to Illinois, a free state, as well as into the Louisiana territory which was covered by the Missouri Compromise of 1820.[62] This federal statute prohibited slavery north of latitude 36° 30'. When the case was carried to the United States Circuit Court, Scott's citizenship in the United States was called into question, and therefore, his right of access to the federal judiciary.

The case was finally argued before the United States Supreme Court in 1856 where the critical issue became Scott's citizenship status. The seven to two majority opinion, delivered by Chief Justice Roger Taney on March 6, 1857, concluded that Scott was not a United States citizen, and consequently not entitled to the jurisdiction of a federal court.

Taney's decision was based on a reaffirmation of the dual nature of citizenship in the United States. Taney insisted that under the Constitution, the Congress has exclusive authority to establish rules for naturalization. He argued that "every person, and every class and description of persons, who were at the time of the adoption of the Constitution recognized as citizens in the several States, became also citizens of this new political body, but none other; it was formed by them, and for them and their posterity, but for no one else." One no longer became a member of the United States by virtue of becoming a citizen of a state after the adoption of the Constitution. Those who were parties to that act by being "then members of the several state communities," also became citizens of the nation thus founded.

Taney concluded that "neither the class of persons who had been imported as slaves, nor their descendants, whether they had become free or not, were then acknowledged as a part of the people," nor were they covered by the provisions of the Constitution.[63] His reasons for this conclusion were, first, that during the founding era Negroes were regarded as an inferior and subjugated race without "rights which the white man was bound to respect."[64] Consequently, they were not among those who became citizens of the newly independent states.[65] According to Taney, Dred Scott, being a Negro, had no national citizenship birthright in the United States, and therefore was not entitled access to the federal courts. The historical deprivation of political rights for Scott's ancestors justified a continuation of that deprivation.

Before a summary of Justice Curtis' dissenting opinion can be presented, it will be necessary to critically examine several key points in Chief Justice Taney's argument. First, his insistence that there were no Negro state citizens either at the time of the Declaration of Independence or at the time of the adoption of the Constitution, was erroneous.[66]

A second significant point concerning Taney's argument was that blacks were uniquely excluded from access to United States citizenship. The principle of *jus soli* was suspended for all blacks and a version of *jus sanguinis* adopted as a sweeping negative determinant of citizenship status. To have had black parents was sufficient grounds for a presumption of noncitizenship.

It is important to note that, although the law often distinguished between free blacks and slaves, Taney did not do so.[67] Free blacks were treated by Taney as though their free status made no difference under the law.

Furthermore Taney insisted that blacks born in the United States could not be admitted to national citizenship through naturalization, since that power granted to the Congress by the Constitution was "confined to persons born in a foreign country, under a foreign Government."[68] He argued that the legal tradition embodied in the state laws, the Declaration of Independence and the United States Constitution reveals:[69]

> ... that a perpetual and impassable barrier was intended to be erected between the white race and the one which they had reduced to slavery, and governed as subjects with absolute and despotic power ... And no distinction in this respect was made between the free Negro or mulatto and the slave, but this stigma, of the deepest degradation, was fixed upon the whole race.[70]

Fehrenbacher rightly concludes that this line of argument led Taney to the extreme position of asserting that "*American Negroes, free and slave, were the only people on the face of the earth who saving a constitutional amendment were forever ineligible for American citizenship.*"[71]

As concerns dual citizenship then, black people, whether slave or free, were ineligible for national citizenship and eligible only for citizenship in states that chose to grant it to them. Their rights and privileges extended no further than those granted by states in which they were residents, and those which were provided by comity among the states.

The third observation to be made about Taney's opinion is that it assumed that national citizenship and state citizenship were two entirely separate political relationships. He argued that just because one is a citizen of a state does not necessarily mean that he holds citizenship in the nation. State citizenship came into existence through the Declaration of Independence, while national citizenship was created by the adoption of the United States Constitution. According to his view, since the ratification of the Constitution no state can confer national citizenship by an act of its own legislature.[72]

When we turn to the more fully developed of the two dissenting opinions, that of Justice Curtis, it seems clear that the most basic disagreement with Taney has to do with the origin of national citizenship. Smith maintained that the central issue between Taney and Curtis was whether citizens of the United States were created by state or national action.[73] While Taney viewed the adoption of the Constitution as a break with the past, Curtis saw greater continuity in the law of citizenship. Taney's perspective led to a conclusion that state and national citizenship were under distinctly separate political jurisdictions after the ratification of the Constitution. However, Curtis argued that national citizenship continued to rest upon citizenship in one of the states.[74] He believed that the only power concerning citizenship delegated to the national government dealt with the power of naturalizing aliens by a uniform rule, according to Article I, Section 8 of the Constitution. From his perspective, free persons born in one of the states become citizens of the United States by virtue of their state citizenship, and according to the requirements and qualifications of that state, not by an act of national authority.[75]

As to the possibility of citizenship for black people, Curtis argued that they were no different from any other person if free, and natives of a state. Curtis pointed out that blacks had been legal citizens of five states under the Confederation and, therefore, citizens of the United States at that time. Black citizens of those states subsequently did become citizens of the United States under the Constitution; Curtis concluded that black people as a race were not excluded from national citizenship.[76]

Justice Curtis' dissenting opinion has the ring of an enlightened and liberal philosophy, especially in its main conclusions. However, as Fehrenbacher observed, it was in fact quite conservative in its assumptions and treatment of the legal tradition. It affirmed the principle of jus soli, but in a very narrow fashion. The right to citizenship according to one's place of birth was understood by Curtis to be limited to the state in which one was born. Thus, blacks born in states granting citizenship to black people were so entitled, while those born in states which restricted citizenship to the white race were thereby denied that status.

Black citizens of one state could not claim the rights of citizenship while traveling in a state which withheld that status from the black race. Nor could a state grant citizenship to any resident, black or white who was born in another state. That was understood by Curtis to involve the power of naturalization which was to be exercised only by the federal government. Fehrenbacher noted that "except for guaranteeing some free Negroes access to the federal courts, the Curtis interpretation of the Constitution would have entailed no significant change in the discriminatory racial arrangements of the time."[77]

To summarize with respect to the concept of dual citizenship, Taney and Curtis represented two quite different points of view. While Curtis' refusal to treat the case in racial terms anticipates a more modern universalization of rights, his understanding of citizenship still represented a conservative view reflecting the tradition of the priority of the states. National citizenship was thought to have been derived from state authority. On the other hand, Taney's framing of the issue and his distortion of fact revealed a strong taint of racial bigotry, reflective of the past, while his treatment of dual citizenship suggests a perspective which was soon to become dominant. His insistence on national citizenship as a separate status derived from national authority by the adoption of the Constitution, was one which had been expressed previously as a minority opinion, but which was to be affirmed decisively by the Fourteenth Amendment.[78]

The Dred Scott decision produced no resolution of the confusion surrounding the status of dual citizenship, and the debate over the primacy of state and national citizenship continued. The tension between these two perspectives was resolved de facto, if not de jure, by the Civil War. The force of arms settled the question in the most ultimate political terms. However, it remained for the Congress, the courts, and the people to translate the results of war into law, constitutional revision and precedent.[79]

Following the Civil War, the first positive step toward the nationalization of citizenship was taken in 1866 when Congress passed the Civil Rights Act on April 9, 1866.[80] The key section of that statute provided:

> That all persons born in the United States and not subject to any foreign power, excluding Indians not taxed, are hereby declared to be citizens of the United States; and such citizens, of every race and color, without regard to any previous condition of slavery or involuntary servitude, except as a punishment for crime whereof the party shall have been duly convicted, shall have the same right, in every State and Territory in the United States, to make and enforce contracts, to sue, be parties, and give evidence, to inherit, purchase, lease, sell, hold, and convey real and personal property, and to full and equal benefit of all laws and proceedings for the security of person and property, as is enjoyed by white citizens, and shall be subject to like punishment, pains, and penalties, and to none other, any law, statute, ordinance, regulation, or custom, to the contrary notwithstanding.[81]

The principle of jus soli, as applied to the entire Union rather than a particular state, was established as the primary determinant of citizenship. Persons born anywhere in the United States were deemed citizens of the nation. State prerogatives had been removed, state citizenship had been clearly separated from national citizenship, and the principle of jus sanguinis had been made a secondary criterion.[82]

Furthermore, the act assigned the responsibility for guaranteeing certain rights previously within the purview of the states to the federal government. Enforcement responsibility and authority were given to federal district courts, United States marshals, and the President, who was authorized to employ "the land or naval forces of the United States, or of the militia" if necessary to enforce the provisions of the act. National citizenship was clearly defined as independent of state citizenship and as transcending the powers of state governments.[83] It should be noted, however, that the rights and privileges guaranteed by the federal government did not include suffrage. That was to be dealt with later.

The Civil Rights Act of 1866 was soon followed by the Fourteenth Amendment to the United States Constitution, approved by the Congress on June 13, 1866 and ratified in July, 1968. It firmly established the main provisions of the Civil Rights Act on Constitutional footing. Section I of the amendment contains key provisions which declare that:

> All persons born or naturalized in the United States, and subject to the jurisdiction thereof, are citizens of the United States and of the State wherein they reside. No State shall make or enforce any law which shall abridge the privileges or immunities of citizens of the United States; nor shall any state deprive any person of life, liberty, or property, without due process of law; nor deny to any person within its jurisdiction the equal protection of the laws.[84]

This language extended the definition of citizenship to include those naturalized by the federal government, as well as those born in the United States. It also dropped the exclusion of Indians found in the Civil Rights Act and provided specific protection from state infringement of the "privileges and immunities" of United States citizens. All United States citizens were guaranteed equality under the law.

Specifying the role of the federal government as guardian of these equally held civil rights of the citizenry over against potential state action was intended to decisively establish the supremacy of national citizenship over state citizenship, and place that relationship beyond the legislative whims of Congress.

As Congressional debates on the amendment reveal, this view of the primacy of national citizenship and the role of the federal government as guarantor of civil rights was not universally held. There were still those who sought to maintain the sovereignty of the states.[85] Although the ratification of the amendment gave evidence of the support for the philosophy it reflected and signaled the ultimate direction of the political tide, defense of the prerogatives of the states died hard.[86]

In fact, five short years after the ratification of the Fourteenth Amendment, the intent of its framers suffered a partial, but significant reversal at the hands of the United States Supreme Court. In a narrow five to four decision in the Slaughter House cases, the court reestablished a distinction between the rights associated with state citizenship and those inherent in national citizenship. In stating the majority opinion, Justice Samuel F. Miller maintained that the first clause of the amendment recognized the existence of two kinds of citizenship: state and national. Then, in clear contradiction of the intent of the framers, he argued that Section I, Clause 2, of the amendment referred only to "privileges or immunities" specifically provided by the federal government in its Constitution, laws, and treaties. In Miller's judgment, Article IV, Section 2 of the Constitution left unchanged those rights traditionally under the purview of the states.[87]

Justice Miller's opinion represented a setback for those who sought to extend national power over the states; however, only a temporary one. As Smith pointed out, the focus of attention in the Slaughter House cases was the "privileges or immunities" clause, which largely neglected the implications of the "due process" and "equal protection" provisions. Smith correctly observed that in these cases the Court "was completely blind" as to how these clauses would impact the future. He concluded that "a great deal of the transfer of control over citizens rights, which the nationalists failed to accomplish through the privileges and immunities clause was accomplished through the due process and equal protection clauses."[88]

However, with respect to dual citizenship, the central issues had been firmly established. Citizenship was primarily that of the United States, achieved either through birth anywhere in the nation, birth to parents who were United States citizens, or through naturalization by federal authority. State citizenship was secondary and essentially a matter of residence.[89] The federal government had assumed responsibility for defining citizenship status in a series of legal actions beginning with Article I, Section 8 of the Constitution and including *Chirac v. Chirac*, the *Louisiana Purchase, Dred Scott v. John F. A. Sanford*, the *Civil War*, the *Civil Rights Act of 1866*, and the Fourteenth Amendment.

NATURALIZATION: THE INTERACTION OF LAW, POLITICAL THEORY, AND THE ETHICAL TRADITION OF CITIZENSHIP

Parallel to the struggle over the primacy of state or national citizenship, and often intertwined with it, was the evolving understanding of naturalization. In practice, naturalization is the *legal means by which one assumes citizenship in a specific political community*. However, the theory of political community and the ethical tradition of citizenship which informed that process determined in large part how naturalization and expatriation were defined in law. Thus, it is possible to discern in the evolution of the legal definition of naturalization the influence of the ethical tradition of citizenship discussed in the previous chapter.

Two Theories of Political Community

In the case of the United States, the dominant theories of political community evolved from British roots. This heritage of the American colonies reflected two perspectives which were extant during the late seventeenth and early eighteenth centuries. These two theoretical viewpoints were in a state of contention within British political and legal thought, and that conflict was carried over into American colonial society. They reflected, respectively, the older feudal tradition of English common law as articulated by Sir Edwin Coke, and the newer contractarian thought of John Locke.

Coke's classic statement on *Calvin's Case*, also known as the *The Case of the Postnati*, was prepared for a specific legal decision in England in 1608.[90] Coke argued that one who is born within the jurisdiction of the king immediately owes "ligeance" or "true and faithful obedience of the subject due to his sovereign."[91] The priority and scope of ligeance to the king was exemplified, according to Coke, by an oath required of every male upon the attainment of his twelfth birthday:

> You shall swear that from this day forward, you shall be true and faithful to our sovereign lord King James, and his heirs, and troth and faith shall bear of life and member, and terrene honour, and you shall neither know nor hear of any ill or damage intended unto him, that you shall not defend. So help you almighty God.[92]

Ligeance was based on a personal relationship to the monarch and was not confined to any particular territorial boundaries.

Coke maintained that the obligation of ligeance to the king was not based on human legal convention or consent, but rather it was required "by the law of nature." This natural law was "infused into the heart of the creature at the time of his creation." It was also incorporated into the law of England: "The law of nature is part of the law of England." Also, since natural law was "immutable," the relationship of ligeance to the King was then, beyond human manipulation. To withhold or modify ligeance would violate the natural law, the law of England, and the subject's own human nature.[93] This perpetual ligeance remained even if the subject left the territorial domain of the king, or if the king's territory were conquered by another monarch.

The king on the other hand, was also compelled by the law of nature to provide a kind of paternal protection for the subject. The ligeance relationship was "the mutual bond and obligation between the king and his subjects" which required the subjects to "obey and serve" and the lord to "maintain and defend" in perpetuity.[94] It is important to emphasize that from this perspective the dual and reciprocal obligations of king and subjects were not grounded in consent by either party.[95]

The other view of the political community that was current in both England and the American colonies reflected to a great degree the more recent ideas of John Locke.[96] Writing in 1689, Locke began with quite different assumptions about the political community. He argued that since men are all creatures of God who are sent into the world to carry out his work, it is logical that they are all equal and free from bonds to each other. In the state of nature no one is subordinate to any other. Under these circumstances "all the power and jurisdiction is reciprocal, no one having more than another."[97]

However, Locke maintained that this state of nature was governed by the law of nature which is reason. The natural law of reason teaches human beings that since all are created as equal and independent beings "no one ought to harm another in his Life, Health, Liberty, or Possessions." Furthermore, Locke argued, when anyone violates this natural law in the state of nature "everyone has the Executive Power" to punish the transgressor.[98]

In order to escape the inconvenience and insecurity of leaving enforcement of the law of reason in the hands of each individual, human beings in a state of nature decided to form political communities which bore the attributes of civil society. This was done through a compact based on mutual consent to delegate to the community the executive power of the law of nature, which each possessed equally. This political community then

> comes to be Umpire, by settled standing Rules, indifferent, and the same to all Parties; and by men having Authority from the Community, for the execution of those Rules, decides all the differences that may happen between any Members of that Society, concerning any matter of right and punishes those Offenses, which any member hath committed against the Society, with such penalties as the Law has established.[99]

Thus, the establishment of a political community led to the establishment of a civil society with a governmental structure reflecting the consent of the majority of the community. Since absolute monarchy was imposed rather than created by consent and voluntary resignation of the individual executive power of the natural law, it was deemed inconsistent with the concept of civil society. No man could be legitimately "subjected to the Political Power of another, without his own Consent."[100]

It logically followed according to Locke's line of thought that governments as constructs of a political community intended to serve certain ends, might be dissolved if they no longer served those ends. It should be clear, that dissolution of a particular government was not tantamount to dissolving the community; the social compact remained. The community was usually dissolved only by conquest from outside, in which case its government could no longer remain, since government is a reflection of the community's interests and dependent upon its support. On the other hand, the community was prior to, and independent of, any particular governmental structure or set of officials.[101]

Governments were dissolved from within when they ceased to serve the ends for which they were established. This might occur as a result of several kinds of destructive events. The legislative function might cease to function, or it might make laws that have not been authorized by the people or that do not protect their interests. The executive power of government, responsible for carrying out laws duly adopted by the legislative power, might neglect to do so, or may act "contrary to his Trust." Furthermore, either the legislative or the executive powers of government might deliver "the People into the subjection of a Foreign Power." When this occurred, "the end why People entered into Society, being to be preserved one intire, free, independent Society, to be governed by its own Laws" was lost.[102]

In short, when government violated its trust in a significant manner, its basis for legitimacy was destroyed and the members of the political community had a right to alter or replace it. The relationship of government to the political community was fiduciary in nature; government's only reason for existence was its role as trustee for the community. When that appointed role was subverted or abdicated, "the trust must necessarily be forfeited, and the Power devolve into the hands of those that gave it, who may place it anew where they shall think best for their safety and security."[103] This might involve constitutional revision or even revolution.

It was only when a prolonged pattern of violations of the trust was perceived by the people that the executive power of the law of nature might be reclaimed by the political community, itself, rather than by individuals.[104] As long as the political community continued to exist the compact remained in effect.[105]

Individuals might, however, according to Locke, withdraw from a political community and join another, if their consent to the social compact was only tacit in nature. So long as they lived within the jurisdiction of the community and enjoyed the protection of its government they might be assumed to have consented tacitly to the compact and were bound to the will of the majority of the community. Any such individual might not withdraw his consent while continuing to reside within the bounds of the community, but was, of course, free to "go and incorporate himself into any other Commonwealth, or to agree with others to begin a new one—in any part of the World, they can find free and unpossessed."[106]

If one participated in an "actual agreement" and consented by "any express Declaration," that person was "perpetually and indispensably obliged to be and remain unalterably a Subject to it and can never be again in the liberty of the state of Nature." The only exceptions to this rule were the calamitous dissolution of the government under which the person lived, and the possibility of being cut off from membership in the community by some public act. Under either of these circumstances anyone was at liberty to join another community and transfer consent to its social compact and government.[107]

A comparison of these two perspectives on political community exemplified by Coke on the one hand and Locke on the other reveal some common assumptions, but more significantly, a number of strong divergences in viewpoint. If we begin with the state of nature we find that both affirmed the existence of a natural law for the "ordering" of human society. Beyond that point, there was a rapid parting of the ways.

In Coke's view the natural law established kings as rulers and the people as subjects under his dominion. Locke on the other hand, argued that the law of nature gave each person the right to interpret the law of nature through reason. Individuals were bound to that law, but retained the prerogative to rationally interpret its meaning.

It followed from these divergent views of the state of nature that Coke and Locke understood the bonds which provide cohesion for a political community in quite dissimilar ways. For Coke, it was the personal link that existed vertically between king and subjects that bound society together, according to natural law. In Locke's case, the political bonds consisted of the voluntary horizontal commitments entered into by free, equal, consenting individuals on the basis of their ability to rationally apprehend the natural law and establish social compacts consistent with its dictates.

The status of government further reflects the conflicting viewpoints of these two men. In Coke's political theory, one particular form of government—monarchy—was consistent with natural law. It was considered to be immutable and eternal. In contrast, Locke viewed government as a convention developed among the members of each political community. In the British feudal tradition, people were expected to be obedient subjects of government, but by Locke's view, the role of government was to obediently and faithfully carry out the wishes of the people.

The implications of these two philosophical perspectives for naturalization and expatriation are apparent. In Lockean thought these were no more than the processes associated with joining or terminating membership in a political community. There was considerable flexibility and latitude in the transfer of one's consent from one community to another. For Coke, allegiance was not under the control of the individual, but was claimed by the king according to natural law. One's birth established political identity within an established natural order.

When we turn to the American colonies it is possible to discern both these perspectives in the treatment of naturalization. Legally and officially Coke's philosophy and the precedent of *Calvin's Case* were still the touchstones for British courts.[108] However, a combination of distance from England, conditions on the American continent, and the experience of the settlers set in motion a gradual erosion of traditional theories and the adoption of the consensual and contractual ideas of the later seventeenth century. The need to attract population to those sparsely inhabited territories made naturalization a compelling public policy issue. This urgency was conducive to deviation from official procedures when they were too restrictive, inflexible, or slow.[109]

In England there were two methods by which aliens could become naturalized British subjects. The first of these involved parliamentary acts of naturalization which could be passed for specific individuals granting them full rights of subjectship. The second method was through royal patents approved by the king, again on an individual basis, but providing only limited rights of residence and property ownership. Since from the beginning England sought to retain political control of its subjects, the colonies were not permitted to create British subjects.[110] Those born under the dominion of the king remained his subjects when resettling in the colonies. However, increasing numbers of non-British settlers heightened the problem of naturalization for the colonial governments.[111] Parliamentary acts and royal patents processed in England for individual aliens in the colonies on the other side of the Atlantic made for a slow and cumbersome means of incorporating new members into the growing political community.

As pressure increased for a more expeditious approach to naturalization for colonial settlers, Parliament passed the first general enabling act in 1740. It required seven years of residence in any of the American colonies, without more than two consecutive months of absence. The act also called for applicants to swear an oath of allegiance to the king and profess adherence to the Christian faith before a colonial chief justice, or any other British colonial judge. Furthermore, a certificate was to be submitted with the signatures of two witnesses confirming that the applicant had received the sacrament in a Protestant or Reformed church in the colonies, or Great Britain, during the three months preceding the filing of the application. Jews and Quakers were exempted from the religious provisions of the act, but Roman Catholics were excluded from naturalization altogether.[112]

In addition to this general act, Parliament also passed two special pieces of legislation in 1756 and 1761 which provided naturalization for aliens who served in the colonies' British military services. Both these acts required periods of residency, oaths of allegiance, and participation in the sacrament under Protestant auspices prior to the granting of full subjectship rights.[113]

Alongside this slowly evolving official process of naturalization controlled by Parliament, the colonies began to develop certain practices of their own which did not conform to any uniform policy. From the beginning of settlement in America, the colonists had accepted aliens into their communities without much concern over fine distinctions between local membership in a colony on the one hand, and the status of British subject on the other.[114] It is understandable that in a political environment dominated by British subjects boundaries of this kind might not be clear.

Under agreements negotiated with the British government, a variety of naturalization policies continued in colonial America. These were purely local until 1740, when an act of Parliament was passed which provided an alternative procedure for granting British subjectship to colonial residents through local courts. This policy represented a combination of centrally determined standards and local administration.[115]

Local naturalization continued alongside the act of 1740 until it was banned in 1773 by an order-in-council forbidding colonial governors from approving acts of naturalization. The reaction in the American colonies to this order was one of anger and resentment at having the power to determine membership in a local political community taken away.[116]

As the tension deepened between the colonies and mother country during the 1770s, differing perceptions of the political community and its constituents lay close to the heart of the conflict. Colonial officials in need of immigrants for military security, labor, and the sale of land, easily assumed that they as British subjects in authority had been granted the right to adopt foreigners into the political community.[117] The practical need for rapidly increasing the colonial population led to a more egalitarian understanding of the community and a more uniform approach to admitting members. Kettner observes:

> In America the foreign immigrant's contribution to the welfare of the community—its military security, its economic prosperity, its rapid and sustained growth—was obvious and highly valued. To limit his rights seemed senseless on grounds of both self-interest and of abstract justice.[118]

Experience and theory informed each other, lending credence to the egalitarian, contractual, and consensual emphases of Locke, depriving of validity Coke's notions of political community as derivative of one's personal and subservient relationship with the king. Coke's theoretical formulations may have captured the essential nature of the old feudal community in Britain, but not the voluntary community of the new world. In the colonies, aliens had made conscious decisions to leave their homes and move to the American continent. They had chosen to align themselves with a particular colony and specific settlement in the process giving their consent to certain governmental arrangements and conditions. This experience of community formation in the colonies created tension with the mother country; it reflected the de facto demise of a unitary political community.

When the colonists attempted to provide a legal justification for the rupture in the political community, they resorted to a combination of Lockean and Cokean concepts. First, they proclaimed their adherence to certain "self-evident" truths which had a distinctly Lockean flavor. These included human equality, natural rights, government based on consent, the fiduciary role of government, and the right of the people to withdraw consent when a government no longer served the ends for which it was established. Then, shifting to Coke's formulations, they accused the British king of violating the bond of allegiance established by the law of nature. They declared that "He has abdicated Government here, by declaring us out of his Protection and waging War against us." This was a decidedly Cokean notion. This charge was then made explicit by detailing a "long Train of Abuses and Usurpations," including "obstructing the Laws of Naturalization."

The colonial leadership set aside Coke's argument that subjects were bound by an immutable and perpetual natural law to maintain their allegiance to the king. After demonstrating the king's defalcations, the colonists shifted to the Lockean notion that allegiance involved the *quid pro quo* of a contractual obligation. If one party defaulted on contract terms, the other was released from further obligation.[119]

Following the Declaration of Independence, the authority for naturalization reverted to the newly proclaimed thirteen separate states. There was little concern for defining the nature of citizenship for those who were formerly British subjects. Volitional allegiance was generally assumed and the outward manifestation of that allegiance was support for the revolutionary cause. It was generally recognized that certain rights of the people and emphasis on law was sufficient for informing and shaping the substance of citizenship. This was the tradition of the British limited monarchy.

However, the naturalization of foreigners was more problematic. Procedures for admitting aliens to new political communities were left to the states. Once again, as was the case prior to 1773, a variety of policies emerged among the states.[120] Kettner identifies three common features in the naturalization requirements among the states which are significant for understanding what was generally assumed about membership in the political community. The first is that applicants were expected to publicly affirm their allegiance to the American states, and in some states they were required to repudiate all foreign loyalties. The second typical requirement involved the character of the applicant. States that had adopted general enabling acts often required letters of reference or certificates of sound morals and conduct. Finally, the most pervasive requirement was a stipulated period of residence. In some cases this was for admission to a first stage of citizenship; in others for the granting of full rights of membership in the political community.[121]

Naturalization and Republican Values:
The Legal and Ethical Traditions

General adherence to a residency requirement was highly significant. This was not intended simply as a demonstration of intent to remain in the state. The assumption behind this condition of citizenship was that foreigners needed a period of resocialization for the inculcation of habits, attitudes, and values consistent with self-governance. One could assume that former British subjects either born in England or in the colonies had acquired these republican virtues, but not so with those from other lands. A period of apprenticeship was necessary to assimilate the principles of responsible participation in the community.[122]

It is in this way that we begin to see the interaction between the legal and ethical traditions of citizenship. The law of residency was employed as a means of inculcating the values and principles which constituted the ethical dimensions of citizenship. This concern for the internalization of political values was understandable as a necessary complement to the claim for legal rights. The Lockean approach to government based on consent tended to produce compacts or constitutions which deal more explicitly with the legal rights of the individual citizen than with ethical obligations to the community. The natural law expressed through reason was more assumed, or mentioned abstractly, as a source of moral obligation. The alien learned how to discern obligations in specific situations only implicitly through life in the community over time. Without the assimilation of values and principles of the ethical tradition of citizenship which evoke a sense of obligation to the community, guided by reason, the assertion of legal rights would assume a disproportionate importance. The exercise of rights had to be conditioned by a commitment to civic virtue.

The acquisition and maintenance of these values and norms associated with the tradition of "ethical" citizenship will be dealt with at greater length in the next chapter, but it is impossible to separate the treatment of the evolving legal provisions for naturalization from an acknowledgment of the influence of the ethical tradition of citizenship.

The Articles of Confederation did not address directly the process of naturalization. This responsibility remained with the individual sovereign states. Only indirectly through the provision for reciprocity was naturalization effected by the document. The most significant implication of the indirect treatment of naturalization through Article IV of the Articles of Confederation was that there was some larger political community which transcended the legally defined boundaries of the thirteen smaller political communities called states. Aliens naturalized in one of these communities were "entitled to all the privileges and immunities of free citizens of all of the others." A sense of community encompassed all thirteen states, stemming from the common political heritage of Great Britain. Inchoate mutual identification ultimately led to a tightening of bonds among the states, and realization took place that admission to a larger shared political community must have priority.

The next step came with the adoption of the United States Constitution which granted Congress the power "To establish an uniform Rule of Naturalization."[123] The generally accepted assumption of the constitutional framers was that naturalization was still conducted and granted by the individual states. This delegation of authority to establish standard qualifications reflected a growing recognition and formalization of the significance of the political community of American states, joined by common geography, mutual interests, and shared political values.

The notion that all states held in common the most important political values, were elements of a larger community, and had a shared ethical tradition, was not universally supported. In fact, strong opposition was expressed by anti-federalist spokespersons during the process of ratifying the constitution. Herbert Storing observed that the anti-federalists held strongly to a belief in the importance of values as the foundation of self-government. He explained that, in their opinion, republican government depended "on civic virtue, on a devotion to fellow citizens and to country so deeply instilled as to be almost as automatic and powerful as the natural devotion to self-interest."[124] This general opinion concerning shared values was not inconsistent with that of the supporters of the proposed constitution. However, a parting of ways emerged over the scale of government at which it would be possible to maintain these values in a coherent fashion.

The anti-federalists insisted that the values of the political community must be homogeneous if they were to be sustained continuously, and if they were to effectively inform the governmental process. One typical anti-federalist, using the pen name *Brutus*, wrote in the *New York Journal* on October 18, 1787:

> In a republic, the manners, sentiments, and interests of the people should be similar. If this be not the case, there will be a constant clashing of opinions; and the representatives of one part will be continually striving against those of the other. This will retard the operations of government, and prevent such conclusions as will promote the public good.[125]

This commitment to homogeneity led in turn to a conviction that the political community must be organized on the scale of *small republics* such as the individual states. Beyond that size, homogeneity of values would be increasingly difficult to maintain.

Given these assumptions, it was logical for anti-federalists to insist that the states, as proper *schools of citizenship*, set the qualifications for membership in the political community and control the process of naturalization. This was especially true with respect to the admission of foreigners, who were viewed as a threat to the purity and similarity of the community's values.[126] For this reason, *Agrippa* and others, during the public debate on the ratification of the constitution, expressed a general reluctance to provide for the naturalization of foreigners at any level and strongly opposed giving this power to the national government.[127] Control of naturalization by Congress, they believed, would make it impossible for each state to preserve its own homogeneous value system since that body would reflect the diversity of the various states.

It seems clear from the anti-federalist literature that misgivings about the dominant federalist perspective arose not over a disagreement about the necessity for homogeneity of all values, but from different perceptions about the extent to which the thirteen states held in common the *most important* political principles. The authors and supporters of the proposed constitution assumed that the states shared a tradition of self-government based on consent, republican in form and limited in its powers, which flowed both from their common British origins and the colonial experience. This uniform ethical tradition was viewed as essential to the larger political community; recognized first by the Articles of Confederation, and more formally in the Constitution. However, anti-federalists such as *Brutus* saw things differently:[128]

> The United States includes a variety of climates. The productions of the different parts of the union are very variant, and their interests, of consequence, diverse. Their manners and habits differ as much as their climates and productions; and their sentiments are by no means coincident.[129]

In this view, the diversity of values and traditions among the states was more prominent than their commonality. Behind this perception was not simply an adherence to the importance of homogeneity for the maintenance of a political community; it was rather commitment to "likeness of a certain kind." Storing described the anti-federalist social ideal as "a society in which there are no extremes of wealth, influence, education, or anything else—the homogeneity of a moderate, simple, sturdy and virtuous people." In contrast to the federalist assumption of self-interest, their vision of the community was one whereby devotion to one's fellow citizens and to community, was as intense and spontaneous as one's concern for self-interest.[130] Recognizing that this particular vision of the homogeneous community was not universally compelling, the anti-federalists were justified in perceiving the regulation of naturalization by Congress as a threat.

A belief in the political necessity for homogeneous values led to a concern on the part of both federalists and anti-federalists about naturalized citizens holding office. During the constitutional debates, both camps supported unequal treatment of former aliens in establishing qualifications for election to Congress and the presidency. It was generally agreed that at least some minimum period of citizenship was desirable prior to national election in order to assure some degree of socialization into the political community. At issue was the proper length of prior citizenship, and the battle lines were not drawn neatly along federalist/anti-federalist lines.

Fear that the foreign born might subvert or distort the existing political consensus, evident throughout the debate on citizenship requirements for the House and Senate, came to a head in a discussion of the presidency.[131] The initial committee report had not recommended a requirement of prior citizenship for the chief executive office, however, a subsequent committee did propose a period of twenty years.[132] This was later changed by a third committee to the present stipulation which states that "No person except a natural born citizen or a citizen of the United States at the time of the adoption of this Constitution shall be eligible to the office of President."[133] As Kettner observed, this prohibition from the Presidency was "the only explicit constitutional limitation" on the potential rights of naturalized citizens.[134] Excepting this, naturalized citizens became full members of the political community.[135]

When we review the legislative treatment of naturalization by Congress following the ratification of the Constitution, three significant patterns are discernible. First, there was a continuing and increasing concern for the proper socialization of the foreign born through a requirement of residency. The first Congressional attempt to establish a uniform rule, the Naturalization Act of 1790, required two years of residence within the United States, at least one year of which had to occur within a single state.[136] Growing apprehension regarding the impact of foreign immigrants led to an extension of the residency qualification to five years in the Act of 1795, and fourteen years in the Act of 1798.

This drastic increase in pre-naturalization residency was attributable to two related but distinct motivations within the Congress. The revision from two to five years in 1795 was largely the result of bipartisan concern for the effects of the waves of refugees from European conflicts following the French Revolution in the early 1790s. Opponents of the French targeted French sympathizers, radicals, and reformers within their own boundaries for repression, sending many into flight from persecution. James Morton Smith described the result for the American states:

> The neutral United States immediately became the haven of refugees. To its shores came discontented Englishmen, aristocratic Frenchmen, German pietists fleeing forced military service, French planters escaping from West Indian uprisings led by Toussaint L'Ouverture, and Irishmen in flight from British repression.[137]

Both Federalists and Democratic-Republicans feared the rapid citizenship of immigrants in large numbers. The Federalists were apprehensive about an influx of democratic reformers, while the Democratic-Republicans were concerned about the aristocratic element among refugees. Five years of residence in the United States seemed to provide a reasonable period of reorientation for both these types of immigrants.

Smith argued that the motivation behind a further increase to fourteen years of residency in 1798 was "a political maneuver by the Federalists designed to cut off an increasingly important source of Republican strength." The Democratic-Republicans had attracted the majority of new foreign immigrants to its ranks, and rebellion in 1798 against the British in Ireland promised to add even greater numbers to those who opposed the Federalist administration. Fearing the political impact of these potential recruits for the opposition party, the more conservative Federalists sought to curtail immigration and discourage naturalization by imposing the four-teen-year period for qualification, five years of which had to occur in the state in which the applicant sought citizenship admission.[138]

The presidential election of Jefferson in 1800 led to reversal of highly restrictive requirements of the Act of 1798. Jefferson attacked its provisions in the opening session of Congress in December, 1801. The Naturalization Act of 1802, restoring the five year residency required by the Act of 1795, was passed quickly and signed into law in April, 1802.[139]

It should be noted that even Jefferson's Democratic-Republicans who had most to gain in political support from the citizenship admission of large numbers of foreigners did not abolish the residency requirement altogether; they maintained it at five years. Although the exaggerated requirements of the Act of 1798 may have been primarily an expression of political games-manship, there was a generally shared concern for adequate inculcation of republican virtues and attitudes through a period of apprenticeship in the political community. Congressional debates on these pieces of legislation reveal a range of attitudes from total opposition to the admission of foreign-ers, to the slightly more restrained belief for the necessity of long periods of residency on the order of nine to fourteen years, to the rather mild, practical judgment that some minimal period of living in the United States would be beneficial prior to citizenship status.[140]

It is clear that the legal definitions of American citizenship were never viewed in isolation from an ethical tradition of citizenship. That ethical tradition was never formally prescribed by law, but nevertheless was as-sumed to be of fundamental importance. Consequently one must hold these two dimensions of the citizenship role together in order to adequately repre-sent the citizenship tradition of the United States.

The adoption of five years of residency prior to naturalization that has prevailed as the standard to this day, reflects not only a compromise among those who wanted more and those who wanted less, but also a largely unques-tioned assumption that the values and traditions of the political community of the United States are as essential as the formal written documents which form, structure, and bind the government. These must be learned and inter-nalized over time, through experience, and the intensity of social interaction that is possible only through residence in the community.

A second pattern of development which is detectable in the first four naturalization acts is an increasing preoccupation with formal certifications of character, allegiance, and adherence to republican government. Although a period of residence was deemed to be the best assurance of consent to the core values of the social compact, through these dozen years provisions requiring formal evidence of worthiness for admission to citizenship were multiplied. In the Act of 1790 the applicant was simply required to submit proof of good character and take an oath to support the Constitution of the United States.[141] Five years later in the Act of 1795, a prospective citizen was required to sign a *declaration of intent* to apply for naturalization, and a statement renouncing all other allegiances three years before becoming a citizen. At the time of admission he or she had to take an oath of support for the Constitution and cast off all other allegiances. Evidence of good character had to be submitted to the court and all titles of nobility had to be renounced.[142] These remained the same in the Act of 1798 except for the declaration of intent which was extended to five years prior to naturalization.

Under the Jefferson administration there was no simplification of these formal certifications of republican virtue. The Act of 1802 retained a declaration of intent three years before naturalization along with a renunciation of other allegiances at that time. When the time for naturalization arrived, the applicant was still required to take an oath of support for the Constitution, renounce titles of nobility, and repudiate foreign allegiances. The Act of 1802 required the court, as before, to certify that the applicant was of good moral character, but in addition was instructed to gain satisfaction that he or she was "attached to the principles of the constitution of the United States, and well disposed to the good order and happiness of the same."[143]

This resorting to more and more formal evidence and certification of worthiness for citizenship seems consistent with the tendency to lengthen residence requirements during this period. They both amounted to defensive reactions intended to preserve a consensus concerning core values of the political community. Both formal and informal means of assuring commitment to republican virtues, consent to the principles of the Constitution, and loyalty to the United States were adopted and expanded.

Thus in a process of evolution during the first thirteen years of the new government the values and concerns which had been prominent in anti-federalist criticism of the new constitution began to surface again. These convictions about the need for homogeneity of values and the importance of good character came to be shared by a larger proportion of the political community as a rising tide of foreign immigration was perceived as a threat to the status quo. Apprehension continued to grow through the first half of the nineteenth century as immigration rates rose sharply and the number of alien paupers seeking refuge in the United States increased noticeably.

This mounting antipathy towards admitting large numbers of immigrants finally found an organized expression in the establishment of the *Native American Association* on July 11, 1837. This organization called for the repeal of the naturalization law and the revocation of all naturalization since, according to Franklin, the existing policy was thought to be "weakening the attachments of natives, and could gain only a sordid allegiance from foreigners."[144] The association adhered to a belief that government from top to bottom should be in the hands of Native Americans and that no political privileges should be granted to aliens without a lengthy period of residence.[145] Memorials were submitted to Congress urging a requirement of twenty-one years of residence in order to qualify for naturalization. Petitions of this kind increased in number through the 1850s as immigration spiraled, but with no success.[146]

A third pattern in the first four naturalization acts was that any alien who was "a free white person" was eligible for admission, subject to meeting the other requirements. Whatever the situation might have been for blacks born within the United States, it was clear that alien persons of color were explicitly excluded from adoption into the political community under these pieces of legislation, even if they were not slaves. This exclusion remained in effect until 1878, when Section 2169 of the *Revised Statutes of the United States* stipulated that "The provisions of this Title shall apply to aliens [being free white persons, and to aliens] of African nativity and to persons of African descent."[147]

Following the *Naturalization Act of 1802*, issues concerning the equality of rights between native born and naturalized citizens emerged again as they had during the debates on the Constitution. The first action occurred in the Congress in 1816 while the House, sitting as *Committee of the Whole*, was considering a bill on the national bank. A motion was offered by Randolph of Virginia, limiting the eligibility for directors of the bank to native citizens. The motion was initially approved, but subsequently attacked by Calhoun who objected that the Constitution recognized no such distinctions except with respect to the presidency. The provision was defeated by a vote of forty-four to sixty-seven on the floor of the House.[148]

The final resolution of the issue of equality of rights passed from Congress to the courts during the 1820s. In 1815, the New York Supreme Court had found that a naturalized citizen could not be tried as an enemy spy, but might be charged with treason.[149] However the most decisive and authoritative decision on the general issue of equality was handed down by the United States Supreme Court in 1824, in Osborn v. Bank of United States. In the majority opinion Chief Justice John Marshall declared:

> A naturalized citizen is indeed made a citizen under an act of Congress, but the Act does not proceed to give, to regulate, or to prescribe his capacities. He becomes a member of the society, possessing all the rights of a native citizen, and standing, in the view of the constitution, on the footing of a native. The constitution does not authorize Congress to enlarge or abridge those rights. The simple power of the national legislature, is to prescribe a uniform rule of naturalization, and the exercise of this power exhausts it, so far as respects the individual. . . . He is distinguishable in nothing from a native citizen, except so far as the constitution makes the distinctions. The law makes none.[150]

Thus membership in the political community achieved through naturalization was definitively established on all but equal footing. The only disparity in status was eligibility for the highest elective office, which was not a significant political disability for the vast majority of naturalized citizens.

CONCLUSION: LEGAL CITIZENSHIP, ETHICAL CITIZENSHIP, AND PUBLIC ADMINISTRATION

This review of the evolution of legal citizenship in the United States leads to several concluding observations which are relevant to the task of defining the normative ethical foundations for American public administration:

1. *If citizenship is to be understood as the normative basis for public administration ethics, the point of reference is most fundamentally national citizenship.* By the last quarter of the nineteenth century, the legal consensus was that the fundamental political community was not state or local, but the larger national community. Citizenship at the state level was not abandoned by any means, but was understood by that time to be *derived from* and *subordinate to* one's rights and obligations determined by the national political community.

2. *Although the struggle over the priority of state or national citizenship and the process of naturalization were carried on in the legal arena and assumed concrete legal forms, the underlying conflict and resolution involved differing sets of political and social values.* The underpinnings of the legal resolution were agreements reached about shared interests, values, culture, and political philosophy. This can be seen most clearly in the development of naturalization law, as the resolution of contending political philosophies concerning the nature of a citizen's rights and obligations in a political community was expressed in legal terms.

3. *It then follows that a full understanding of citizenship in the United States must include both legal and ethical traditions, but the ethical must be assigned primary importance.* The legal forms are important, not as full and final content of citizenship, but only as means of focusing attention on the more fundamental evolution of a stream of values and principles which give essential shape and content to the role of citizen. Specific laws, in and of themselves, give little direct insight into the deeper ethical process of conflict and resolution.

4. *Public administration, then, should seek its normative ethical identity in this evolving ethical tradition of citizenship.* It is this tradition which reveals the subtlety and texture as well as the theoretical grounding of the rights and obligations of citizenship which are entrusted to the public administrator as fiduciary citizen. For example, by examining the conflict and resolution of values and principles underlying the priority of national citizenship, the public administrator can comprehend more fully the obligation to uphold a set of broader national rights and obligations of the citizen over any more limited and provincial views which might be asserted by local authorities and vested interests. Similarly, reflection upon the development of naturalization law illuminates the Lockean theory of political community underlying the dominant United States perspective. It is clear from this perspective that any fiduciary of the citizenry is *ultimately* obligated to uphold the sovereignty of the people, rather than the sovereignty of any given set of political leaders or administrative authorities.

We will now move on to examine the ethical tradition of American citizenship and its implications for public administration ethics in the following chapters.

REFERENCES

1. JAMES H. KETTNER, *The Development of American Citizenship, 1608–1870* (Chapel Hill, North Carolina: University of North Carolina Press, 1978), p. 65.
2. These are discussed in the second section of this chapter on naturalization.
3. KETTNER, *The Development of American Citizenship*, p. 219. *See also* ROGER HOWELL, *The Privileges and Immunities of State Citizenship* (Baltimore: Johns Hopkins Press, 1918), pp. 10–13.
4. ROBERT FRANCIS SEYBOLT, *The Colonial Citizen of New York City* (Madison, Wisconsin: University of Wisconsin Press, 1918) pp. 3, 28.
5. *See Declaration of Independence*, concluding paragraph.
6. A report of a commission established by the 59th Congress (1906–1907) asserts that "There can be no doubt that they described the holders as citizens of the State issuing the passport and that they were given to naturalized as well as native citizens." The report goes on to remind the reader that, since 1789, passports issued by the Secretary of State have always stated that the persons described were citizens of the United States. . . ." United States House of Representatives, 59th Congress, second session, document no. 326, *Citizenship of the United States: Expatriation and Residence Abroad* (Washington, D.C.: 1906), p. 9.
7. Discussed in the second section of this chapter on naturalization.
8. KETTNER, *The Development of American Citizenship*, p. 213.
9. Quoted in Frank George Franklin, *The Legislative History of Naturalization in the United States From the Revolutionary War to 1861* (Chicago: University of Chicago Press), p. 2.
10. *Ibid.* and KETTNER, *The Development of American Citizenship*, p. 179, 219.
11. KETTNER, *The Development of American Citizenship*, p. 219.
12. HOWELL, *The Privileges and Immunities*, p. 13 and KETTNER, *The Development of American Citizenship*, p. 219.
13. *Articles of Confederation.* Widely available.
14. GEORGE BANCROFT, *History of the United States of America* (New York: D. Appleton and Co., 1885), pp. 206–207.
15. DUANE DOUGLAS SMITH, "The Evolution of the Legal Concept of Citizenship in the United States" (Unpublished Ph.D. dissertation, Ohio State University, 1936), pp. 11–12.
16. KETTNER, *The Development of American Citizenship*, p. 221; FRANKLIN, *The Legislative History of Naturalization*, pp. 14–15; HOWELL, *The Privileges and Immunities*, pp. 13–14.
17. ALEXANDER HAMILTON, JAMES MADISON, AND JOHN JAY, *The Federalist Papers* (New York: New American Library, 1961), pp. 269–270.
18. *See* SMITH, "The Evolution of the Legal Concept," pp. 8–11 on the use of these terms. *See also* KETTNER, *The Development of American Citizenship*, p. 221n for comments on this terminology, and pp. 79, 83, 87–89, for a discussion of "freemanship" as analogous to "citizenship" in the colonial era.
19. KETTNER, *The Development of American Citizenship*, p. 224.
20. *Ibid., See* chapter 7, "The Idea of Volitional Allegiance" pp. 173–209, for a full discussion of the theoretical underpinnings of this perspective. *See* pp. 183–184 on the particular point treated here.
21. JOHN P. ROCHE, *The Early Development of United States Citizenship* (Ithaca: Cornell University Press), pp. 3–4.
22. JAMES MADISON, *The Federalist Papers*, p. 270. *See* KETTNER, *The Development of American Citizenship*, pp. 214–218 and United States House of Representatives, *Citizenship of the United States*, pp. 8–9, for examples of variations among the states.
23. FRANKLIN, *The Legislative History of Naturalization*, p. 18. *See also* KETTNER, *The Development of American Citizenship*, p. 221n for a specific case citation.
24. *See* discussion of Bayard v. Singleton and Camp v. Lockwood in KETTNER, *The Development of American Citizenship*, pp. 222–224.
25. *Secret Journals of the Acts and Proceedings of Congress, From the First Meeting Through to the Dissolution of the Confederation, By The Adoption of the Constitution of The United States.* Volume I (Boston: Thomas B. Wait, 1821), pp. 258–259.
26. *See* Madison's summary of Randolph's views in JAMES MADISON, *Notes of Debates in the Federal Convention of 1787* (Athens, Ohio: Ohio University Press, 1976), p. 31, on the general role of the national legislature. See also p. 128 for a specific reference to naturalization and p. 121 for discussion of William Patterson's "New Jersey Plan."

27. ROCHE, *The Early Development*, pp. 5–6; KETTNER, *The Development of American Citizenship*, pp. 224–225.
28. SMITH, "The Evolution of the Legal Concept," pp. 14–15.
29. *See* HOWELL, *The Privileges and Immunities*, pp. 16–104, for a review of court cases dealing with the comity clause.
30. Quoted in *Ibid.*, p. 33.
31. FRANKLIN, *The Legislative History of Naturalization*, pp. 33–38.
32. *United States Statutes at Large*, Volume I. Richard Peters, ed. (Boston: Little, White, Brown and Co., 1853), pp. 103–104. *See also* FRANKLIN, *The Legislative History of Naturalization*, p. 48.
33. *United States Statutes at Large*, Volume I, pp. 414–415.
34. FRANKLIN, *The Legislative History of Naturalization*, pp. 68–70.
35. ROCHE, *The Early Development*, p. 11.
36. FRANKLIN, *The Legislative History of Naturalization*, pp. 67–68.
37. ROCHE, *The Early Development*, p. 11.
38. *United States Statutes at Large*, Volume I, pp. 566–569.
39. FRANKLIN, *The Legislative History of Naturalization*, pp. 92–93.
40. *United States Statutes at Large*, Volume I, p. 567.
41. ROCHE, *The Early Development*, p. 12.
42. *United States Statutes at Large*, Volume I, pp. 153–155; FRANKLIN, *The Legislative History of Naturalization*, pp. 97–109; ROCHE, *The Early Development*, p. 14.
43. KETTNER, *The Development of American Citizenship*, p. 248.
44. For a more detailed and comprehensive review of this history *See* SMITH, "The Evolution of the Legal Concept," chapters 3, 5, 6, and 7. *See also* KETTNER, *The Development of American Citizenship*, chapter 9.
45. Collet v. Collet, 2 Dallas, 294 (United States 1792).
46. KETTNER, *The Development of American Citizenship*, p. 329.
47. Chirac v. Chirac, 2 Wheaton, 259, (United States 1817).
48. *United States Statutes at Large*, Volume I, p. 414.
49. KETTNER, *The Development of American Citizenship*, pp. 249–250.
50. *Ibid.*, p. 250.
51. ROCHE, *The Early Development*, p. 1, 2.
52. *See* EVERETT SOMERVILLE BROWN, *The Constitutional History of the Louisiana Purchase, 1803–1812* (Berkeley: University of California Press, 1920), for a detailed discussion of these constitutional issues.
53. United States House of Representatives, 57th Congress, second session, *State Papers and Correspondence Bearing Upon the Purchase of the Territory of Louisiana*, document no. 34 (Washington, D.C.: U.S. Government Printing Office, 1903), p. 254.
54. BROWN, *The Constitutional History*, chapters 4 and 5.
55. Unites States House of Representatives, *State Papers and Correspondence*, "Articles of Exchange of Possession," p. 286.
56. SMITH, "The Evolution of the Legal Concept," pp. 76–77; Kettner, *The Development of American Citizenship*, pp. 13–15.
57. 1 Peters, 511 (United States 1828)
58. *See* KETTNER, *The Development of American Citizenship*, p. 253, for other applications of this principle.
59. WILLIAM W. FREEHLING. *Prelude to Civil War, The Nullification Controversy in South Carolina, 1816–1836* (New York: Harper & Row, 1966), pp. 311–321.
60. FRANKLIN, *The Legislative History of Naturalization*, chapter 9. Expatriation is the opposite process concerning one's rights to abrogate the obligations of political allegiance. Length considerations will not permit a treatment of the evolution of expatriation theory and practice in this text; instead the reader is referred to I-MIEN TSIANG, *The Question of Expatriation in America Prior to 1907* (Baltimore: Johns Hopkins Press, 1942) and United States House of Representatives, 59th Congress, *Citizenship of the United States: Expatriation and Residence Abroad.*
61. *Ibid.*, pp. 260–263.
62. Scott v. Sanford, 19 Howard, 393 (United States 1857). *See* DON E. FEHRENBAHER, *The Dred Scott Case, Its Significance in American Law and Politics* (New York: Oxford University Press, 1978), for a comprehensive analysis of the case; in particular chapter 15 for a critical analysis of Taney's decision.
63. Scott v. Sanford, p. 407.

64. *Ibid.*, pp. 409–410.
65. *Ibid.*, pp. 411–412.
66. *Ibid.*, pp. 572–575. As Justice Curtis noted—"at the time of the ratification of the Articles of Confederation, all free native-born inhabitants of the States of New Hampshire, Massachusetts, New York, New Jersey, and North Carolina, though descended from African slaves were not only citizens of those States, but such of them as had the other necessary qualifications possessed the franchise of electors, on equal terms with other citizens.' Congressman Daniel W. Gooch, in attacking Taney's decision, cited these same states and argued that these facts were generally known. (Pamphlet entitled "The Supreme Court and Dred Scott, Speech of Honorable Daniel W. Gooch of Massachusetts." Delivered in the United States House of Representatives, May 3, 1860. *See also* DAVID M. POTTER, *The Impending Crisis, 1848–1861* (New York: Harper & Row, 1976), p. 275.
67. For example, in arguing that the Constitution itself acknowledged the inferior status of black people, Taney cited two clauses which refer specifically to slaves, not to blacks in general. *See* 19 HOWARD, p. 411; *also* FEHRENBACHER, *The Dred Scott Case*, p. 343.
68. 19 HOWARD, p. 417.
69. 19 HOWARD, p. 426.
70. *Ibid.*, p. 409.
71. FEHRENBACHER, *The Dred Scott Case*, p. 357.
72. *Ibid.*, p. 405.
73. SMITH, "The Evolution of the Legal Concept," p. 98.
74. 19 HOWARD, pp. 578–579, 588.
75. *Ibid.*, pp. 579, 588.
76. *Ibid.*, pp. 572–576.
77. FEHRENBACHER, *The Dred Scott Case*, p. 408.
78. SMITH, "The Evolution of the Legal Concept," p. 109. *See* cases he cites here.
79. KETTNER, *The Development of American Citizenship*, pp. 340–341.
80. ROCHE, *The Early Development*, p. 24; KETTNER, *The Development of American Citizenship*, p. 342.
81. *United States Statutes at Large*, Volume 14, George P. Sanger, ed. (Boston: Little, Brown & Co., 1868), pp. 27–29.
82. ROCHE, *The Early Development*, p. 24. Indians still under tribal authority were excluded on the grounds that they were not regarded as "part of our people." *See* SMITH, "The Evolution of the Legal Concept," pp. 130–131 for a discussion of this provision. *See also* ROCHE, *The Early Development*, pp. 25–26 on this general point. Jus sanguinis had been incorporated into the Naturalization Act of 1855 which provided that persons born outside the United States to fathers who were United States citizens were deemed citizens of the United States. With some minor modifications this principle is still used as secondary source of natural born United States citizenship.
83. KETTNER, *The Development of American Citizenship*, pp. 341–342. *See* SMITH, "The Evolution of the Legal Concept," pp. 125–135 for a summary of the Congressional debates on the issues raised by this act. For an analysis of the debates, *see also* "Our Declaratory Fourteenth Amendment" in HOWARD JAY GRAHAM, *Everyman's Constitution* (Madison: State Historical Society of Wisconsin, 1968), pp. 295–336.
84. ALFRED H. KELLY AND WINIFRED A. HARBISON, *The American Constitution, Its Origins and Development* (New York: W.W. Norton & Co., 1948), appendix 2, p. 857.
85. *See The Reconstruction Amendment Debates* (Richmond: Virginia Commission on Constitutional Government, 1967), especially pp. 150–151, 153–155, 216, 223–224.
86. *Ibid.*, *See*, for example, debates on the "Klux Klan" bill in 1871, pp. 492–498.
87. SMITH, "The Evolution of the Legal Concept," pp. 159–163; KETTNER, *The Development of American Citizenship*, pp. 345–348.
88. SMITH, "The Evolution of the Legal Concept," p. 166.
89. KETTNER, *The Development of American Citizenship*, p. 349; Roche, *The Early Development*, p. 26.
90. THOMAS BAYLY HOWELL, ed., *A Complete Collection of State Trials* Volume 2 (London: T.C. Hansard, 1816). The case begins on p. 559; Coke's statement is on p. 607.
91. *Ibid.*, pp. 613–614.
92. *Ibid.*, p. 618. *See also* JAMES H. KETTNER, *The Development of American Citizenship*, pp. 17–18, note no. 18.

93. Howell, *The Privileges and Immunities*, pp. 629–630.
94. *Ibid.*, p. 614.
95. I-MIEN TSIANG, *The Question of Expatriation*, pp. 13–15.
96. FRANK M. COLEMAN'S argument in *Hobbes and America, Exploring the Constitutional Foundations* (Toronto: University of Toronto Press, 1977) that Hobbes' thought was the real guiding philosophy behind the United States Constitution, Locke's work being only a "lackluster" variant of Hobbesian thought, is an issue that transcends the subject of citizenship. Suffice to say for purposes of this discussion that Coleman did not appear to succeed in demonstrating more than the obvious fact that Madison employed certain concepts that were common to both Hobbes and Locke. Coleman ignored or downplayed some significant differences between them which deserve more careful treatment. Also, the Lockean influence on the Declaration of Independence, a highly significant document for the ethical tradition of citizenship, was not dealt with by Coleman. Most disturbing is the fact that although Coleman's citations are from Peter Laslett's edition of Locke's *Second Treatise*, he did not seriously address the formidable case developed by Laslett for no direct or dominant influence of Hobbes on Locke. Laslett argued that the similarity between Hobbes and Locke are the result of only indirect influence. He concluded that there is "an exquisite contrast" between these two philosophers. *See* PETER LASLETT, ed., *Locke's Two Treatises of Government* (London: Cambridge University Press, 1960), in particular pp. 67–78.
97. LASLETT, *Locke's Two Treatises*, pp. 287–289.
98. *Ibid.*, pp. 289–293.
99. *Ibid.*, pp. 341–342.
100. *Ibid.*, pp. 344–349.
101. *Ibid.*, p. 424.
102. *Ibid.*, pp. 425–431.
103. *Ibid.*, pp. 384–385, 389–390, *See also* Laslett's analysis of Locke's use of the terms *contract, compact,* and *trust,* pp. 111–114.
104. *Ibid.*, p. 433.
105. *Ibid.*, pp. 445–446.
106. *Ibid.*, pp. 362–367.
107. *Ibid.*, p. 367.
108. KETTNER, *The Development of American Citizenship*, pp. 9, 45.
109. *Ibid.*, pp. 60, 106.
110. FRANKLIN, *The Legislative History of Naturalization*, p. 17.
111. KETTNER, *The Development of American Citizenship*, p. 66.
112. *Ibid.*, p. 74.
113. *Ibid.*, pp. 76–77.
114. *Ibid.*, p. 83.
115. *Ibid.*, pp. 99–103.
116. *Ibid.*, p. 105.
117. *Ibid.*, pp. 66, 106.
118. *Ibid.*, p. 127.
119. *Ibid.*, pp. 18–19, 165–167.
120. For examples of state legislation *See* United States House of Representatives, 59th Congress, *Citizenship of the United States*, pp. 8–9.
121. KETTNER, *The Development of American Citizenship*, p. 218.
122. *Ibid.*, pp. 218.
123. HERBERT J. STORING, ed., *The Complete Anti-Federalist.* 7 volumes (Chicago: University of Chicago Press, 1981), Volume 1, p. 20.
125. *Ibid.*, Volume 2, p. 369.
126. *Ibid.*, Volume 1, p. 21.
127. *Ibid.*, Volume 4, pp. 85–86, 89. *See also* p. 68 for Storing's observation that "Agrippa" was probably James Winthrop of Massachusetts.
128. CECILIA M. KENYON, ed., *The Antifederalists* (New York: Bobbs-Merrill, 1966), pp. xxiv–xxx.
129. STORING, *The Complete Anti-Federalist*, Volume 2, pp. 369–370.
130. *Ibid.*, Volume 1, p. 20. *See also* KENYON, *The Antifederalists*, p. xxxix, and *The Federalist Papers*, no. 10 on federalist views of self interest.

131. MADISON, *Notes of Debates*, pp. 418–422, 437–442.
132. *Ibid.*, pp. 392–393, 509.
133. *Ibid.*, pp. 575. *See also United States Constitution*, article II, section 1.
134. KETTNER, *The Development of American Citizenship*, p. 230.
135. ALEXANDER BICKEL'S contention in "Citizenship in the American Constitution," 15 *Arizona Law Review*, 370 (1973), that "citizenship was nowhere defined in the original Constitution" because "It was not important" is puzzling when the document is examined within this historical context. At that time, citizenship was largely assumed to be defined in continuity with British subjectship, with its legal determination being almost exclusively a state concern. The implications of naturalizing large numbers of nonBritish aliens were just beginning to emerge as a new and significant problem to be addressed. The federalist/anti-federalist debates over the role of the general government in naturalization and the rights of naturalized citizens were expressions of an ensuing struggle to define the nature of the political community in the face of changing conditions. In times of change, implicit assumptions often require explicit formulation. Traditions become modified as they are replaced with formal policies to account for the new situation. It was not, as Bickel suggests, that citizenship was unimportant, but only that its meaning at the national level was not yet ripe for statement as formal policy. That ripening process occurred through a subsequent series of congressional acts, court decisions, constitutional amendments, and, of course, a civil war. Aside from these broader historical considerations that are essential to an adequate treatment of citizenship and the United States Constitution, there is also evidence that citizenship was important to the framers in the explicit provisions of the document itself. In developing his argument that citizenship was an unimportant concept to the authors of the Constitution, Bickel makes an astonishing statement. He observes that the authors made nothing depend on citizenship explicitly "aside from a few offices: President, Congressman, Senator, but notably not judge." These "few offices" happen to be those of the elected representatives of the citizenry at the national level.
136. *See* FRANKLIN, *The Legislative History of Naturalization*, pp. 34–48, for a summary of the debate.
137. JAMES MORTON SMITH, *The Alien and Sedition Laws and American Civil Liberties* (Ithaca, New York: Cornell University Press, 1956), p. 23.
138. *Ibid.*, See pp. 22–34 for a legislative history of this act.
139. FRANKLIN, *The Legislative History of Naturalization*, pp. 97, 107–109.
140. THOMAS HART BENTON, ed., *Abridgment of the Debates of Congress*. Volume 1 (New York: Appleton, 1857), pp. 184–190. *See also Annals of Congress*. 3rd Congress, 1st session, pp. 1063–1064.
141. *United States Statutes at Large*, Volume 1, pp. 103–104.
142. *Ibid.*, pp. 414–415.
143. *Ibid.*, Volume 2, pp. 153–155.
144. FRANKLIN, *The Legislative History of Naturalization*, p. 191.
145. *Ibid.*, p. 194.
146. *Ibid.*, pp. 198, 215, 247, 278. According to Richmond Mayo Smith, *Emigration and Immigration* (New York: Charles Scribner's Sons, 1890), pp. 41–42, immigration increased from 10–12,000 in the 1820's to 100,000 in 1842, and to 400,000 in 1854.
147. United States House of Representatives, *Citizenship of the U.S.*, p. 182.
148. FRANKLIN, *The Legislative History of Naturalization*, pp. 131–133.
149. KETTNER, *The Development of American Citizenship*, p. 254.
150. United States Supreme Court, 9 Wheaton, section 827, p. 1824.

3
THE AMERICAN TRADITION OF ETHICAL CITIZENSHIP

In the first chapter of this book a distinction was drawn between legal citizenship and ethical citizenship. The proposition was advanced that the ethical foundations of the public administrative role are to be discovered in the tradition of ethical citizenship. It was suggested that in order to adequately understand citizenship in the United States, one must grasp the dynamic interaction between the legal and ethical perspectives as they have unfolded historically. Chapter two outlined the evolution of the legal definitions of citizenship in the United States, and began illustrating the impact of ethical tradition on legal tradition.

In this third chapter, the primary focus shifts to an examination of the ethical traditions of citizenship. The key assumption here is that this informal multichanneled stream of values, principles, beliefs, and ideas has functioned as a healthy corrective force against the relatively low legal perspective of citizenship embodied in the United States Constitution and statutory law. Furthermore, it is in probing and reflecting upon the elements of this tradition that we may arrive at some normative basis for public administration ethics.

THE ETHICAL AND LEGAL TRADITIONS:
TWO SOURCES OF REGIME VALUES

The thesis developed here is that informal traditions associated with ethical citizenship have tended to democratize American governmental institutions by encouraging participation of the citizenry beyond what the Federalists would have thought desirable. In the historical development outlined in chapter two, the power of the ethical tradition is clearly reflected in the impulses, ideas, and values of those who sought to change the legal structures and provisions associated with United States citizenship.

These streams of thought and belief have provided sources of moral obligation to complement the emphasis on rights in the legal definitions of citizenship. By acting upon these inclinations and obligatory feelings in changing both statutory law and the Constitution, citizens have widened the possibilities further for more extensive citizen participation by having more people involved in government. Participation in reform politics has produced much more participation.

The notion that it is important to include both legal and ethical, formal and informal dimensions in order to comprehend adequately the nature of citizenship in the United States is shared by scholars. Martin Diamond has argued that, to fully understand the American regime it is essential to identify the "American idea of what is advantageous and right for humans" or what is "advantageous and just." One finds this idea not in the Aristotelian manner, by examining the laws which are adopted to inculcate virtues, says Diamond, but by looking beyond the law. Since the assumptions behind the architecture of the United States Constitution eschew attempts to change human nature through legal means but are intended to shape the outcomes of collective conduct, one must not depend entirely upon an analysis of the Constitution and its interpretations in order to identify the regime values which inform citizenship.

While this view is shared by others it is to be contrasted with John Rohr's approach in *Ethics for Bureaucrats: An Essay on Law and Values.*[1] Rohr argues that American regime values are best found in the Constitution and its interpretations by the United States Supreme Court. The position adopted here does not amount to a rejection of Rohr's case for regime values as the appropriate basis for public administration ethics, but rather it is an argument for understanding the source of these values more broadly than by what is stated in the Constitution and its interpretation by the Supreme Court. Freedom, equality, and property may well be the abiding values of the Constitution, but they are not exhaustive of the values of the American regime.

As Diamond has suggested, one must immediately place the Declaration of Independence alongside the Constitution, as well as a number of informal elements of the American political regime. He included among these

the Anti-Federalist 'virtuous republic' tradition, or Puritanism with its original high-pitched piety, or the high-toned Anglicanism that long persisted in this country, or vestiges of the English aristocratic tradition, or, more recently, elements derived from powerful intellectual currents in the contemporary world, or from the many other possibilities that crowd into a particular 'idea' in practice.

Consistent with the central argument of this book is Diamond's contention that the function of these informal strands of the American idea can only be understood when they are "seen in tension" with "the principles, institutions, and processes of the Constitution."[2] It is the dynamic interaction between American legal institutions and this informally held ethical tradition of citizenship which has slowly opened government to greater participation and a broader range of participants.

Supreme Court Justice Thurgood Marshall gave forceful expression to this tension between the Constitution and the more democratic values in our ethical tradition with his claim that the original plan for our government was "defective from the start" and took "two turbulent centuries " to correct.[3] He went on to explain that during that time the Civil War and four constitutional amendments (the thirteenth, fourteenth, fifteenth and nineteenth) were required to democratize our legal structure of government.[4]

The argument advanced here is that the pressure for those changes was rooted in several streams of values which have been strong and continuous elements of the American political tradition—regime values not originally embodied in formal constitutional provisions. Joseph Cropsey supported the necessity for this broader approach if the regime values which inform United States citizenship are to be identified and understood. He argued for consulting "the documents of our political life" as well as other sources: "Both together—the Constitution, laws, judicial opinions; and the Declaration of Independence and great public utterances of eminent men—articulate the conception that constitutes the American regime." He maintained that "Regime is what we stand for, the expression of what our goals are. . . ."[5]

Similarly, Loren Beth provided the only adequate way of understanding the Constitution as the source of regime values by maintaining that the appropriate understanding of "constitution" in the United States is the characteristically British view advanced by Lord Bryce in his commentary on late nineteenth century American government:

> He saw the American constitution not merely as the document written in 1787, but as the whole set of written and unwritten rules and practices which govern the way our political system operates. Thus one writer can realistically assert that "it is doubtful whether any mature Constitution can be said to be wholly . written in a legal and authoritative sense."[6]

This chapter will examine these broader foundations of ethical citizenship in the experience of forming voluntary associations, Puritan thought, Antifederalist perspectives, and Jeffersonian ideas.

THE HISTORIC ROOTS OF ETHICAL CITIZENSHIP
IN THE UNITED STATES

The Experience of Citizenship

In the 1830s, Alexis de Tocqueville, a young Frenchman, concluded after nine months of travel in the United States and Canada, that widespread involvement in political affairs through the formation of associations was one of the notable facts of life in America:

> There is only one country on the face of the earth where the citizens enjoy unlimited freedom of association for political purposes. This same country is the only one in the world where the continual exercise of the right of association has been introduced into civil life and where all the advantages which civilization can confer are procured by means of it.[7]

This inclination to form associations for political purposes grew out of shared assumptions about the consensual nature of authority and the voluntary nature of public action, which were consistent with the practical need to solve the common problems of collective life in a frontier setting. Thus, ideas *and* experience, context *and* principle, interacted to produce a uniquely American ethical tradition of citizenship which often went beyond the legal definitions of what it meant to be a citizen.

Tocqueville noted that the citizen of the United States was socialized from infancy to "rely upon his own exertions" and view "social authority with an eye of mistrust and anxiety." Children in school learned to obey rules in their games which they themselves had created. People in America, noted Tocqueville, become accustomed to forming an extemporaneous deliberative body and taking action to deal with such mundane problems as traffic jams. He suggested that this "extemporaneous assembly gives rise to an executive power which remedies the inconvenience before anybody has thought of recurring to pre-existing authority superior to that of the persons immediately concerned."[8]

Tocqueville went on to observe that in politics in the United States "men combine for great undertakings, and the use they make of the principle of association in important affairs *practically* teaches them that it is in their interest to help one another in those of less moment." (Emphasis added.) Thus, in the process of participating in governing themselves citizens learned to think about and work toward the common good. According to Tocqueville, associating in the political process "draws a number of individuals at the same time out of their own circle; however they may be naturally kept asunder by age, mind, and fortune, it places them nearer together and brings them into contact. Once met, they can always meet again."[9]

Voluntary political associations organized around shared ideas, according to Tocqueville, constituted a significant force in the legislative process because they functioned like "a separate nation in the midst of a nation, a government within the government." Although they possessed no official authority, they "have an appearance of nationality and all the moral power that results from it." Tocqueville recognized the significant de facto role of these associations: "It is true that they have not the right, like others, of making the laws; but they have the power of attacking those which are in force and of drawing up beforehand those which ought to be enacted."[10]

Tocqueville acknowledged that the active nature of American citizenship did not always produce the best immediate results. He admitted that, "It is incontestable that the people frequently conduct public business very badly," however he hastened on to observe that the ultimate long-term benefits outweighed particular instances of misjudgment. The reason for this final positive assessment was that "it is impossible that the lower orders should take part in public business without extending the circle of their ideas and quitting the ordinary routine of their thoughts." Citizens learned from the political process in which they involved themselves.[11] Practical experience in the relatively open social and political environment of the United States cultivated democratic habits and served to transmit democratic ideas.

Ralph Barton Perry developed this basic thesis with particular reference to the frontier experience of those who migrated westward to establish new settlements. He observes the ready applicability of Lockean social compact theory to those who traveled across the continent to live in places where no previous government existed.[12] Having no preestablished form of organization, the settlers realized its necessity and set about converting themselves "at once from a mere aggregation of chance arrivals into a political and legal entity." Perry quoted from the journal of one pioneer who described this process:

> After a particular route has been selected to make the journey across the plains, and the requisite number have arrived . . . their first business should be to organize themselves into a company and elect a commander . . . An obligation should then be drawn up and signed by all the members of the association, wherein each one should bind himself to abide in all cases by the orders and decisions of the captain, and to aid him by every means in his power . . . and they should also obligate themselves to aid each other, so as to make the individual interest of each member the common concern of the whole company.[13]

Perry points out that all of the essential elements of social compact theory are present in this kind of agreement.

Schlesinger reported the blossoming of these early experiences of constructing associations throughout the eighteenth and nineteenth centuries. He suggested that the increase in associational activity in America parallels the development of "democratic self-confidence and the greater complexity of social and economic life."[14] Schlesinger concluded that these associations have provided Americans with "their best schooling in self-government." It is through these associations that they have learned how to consult with each other, select leaders, resolve conflict, and accept the will of the majority. Schlesinger maintained that "By comparison, the much-vaunted role of the New England town meeting as a seedbed of popular government seems almost negligible."[15] Although invidious comparisons of this kind miss the more fundamental significance of the similarity of function in cultivating an ethic of citizenship, the importance of experience derived from unofficial voluntary associations is difficult to exaggerate.

Experience *and* ideas are the key ingredients of the American ethic of citizenship. It is to the ideas that we turn next. The material that follows is not intended as an exhaustive intellectual history of ethical citizenship; rather it includes a selection of three bodies of thought that are clearly central to this tradition in the United States: Puritanism, Anti-federalist ideas, and Jeffersonian thought.

The Puritan Perspective on Ethical Citizenship

In November 1620 a band of one hundred two separatist Puritans arrived off the coast of Massachusetts aboard the *Mayflower* after a gale-battered three month crossing of the Atlantic. Having landed north of the territory controlled by the Virginia Company, the patent granted by it was without legal authority. There had also been incidents of rebellion among some of the men while at sea. Therefore in order to establish some basis for orderly existence together, on November eleventh on board ship in Provincetown Harbor the forty-one free adult males among these Pilgrims drew up and signed a brief agreement which we know as the *Mayflower Compact*.[16]

One member of the party explained that "it was thought good there should be an association and agreement that we should combine together in one body, and submit to such government and governors as we should by common consent agree to make and choose, and set our hands to this that follows word for word."[17] What followed were two brief paragraphs modeled on the *covenants* or *combinations* of the Puritan Separatist congregations. After an acknowledgment of loyalty to both God and King James, the Plymouth settlers swore to:

> solemnly and mutually in the presence of God and one of another, covenant, and combine ourselves together into a civil body politic, for our better ordering and preservation, and furtherance of the ends aforesaid; and by virtue hereof to enact, constitute, and frame such just and equal laws, ordinances, acts, constitutions, offices from time to time, as shall be thought most meet and convenient for the general good of the colony: unto which we promise all due submission and obedience.[18]

Heath observed that it is noteworthy that the Puritan concept of self-government stands out so clearly in this document at a time when the divine right of kings was so commonly assumed.[19]

Kendall and Carey reenforced this observation in their analysis of the

Mayflower Compact as the earliest expression of the American political tradition, the central commitment of which is "self-government by a virtuous people." They found there the notions of "just and equal laws," a concern for the general good, the body politic as a deliberative community, and equal consent as a basis for political authority.[20]

Doctrine and Experience

Lawrence Scaff argued that in the United States the language of citizenship originated with Puritanism.[21] He emphasized that it was the combination of *ideas* and *experience* in the Puritan communities of the new world which "produced the novel conception of citizenship as the natural condition of human association, not merely a conferred privilege or abstract principle."

The Puritans in America were confronted with the necessity for improvisation in a colonial setting rather than having to resist the constraints of a traditional society founded on feudalism. It is understandable then, as Scaff points out, that "citizenship came to be viewed as the expected, normal condition of association, rather than as a contractual stipulation or a transformation of human society." Scaff went on to state that, "In this respect, American experience superseded both Locke's formalized contractarianism and Rousseau's utopian vision of civil commitment."[22]

While it is clear that Puritan doctrine, especially that of vocation, was the source of this view of the naturalness of citizenship, it is also evident that the context of the new world was crucial. The colonies provided an opportunity for doctrine and situation to interact with each other to produce the experience of active citizenship.

Puritan theology provided an interpretive framework through which the colonial experience could be understood. Walzer noted that the Puritan "saint" became synonymous with "citizen." He argued that "the same sense of civic virtue, of discipline and duty, lies behind the two names." Walzer maintained that both terms indicate groups of private persons who are integrated into the political order in a new way— "an integration based upon a novel view of politics as a kind of conscientious labor." In sum it can be said that "conscience and work entered the political world together...."[23]

Responsibility for continually reforming and shaping the world was vested in the saints. Political involvement was viewed as a creative activity in which they were privileged and obliged to participate. Walzer indicated that Puritan political activity was based on the assumption that "all subjects were knowledgeable and active citizens rather than naive political children...."[24] Reenforcing this premise was the need to test one's divine election through a vocation. By publicly engaging in good works, the saint might provide a demonstration of God's agency in the world. The political order was the most public arena in which a Puritan vocation might be worked out.[25]

Although the Puritan view of citizenship was linked to these religious beliefs, its logical underpinnings were not necessarily dependent upon adherence to religious doctrine. For example, the 18th century American Puritan John Wise, a transitional figure between earlier Puritan thought and the political philosophy which later informed the American revolution, based his understanding of the relationship of citizens to the state on what he believed to be right reason and observable fact.[26] He argued that it was "obvious to view" that human nature includes a principle of self-love, or self-preservation; a tendency toward sociability and "an affection or love to mankind in general." Through the exercise of reason human beings are led to balance self-love with concern for others and the welfare of society. Perry noted that these grounds for the position developed by Wise had democratic implications of a revolutionary nature because of "their equally valid applications to political institutions."[27]

Wise believed that individuals are capable of distinguishing between their own private interests and the common good, and then choosing the latter. He maintained that it is this ability to deny one's own self-interests for the sake of the common interest which makes it possible for a political community to emerge. Wise explained that all people are equal by the law of nature "till man has resigned himself with all his rights for the sake of a civil state."[28] Thus we enter into a "covenant" to insure that reason prevails, the common good is upheld, and "public rule and order" are maintained.

The concept of covenant was of central importance in Puritan thought concerning citizenship. Covenants established a collective discipline in place of the older hierarchies.[29] The covenant was the foundation of "a political society, framed according to rational principles and legislated into being by citizens for their own liberty and welfare."[30] The covenant was seen as emerging from *natural* human propensities for association and concern for others, but was also understood as a means of establishing "a new order *not natural* and inevitable but artificial and purposive."[31](Emphasis added.)

The covenant was viewed as an instrumental document subject to revision or total reconstruction, by the citizens whose sovereignty always remained behind any political arrangements. The people could delegate the exercise of that sovereignty according to the provisions of a particular covenant, but "when the subject of sovereign power is quite extinct, that power returns to the people again."[32]

Thus a view of the citizenship role emerged among American Puritans which emphasized the positive and constructive nature of political activity. It placed responsibility for the commonweal in the hands of individuals who enter into covenants with each other as equals in order to establish order and protect liberty. Citizens were viewed as the architects and builders of the political community. With their capacity for reason and their sociable inclinations they were thought to be able to balance self-love with regard for their fellows. Puritan citizens were obligated to participate in democratic debate, exchange diverging opinions, but finally act for the common good, even if this required denying personal interests.

Unlike the Madisonian view of human nature with its belief in the dominance of passions, this perspective embodied a trust in human reason and cooperation. The political community was to be maintained ultimately by natural human inclinations rather than institutional structure. According to Scaff, the Puritan citizen was "simply naturally sociable man combined with others like himself and united through 'covenants' that created political authority." He continued: "The gap between nature and citizen was small indeed, symbolized not by a change in internal human qualities but only by the overt, external act of association."[33] This view of citizenship endows the common member of the political community with a weightier, more direct, more active, and more consistent role in governing than that of either Madison or the twentieth century democratic elitists.

Of course, this view of the "natural" qualities of human nature is a highly debatable one. It seems reasonable to argue for the possibility of cultivating something like the Puritan view of the citizenship role without subscribing to the specific anthropology which accompanied it. One might well believe that human nature is flexible and moldable without adopting the notion that it is inherently predisposed to cooperative activity directed toward the common good. When John Wise insisted that the view of human nature he articulated was "obvious to view" he may have simply been reporting observations of the style of human interaction which had been fostered by the teachings, environment, and history of Puritan communities. His doctrine of human nature may well be the product of American Puritan experience rather than its cause, and evidence for the malleability of human nature rather than its natural predisposition to rational cooperation.

The experience of self-government in the Puritan churches was a training process for the citizenship role which was carried over into the larger political order. Even before the establishment of congregations in the new world, Kendall and Carey viewed the crafting of the Mayflower Compact as an anticipation of the New England town meeting. In the deliberative process which produced that compact they saw the "weighing and criticizing each word until *the* word is found that expresses what will later be called in America the sense of the meeting."[34] Concerning the congregational pattern which developed subsequently, Price suggested that "The original town meeting was, of course, government by the Puritan congregation and its elders, who were the legal authority in many towns until the disestablishment of the churches in the 1820s and 1830s in Connecticut and Massachusetts."[35]

Working out covenants for governing themselves in very small scale organizations such as congregations must have been conducive to active participation, to the exchange of diverse points of view, to learning how to manage conflict, and to experimentation with governance structures and policies. Perry Miller maintained that the Puritan congregation in New England "was unlike anything the world had ever beheld." He described these unique organizations as follows: "The core of each town was a church, composed of those who had given proof that they were visibly sanctified, joined together by a covenant into which they entered of their own will, who elected the minister and voted upon admissions and excommunications."[36]

In these very proximate organizations which were understood as related to the larger political community, individuals learned the necessity for tempering self-interest with concern for the whole. They served purposes similar to those of the *ward republics* as civic training schools in Jefferson's proposal for a participatory citizenship.

Puritanism and John Locke

Although some of these ideas have a certain Lockean ring, especially those of John Wise, Cook maintained that there is no evidence that Wise had read Locke, but that he more likely drew on the thought of the church fathers and the Greek classics, as well as common ideas of the time.[37] Since Locke was of British Puritan stock and his early surroundings and schooling were dominated by Puritan influences, it should not be surprising to find a similar cast to his ideas.[38] However, Scaff insisted that although the Puritan view of citizenship drew from similar intellectual sources, particularly in the fully developed form found in Wise, it is significantly different from Locke's formulation.[39] Although there are parallels between the Puritan notion of a covenant among reasoning free individuals and the Lockean social compact, there are important differences. The limited instrumental nature of government in the case of Locke is seen clearly in these words: "The great and chief end therefore, of men uniting into Commonwealths, and putting themselves under Government, is the Preservation of their Property."[40]

One finds similar expressions in Wise, for example: "The chief end of civil communities, is, that men thus conjoyned, may be secured against the injuries, they are liable to from their own kind . . ."[41] However, there is a significant difference here. In both cases, equal rational individuals give up their natural liberty, in one case for the protection of property, and in the other for protection from injury. From that point, the two perspectives diverge significantly. Puritan thought focused much more on the common good in broader terms.

The words of Thomas Hooker reveal this communitarian side of Puritanism. Hooker maintained that whoever entered society through a covenant "must willingly binde and ingage himself to each member of that society to promote the *good of the whole*, or else a member actually he is not."[42] (Emphasis added.) Even stronger language was adopted by Wise:

> A civil state is a compound moral person. Whose will (united by those covenants before passed) is the will of all; to the end it may use, and apply the strength and riches of private persons towards maintaining the common

peace, security, and well-being of all, which may be conceived as tho' the whole state was now become one man; in which the aforesaid covenants may be supposed under God's providence, to the divine Fiat, pronounced by God, let us make man.[43]

However, Ralph Barton Perry suggested that this kind of language must not be misunderstood. Individuality was not to be dissolved into a totalitarian political mass. The American Puritan citizen remained a thinking individual who as a *member* of the political community sought the common good: "The public interest, then, is the will, not of the collectivity as such, but of each and every individual person when these are in agreement in willing the good of all."[44]

To summarize, while Locke saw the role of the social compact as a necessary instrument for the protection of individual liberty and property, the Puritan covenant was rooted in the natural sociability of rational individual human beings and the priority they would naturally attribute to the common good over personal interests; public over private. The Puritan view manifested both a more positive and natural understanding of the origins of civil society while the Lockean formulation reflected a more negative and artificial perspective; government as a social invention to avoid the negative consequences of remaining in a state of nature. Puritanism found substantive good in government based on the covenant, while Locke saw only instrumental value in the social compact.

Scaff concluded from these differences that the tendency of scholars to focus on Lockean thought as the exclusive framework for understanding citizenship in the United States has led too easily to conclusions based on the limitations and essential weaknesses of the citizen role in the liberal state. From his analysis of Puritan thought, Scaff pointed out that "the American understanding of citizenship does not fit neatly into Lockean language, but has developed in a new and independent direction." He described that uniquely American approach to citizenship as follows:

> The special tension between individualism and political membership, between action and order, is never resolved in American political thought. If it were, we would surely regret the loss, for it sets in motion attempts to fulfill in practice the provision of rights and the claims for autonomy and improvability that constitute the full idea of citizenship.[45]

Puritan thought put its own imprint on ideas that were current and which influenced Locke's thinking also.[46] Ralph Barton Perry described the American Puritan citizen that emerged:

> The citizen is . . . both disinterested and interested, both impartial and partial. He is a judge of public good and at the same time the exponent of his own private stake in that good. As disinterested, he uses his faculties of sympathy

and imagination to understand the interests of others; and adopting these represented interests together with his own, he then proceeds precisely as in enlightened self interest. The choosing will which emerges, and which by limitation, rearrangement, and subordination transforms conflict into harmony, is a will in which all interests are taken account of and disarmed. The chooser, thus qualified, is more than a person; he is a statesmanlike or moral person. His reconstituted will expresses the interest of enlightened benevolence.[47]

Democracy and Puritan Citizenship

The connections between Puritan ideas concerning citizenship and American democratic thought seem to have been strong. Miller pointed to the limitation of magistrates, the commitment to a government of laws rather than men, the possibility of having the covenant annulled if its terms were violated, and the right of the people to resist such infringements in Puritanism. He then asserted that "these principles were declared no less emphatically in Puritan theory than in the Declaration of Independence."[48]

The consistent underlying purposes toward which Puritan thought and action were directed were also fundamental to democratic theory. Miller described these as oriented toward pushing back the realms of life which are determined by inexorable law in order to establish "an order founded upon voluntary choice, upon the deliberate assumption of obligation, upon unconstrained pacts, upon the sovereign determination of free wills."[49]

These purposes in turn grew out of deep beliefs in the dignity of the individual "irrespective of his place in any ecclesiastical, political, social, economic, or other institution."[50] In both Puritanism and democratic theory the fundamental entity was the individual person possessed of rationality and conscience, but bound to his or her fellow human beings by natural inclination and "higher truths." It was assumed in both cases that these truths were not to be dispensed of and interpreted exclusively by some higher orders of humanity such as monarchs or priests, but were accessible to anyone. Both democratic thought and Puritanism encouraged popular education which encouraged citizens to develop their minds. The result in both the Puritan and the democratic traditions was an encouragement of intellectual self-reliance in seeking the truth, as well as an obligation to do so. Perry argued that this respect for the human individual was the "deepest bond between Puritanism and democracy. . . ."[51]

Perry further asserted that the dignity attributed to the individual in both bodies of thought led to an affirmation of two specific values: *happiness* and *equality*. Puritanism emphasized the achievement of wealth and earthly happiness as God's reward for thrift and energy, both signs of godliness in one's life. Liberal democratic theory on the other hand, supported the enlightened pursuit of personal happiness as being at one and the same time conducive to the happiness of others.[52]

Following logically from their parallel commitments to the dignity of the individual and the belief in individual access to the power of reason, both Puritan and democratic thought embodied the value of equality in the principle of contract. In Puritanism, individuals stood as equals under God, who were able to enter into covenants concerning how they would govern themselves in the temporal sphere. Thus, no one occupied positions of authority unless so designated by the community, and then only because of greater piety and learning, not because of inherent rights to office. The concrete expression of this belief in equality was the congregational polity of Puritan churches.

In American democratic thought, the state has been understood as essentially a contract among free and equal consenting individuals, each possessing reason and the executive power of the law of nature. Again, persons hold office only on the basis of rational choice by individual members of the political community, presumably based on wisdom and experience rather than any right to office.[53]

Having generalized about the democratic tendencies of Puritanism, it is important to note that these were not universally true of all Puritan communities. It appears that the democratic spirit was strongest among the Puritan separatists whose impatience with the episcopal polity of the Church of England drove them toward independence from hierarchical authority. Thus the clearest and strongest early expression of democratic values was to be found in those separatist Pilgrims who, before landing at Plymouth, drafted the Mayflower Compact in 1620. By contrast, the Massachusetts Bay Colony, established in 1630, adhered to a congregational polity, but rejected both separatism and democracy.[54] As Rossiter noted, for all practical purposes, "In the very act of crossing the Atlantic, these nonseparatist Puritans became separatist Congregationalists."[55]

Perry maintained that the full democratic implications of congregationalism were more fully realized in Connecticut than in Massachusetts. It was there that *The Fundamental Orders of Connecticut*, sometimes referred to as the first written constitution of modern democracy, was drafted in response to a sermon by the Puritan Thomas Hooker, and delivered before the General Court of Hartford on May 31, 1638.[56] Although the extent of both Hooker's and Connecticut's democratic leanings are a matter of debate, it seems clear that one can at least see "the forces of liberty inherent in Puritanism . . ." in Hooker and definite steps toward democracy in the founding of Connecticut.[57]

Another significant link between Puritan thought and the American democratic tradition was represented by Roger Williams, often recognized as the founder of Rhode Island in 1644. Williams' thinking was bold and radical in its development of Puritan theology. He carried the belief in the dignity of the rational individual to its logical conclusion. Williams first insisted on the clean separation between church and state, since the state had no business governing the consciences of equal individuals with the capacity to reason for themselves about matters of doctrine. According to Williams, it was the role of the church and its clergy to persuade through power of reason and wisdom, using scripture as its point of reference; not to rely upon civil authority to gain adherence through coercion.[58]

Williams placed the principle of popular government alongside that of religious liberty. In March 1644 Williams obtained a patent from the Commissioners of Plantations which provided for a new colony based on a union of independent towns. However, it was not until 1647 that a government was actually organized under the patent. Rossiter summarized the remarkable features of this first governmental structure of Rhode Island:

> (1) it was adopted by an assembly attended by "the major parte of the Colonie" and was thus one of the few constitutions in history to proceed directly from the people; (2) it was couched in the language of an explicit civil compact; (3) the form was declared to be *"Democraticall;* that is to say, a Government held by ye free and voluntarie consent of all, or the greater parte of the free inhabitants;" (4) it recognized the rights of the originally independent towns by establishing a pattern of incipient federalism that was strengthened by subsequent laws and town charters; (5) it made further concessions to the towns by inaugurating a primitive system of initiative, referendum, and recall; and (6) it instituted an extensive code of laws and liberties based directly on those of England.

In addition, there were interesting provisions that established the concept of public office as a duty as well as a trust, and liberty of conscience in all things not specified by law.[59] The result, according to Rossiter, was that colonial records indicate "Rhode Island was the closest thing to democracy in seventeenth-century America . . . And they testify also that Roger Williams was the one man most responsible for this triumph of liberty."[60]

If one looks for direct links between Puritan thought and the American Revolution as the major move toward the democratization of the New World, one clear influence can be found in John Wise, previously discussed. Cook argued that his acknowledgment of human natural rights and enthusiastic support for democracy in John Wise's *A Vindication of the Government of New England Churches* (1717) anticipated the period of revolutionary ferment by about 50 years.[61] Cook noted that the earliness of his contribution and its later influence has been appreciated too little. *A Vindication* went through two new printings of five hundred copies each during the 1770s just prior to the Revolution. Subscribers to the second printing in 1772 included the commander of minutemen at Concord; Timothy Pickering, lawyer, adjutant-general, and quartermaster-general of the Continental Army; and two colonels who bought twelve copies each. The number of military men among the subscribers almost equalled the number of ministers. Laymen purchased almost seven times as many as ministers. The democratic ideas espoused by John Wise in 1717 were warmly received by the makers of revolution.

Summary

Through this brief review of Puritanism it is possible to identify five contributions to the tradition of ethical citizenship in the United States which have influenced American political history and continue to inform our thinking about the future:

1. *Puritanism held to a positive valuation of the political process as the means for achieving the common good.* Through rational deliberation the congruence of both individual interests and the collective interests of the community could be discovered.

2. *Puritan theology valued the political process because of its emphasis on the dignity of the individual.* Individual dignity was reflected in the assumed ability to balance self interests with obligation to the common good. This was understood as possible through human capacity for reason, the centrality of moral conscience in individual life, and the naturally sociability of human beings.

3. *The concept of the covenant in Puritan thought provided a way of understanding the basis for self-government among individuals possessing the attributes described in item number one.* Presumed equals had a right and obligation to develop standing agreements about how collective life was to be carried out. These could be altered or abolished when they no longer served the common good. Sovereignty remained with the individual members of the community.

4. *Doctrine reflected in the first two items interacted with experience in the new world to produce self-governing communities which were relatively democratic, if never fully so.* Isolated congregations had no choice but to enter into experimentation with actual self-governance in the absence of any other proximate and effective authority; theory had to be put into practice.

5. *The Puritan experience yielded concrete artifacts such as the Mayflower Compact, the Fundamental Orders of Connecticut, the Rhode Island "laboratory" of democratic government, and the town meeting as an outgrowth of the self-governing congregations.* These artifacts served as models and points of reference for further experimentation, and milestones in the progress toward democratic government. They represented encouraging evidence of the validity of self government.

Anti-Federalism and Ethical Citizenship

Since the winners in any contest receive more attention than those who lose, it is not surprising that so much is known about the men who designed, drafted and advocated adoption of the United States Constitution, but little about those who opposed it. From examining the typical treatment of the Constitution in government and public administration courses, one gains little sense of the "other side"—the "losers"—in that important struggle. In fact, the focus on the *Federalist Papers* and their authors—Hamilton, Madison, and Jay—fails to impart any sense of struggle at all. Nevertheless, the struggle was there; the United States Constitution was born in intense conflict.

The tension between two competing perspectives in the American political tradition became sharply focused during the Constitutional Convention of 1787 with the emergence of what came to be known rather quickly as the Federalist and Anti-federalist camps. The Federalists were of course, proponents of Madison's general approach, originally known as the *Virginia Plan.*[62] Anti-federalists, on the other hand, opposed Madison's proposal for a new governmental structure. They included well-known figures such as Patrick Henry, George Mason, and Richard Henry Lee along with many less familiar persons such as Mercy Otis Warren.

The differences between these two perspectives surfaced during the convention in Philadelphia and were developed further by various spokespersons during the debates over ratification of the proposed new United States Constitution. Hanson argued that the opposing views advanced by these two competing factions can be understood best as a clash over the nature of republican government since "republicanism provided an ideological framework common to nearly all of the various factions of this period."[63] The conflict, according to Hanson, was not one between totally different political philosophies such as aristocracy and democracy. Neither of these was popular in the United States at that time. Rather, it was a struggle pitting the Federalist revision of republican theory against the Anti-federalists' more traditional view.[64]

Hanson maintained that the traditional philosophy of republicanism that emerged during the colonial era was fundamentally oriented to a central purpose of government rather than some particular form. That purpose was the pursuit of the general welfare, sometimes referred to as the *public good,* or *good of the whole.* This language was derived from Latin roots of the word *republic — res republic*—meaning "of the public," or "commonweal." In more specific terms, the public good was understood as "mixed" government founded on a balance among the various interests and orders of society.[65]

According to Hanson, the view of citizenship which typified this perspective on republicanism reflected classical thought. Citizenship in such a political community required virtue that amounted to a commitment to give priority to the common good over one's own selfish interests. It was expected that the good citizen would manifest certain specific virtues such as honesty, fairness, and courage in serving the commonweal. The underlying assumption was that virtue offered the ultimate protection against invasion and faction, the two most serious enemies of republican government.[66]

Liberty was understood as another essential attribute of a republic, in the traditional sense. However, Hanson argued that this did not refer to *civil* liberty, but liberty to participate in public affairs. Participation was understood as directed toward "the common interest of all in a public sphere ... in which there was no domination, i.e., no imbalance of interests."[67] The *good republic* was thought to be one which provided the right to freely enter into the process of governance, while the virtuous citizen was viewed as one who used that right for the good of all.

Hanson represented the Constitutional struggle as one between Anti-federalists who held to the traditional view summarized above, and Federalists who challenged it with a newer perspective.[68] According to his analysis, the Federalists' "new science of politics" was strongly influenced by the Scottish enlightenment and its passionate theory of interests as expressed by scholars such as David Hume. For Hume, people were essentially "dangerous egoists driven by passion and self interest." Hume maintained that it was possibile to restrain impulses through virtue, but that the meaning of virtue was to be transformed from excellent practices, or desirable character traits, to rules which must be obeyed.[69]

Under the sway of this kind of thinking that was reflected in Federalist No. 10, the Federalists were moved to devalue the significance of virtue in its classical sense. If human nature was driven essentially by self-interested "passion," "mutual animosity" is to be expected, and one should not be surprised if human beings are "much more disposed to vex and oppress each other than to cooperate for their common good." Madison argued that various *factions* would emerge among the citizenry as expressions of these destructive and anti-social emotional impulses. They would tend to engage in constant conflict leading to instability in society and ultimately to tyranny, as the only resort for the restoration of order. In the face of these attributes "sown in the nature of man," virtue perceived as character stood little chance of maintaining conduct oriented toward the public good.[70]

According to Hanson, the Federalist approach to republican government diverged significantly from the traditional view, and therefore from that of Anti-federalists. Their approach was to rely mainly on certain arrangements of governmental structure, and rule-making concerning relationships among parts of the structure rather than on any assumptions concerning the virtue of the people as a whole. The Federalist approach embodied in the United States Constitution sought to control the effects of factions since it was impossible to remove their causes—causes inherent in human nature.

The United States Constitution, adopted by the Philadelphia convention in 1787, reflected this concern with structure and rules to assure stability and order in its provision for a separation of powers; a system of checks and balances; a largely indirect electoral process; differential constituencies for the President, the House and the Senate; and a delineation of federal and state jurisdictions. Rather than relying on the public wisdom of a virtuous citizenry, the Federalists sought to create balanced government by buffering the governing process from the passionate expression of interests through these mechanisms. Interest was juxtaposed with interest in a self-correcting and stabilizing structure of fragmented authority and overlapping jurisdictions. Thus the "new science of politics" was substituted for traditional republicanism, according to Hanson.[71]

Although this characterization of the constitutional conflict presented by Hanson is generally accurate, once again it is important to understand that the conflict between Federalists and Anti-federalists was not as sharply delineated in principle as one might be tempted to conclude. Borden maintained that the Anti-federalists wavered over the Americans' ability to govern themselves solely through the virtuous character of the citizenry. He also suggested that although the Federalists manifested a largely Hobbesian view of human nature, they were also committed to the British heritage of popular sovereignty.[72]

Similarly, Horwitz emphasized the extent to which the Anti-federalists had departed from the communal values of classical republican tradition and joined the Federalists in a preoccupation with individual liberty.[73] Both Hanson and Storing pointed out that the Federalists had to allow the existence of enough virtue of character among the populace to justify their ability to select wise leaders through elections.[74] Thus, the positions of both perspectives contained certain elements of the other which blurred the skirmish lines between them, even though significant differences remained.[75]

In the end the general approach and emphases advocated by the Federalists carried the day in the adoption and ratification of the Constitution. The Anti-federalists, with their more traditional republican views, fought persistently against the acceptance of the new Constitution. They lost most major issues, the only significant concession being an agreement to add a bill of rights after ratification.

It is fair to say that even if the Anti-federalists lost during the initial constitutional struggle, their ideas have never really vanished from American political debate. Ketcham observed that "the Jeffersonian triumph of 1801 with its manifold anti-federalist overtones," the adoption of the Bill of Rights, and the acceptance of the new constitution by former anti-federalists, once it was adopted, "all attest to the vigor and influence of anti-federalism and its ability to find fulfillment even under the document opposed so vehemently in 1787-88." He concluded that "Anti-federal ideas have also surfaced again and again in various guises among later generations of Americans. Those ideas, as well as the enticing prospects held out by Publius, are a vital element in the American political tradition and are properly viewed as part of the philosophy of the Constitution."[76]

The late Herbert Storing, leading editor of Anti-federalist documents, offered similar observations: "If, however, the foundation of the American polity was laid by the Federalists, the Anti-Federalist reservations echo through American history; and it is in the dialogue, not merely in the Federalist victory, that the country's principles are to be discovered."[77]

And Kenyon also maintained that "the Anti-federalist complex of ideas is worth serious attention." She explained that, "Their influence was not cut off with the defeat of 1788." In fact, she suggested that "their opposition to centralized federal power has been passed on from generation to generation until the present time." She concluded: "their ideas are an essential part of the American tradition."[78]

These scholarly observations support the central thesis of this book concerning the existence of a stream of values, norms, beliefs, and political perspectives which have been employed to democratize the legal definitions of American citizenship. They have been referred to herein as the ethical tradition of citizenship. One significant part of that stream is the cluster of republican values within Anti-federalism. Although it has been acknowledged that Anti-federalism was not completely homogeneous, it is true that there are certain core concepts that characterized a significant consensus within that movement and tradition. It is necessary for our purposes to identify and elaborate briefly those key ideas in the following sections.

The Sovereignty of the People

At the very heart of Anti-federalist thought was a firm and unyielding commitment to popular will as the central orienting force for government. Anti-federalists recognized the necessity for delegating some authority to their chosen rulers, but did so grudgingly and reluctantly. This authority took the form of limited, stipulated powers, and, as under the Articles of Confederation, indicated concern for safeguarding the ultimate sovereignty of the people.

As the pseudonymous Anti-federalist, *Brutus*, wrote to the editor of the *New York Journal* on October 18, 1787:

> In every free government, the people must give their assent to the laws by which they are governed. This is the true criterion between a free government and an arbitrary one. The former are ruled by the will of the whole, expressed in any manner they may agree upon; the latter by the will of one, or a few.[79]

The Anti-federalists saw the Federalist Constitution as delegating far too much authority to the few, and removing their election, as well as their accountability for conduct in office, too far from the direct influence of popular will.

Centinel, identified as a Pennsylvania Anti-federalist, argued in the Philadelphia *Independent Gazateer* and the *Freeman's Journal* in October 1787 that the Federalist proposal did not amount to popular sovereignty.[80] He questioned the adequacy of the system of opposing interests that the Federalists offered that were to be regulated by a set of checks and balances and were to "answer the great purposes of civil society." Seeing the proposed Constitution as too complex and too oriented towards distancing the mass of people from governance, Centinel insisted that free government could exist only where those entrusted with power were held "in the greatest responsibility to their constituents . . ." and where "the people are the sovereign and their sense or opinion is the criterion of every public measure. . . ." Without this direct link of responsibility, "the nature of the government is changed and an aristocracy, monarchy, or despotism will rise on its ruin."[81]

Some Anti-federalists saw the variance between their own understanding of human nature and that of the Federalists as posing a problem for popular sovereignty. Robert Yates and John Lansing responded to the rather negative view of human nature reflected in the letters of Publius by suggesting that "the supposition of universal venality in human nature is little less an error in political reasoning than the supposition of universal rectitude."

They then went on to point out the inconsistency within the Federalists' own position by noting that, "The institution of delegated power" to which the Federalists adhered, "implies that there is a portion of virtue and honor among mankind, which may be a reasonable foundation of confidence."[82] The aristocratic bias implicit in the Federalist assumption of the possibility of virtue among "men of the better sort," while at the same time assuming the lack of virtue among the mass of people, was not lost on the Anti-federalists.

Over against the Federalist attempts to devise a set of structural arrangements and procedural rules designed to buffer government from direct influence by an inherently untrustworthy, irrational, and self-seeking citizenry, the Anti-federalists vigorously asserted their commitment to popular sovereignty. There were certain essential ingredients in a self-governing republican government which they advanced and we will next turn to a treatment of those provisions.

Elected Leaders Must Directly Represent the People

Although it is possible to find language to the contrary, the dominant Anti-federalist view of representation is one often referred to as the *delegate* definition, generally associated today with John Stuart Mill. This understanding of the role of the elected representative calls for responsiveness to the wishes of constituents. The representative does not ask "In *my* judgment, what is best for the people who elected me?" as would be the case for one acting from the view of representation often termed the *trustee* perspective, generally attributed to Edmund Burke. Rather, the Millian representative focuses on what his *constituents* believe to be in their best interests, and what they have instructed him to do, whether he agrees with it or not.[83]

Ketcham suggested that the Anti-federalist perspective comes most clearly into focus at this point—"in its understanding of what representation and government by consent could really mean." He continued: "Instead of seeking to insulate officials from popular influence [as Publius did] . . . Anti-federalists sought to insure the public good by requiring close association."[84]

The Anti-federalists reacted against what Hanson described as the "decidedly Burkean view of representation" held by the Federalists.[85] The Anti-federalists saw the Federalist argument for selecting the "best men" who would exercise wise judgment on behalf of their constituents as turning government over to what they referred to as *the natural aristocracy*.[86] According to Storing, the Anti-federalists were explicitly opposed to "brilliant talents" and "great abilities" as criteria for representatives. Thus he quoted the Antifederalist *Cato* as saying: "Great abilities have generally, if not always, been employed to mislead the honest unwary multitude, and draw them out of the plain paths of public virtue and public good."[87]

The Anti-federalists were much more concerned "to keep the representative responsible, in the rather narrow meaning of that term, that is, directly answerable to and dependent on their constituents." Storing explained further that, "This is the reason for the concern with short terms of office, frequent rotation, and a numerous representation."[88]

The Anti-federalist minority report at the Pennsylvania Convention expressed the concern of those delegates for establishing methods for selecting representatives so "as to prevent their neglecting or sacrificing the views and interests of their constituents, to their own pursuits."[89] Their fear was that the Federalist Constitution provided an insufficient number of representatives, and transferred too much power to a remote central government to keep Federal elected officials strictly accountable to the people.

Similarly, Melancton Smith, speaking at the New York ratifying convention, argued that "government which is directed by the will of any one or a few, or any number less than is the will of the community, is a government for slaves." He went on to describe representation as the scheme by which the people "*deputed* others," denoting an understanding of the representative as an agent, or delegate, of the electors.[90]

Necessity for Close Proximity Between Ruler and Ruled

Consistent with the *delegate* view of representation, the Anti-federalists insisted on a close relationship between electors and those who would represent them. One who would represent others must be physically close enough to understand and share their values, opinions, sentiments, and aspirations. Only then could trust and goodwill be cultivated, and effective deliberation between the representative and the constituents be maintained.

This kind of relationship was thought to require a high ratio of representatives to population, as well as proximate government authority. A representative could not adequately reflect the perspectives of his constituents unless they were relatively few in number and in regular contact with him. Thus the Anti-federalists were opposed to the method of providing representative government in the proposed constitution. The constituencies were considered too large, too much governmental authority was removed from the states and assigned to the national government, and the members of the Senate were to be elected indirectly.

George Mason argued at the Philadelphia Convention that it was essential that the people elect their own representatives, rather than having them selected by state legislatures, as was proposed for the Senate. This was because "The requisites in actual representation are that the Representatives should sympathize with their constituents; should think as they think, and feel as they feel; and that for these purposes should even be residents among them."[91] This bond of close proximity, and similar views and values, was considered the only way the basically virtuous human nature of the people would be able to impact on government continuously. The representative would then mirror his constituents as precisely as possible. Ketcham explained: "If the basic decency in human nature most evident among ordinary people at the local level amid family, church, school, and other nourishing institutions, could impinge directly and continuously on government, then perhaps it too might be kept virtuous and worthy of confidence."[92]

Storing noted the essential link between this emphasis on a close relationship and similarity of views between the people and their representatives. If the crucial problem was understood as keeping the representatives directly responsible to the citizenry, Storing maintained that the Anti-federalists knew that mechanical devices such as rotation in office, short terms, and numerous representation were not sufficient. Rather they recognized that, "Effective and thoroughgoing responsibility is to be found only in a likeness between the representative body and the citizens at large." Storing went on to quote Melancton Smith's insistence that representatives "should be a true picture of the people; possess the knowledge of their circumstances and their wants; sympathize in all their distresses, and be disposed to seek their true interests."[93]

The Citizenry Must Possess Certain Characteristics

It logically follows that if elected representatives are to reflect the values and interests of their constituents there must be homogeneity among the electors. Brutus stated the argument succinctly as follows:

> In a republic, the manners, sentiments, and interests of the people should be similar. If this be not the case, there will be a constant clashing of opinions; and the representatives of one part will be continually striving against those of the other. This will retard the operations of government, and prevent such conclusions as will promote the public good.[94]

Similarity was essential for the unified expression of the will of the people to their representatives which, in turn, was necessary in order to maintain popular sovereignty.

One crucial dimension of homogeneity was thought to be equality of socioeconomic status. In a true republican government there should not be extreme differences of wealth, influence, education, or anything else which would create conflicting interests.[95] Centinel argues that "a republican, or free government, can only exist . . . where property is pretty equally divided. . . ." Otherwise, if great inequalities exist, aristocracy was considered certain to emerge.[96]

Consonant with these concerns for homogeneity and equality was a belief in the particular importance of people of "the middle sort or yeomanry of the country" being adequately represented in government.[97] Since some class differences in society were admitted to be unavoidable, it was the middle classes that were thought to provide a kind of egalitarian anchor between the rich and poor. In his extended debate with Hamilton during the New York ratifying convention, Melancton Smith developed the Anti-federalist case on this point:

> The same passions and prejudices govern all men. The circumstances in which men are placed in a great measure give a cast to the human character. Those in middling circumstances, have less temptation—they are inclined by habit and the company with whom they associate, to set bounds to their passions and appetites—if this is not sufficient, the want of means to gratify them will be a restraint—they are obliged to employ their time in their respective callings— hence the substantial yeomanry of the country are temperate, of better morals and less ambition than the great.

Smith then acknowledged a bit later in the same speech that the upper class must be included in the representative bodies of government, for "they would be more dangerous out of power than in it" since, not only would they be "factious," dissatisfied, and disruptive, but it would be unjust to exclude them. In his view, it would be necessary to have enough of the middle class to control them. He maintained that:

> A representative body, composed principally of respectable yeomanry is the best possible security to liberty. . . . When the interest of this part of the community is pursued, the public good is pursued; because the body of every nation consists of this class. And because the interest of both the rich and the poor are involved in that of the middling class. . . . When therefore this class in society pursue their own interest, they promote that of the public, for it is involved in it.[98]

Civic virtue was another essential characteristic of the citizenry drawn from the republican tradition. Contrary to the Federalists' reliance on a virtuous elite, the Anti-federalists looked to the people as a whole, but particularly the middle classes, for civic virtue.[99] Storing explained that: "Republican government depends on civic virtue, on a devotion to fellow citizens and to country so deeply instilled as to be almost automatic and powerful as the natural devotion to self-interest."[100] Implicit in these words is the centrality of two particular civic virtues: commitment to the public good and to liberty. The former suggested an orientation to government that carried the citizen beyond a preoccupation with limited personal interests, and the latter an inclination to participate in the process of governance as a way of seeking the good of all.[101]

Storing quoted from three Anti-federalists—*Candidus, Alfred,* and *Plebian*—who identify the crux of the conflict between themselves and the Federalists as emerging from a fundamental difference in views about the role of virtue. The Federalists sought solutions to the problems encountered under the Articles of Confederation through rearranging the structure of government. However, the Anti-federalists believed that the difficulties were not primarily the result of an ineffective governmental design, but rather "the want of public virtue, in preferring private interest to every other consideration."[102]

The Anti-federalist contention was that the kinds of checks and balances, separation of powers, and multiple constituencies designed into the proposed constitution simply created unnecessary complexity. This preoccupation with mechanical devices to assure free government would only hinder the full participation of the middle classes, thus encouraging erosion toward aristocracy. As the Anti-federalists saw it, this approach simply failed to recognize the essential importance of virtue to the functioning of republican government. Storing summarized as follows: "The Anti-Federalists saw, although sometimes only dimly, the insufficiency of a community of mere interest. They saw that the American polity had to be a moral community if it was to be anything, and they saw that the seat of that community must be the hearts of the people."[103]

The Importance of Participation
for Citizenship Education

The Anti-federalists adhered to the *possibility* of cultivating civic virtue, although they did not insist on its inherent presence in human nature. Therefore, civic education as a means of cultivating public virtue was an essential component of their republican philosophy. This tenet of Anti-federalist thought comes through clearly in their writings.

Mercy Otis Warren, in addressing the threat to republican government from the corrupting attractions of European luxury, insisted that the crucial task was not isolating Americans from foreign influence; rather it lay in the public and private education of the youth. The danger to republicanism was not external, she maintained, but, according to Storing, "in the restless ambition and avarice in the heart of every man and every people; and that is where it must be met, principally by education."[104]

Some Anti-federalists offered specific proposals for civic training schools, but most saw participation in the polity itself as the principal educative process for citizenship.[105] Storing indicated that, "The small republic was seen as a school of citizenship as much as a scheme for government." He pointed out that a far more important part of the Anti-federalist insistence on a bill of rights was the educational function it would perform. By regularly reminding citizens that the purpose of republican government was to preserve liberty, a rights bill would provide continual civic education.[106] The Anti-federalist who adopted the pen name *The Federal Farmer* argued this case at length:

> We do not by declarations change the nature of things, or create new truths, but we give existence, or at least establish in the minds of the people truths and principles which they might never otherwise have thought of, or soon forgot. . . . Men, in some countries do not remain free, merely because they are entitled to natural and unalienable rights; men in all countries are entitled to them, not because their ancestors once got together and enumerated them on paper, but because, by repeated negociations and declarations, all parties are brought to realize them, and of course to believe them to be sacred. Were it necessary, I might shew the wisdom of our past conduct, as a people in not merely comforting ourselves that we were entitled to freedom, but in constantly keeping in view, in addresses, bills of rights, in newspapers, &c. the particular principles on which our freedom must always depend.[107]

Similarly, the Anti-federalist *Cato*, thought to be the pseudonym of Governor George Clinton of New York, found civic educational value in the experience of serving in elective office. One of the strengths of democratic government was that "it affords to many the opportunity to be advanced to the supreme command, and the honors they thereby enjoy fill them with a desire of rendering themselves worthy of them; hence this desire becomes part of their education, is matured in manhood, and produces an ardent affection for their country. . . ." Cato concluded that these benefits would be optimized by holding annual elections.[108]

The Anti-federalist emphasis on participation as the most effective form of civic education rested on the belief in a formative interaction between governmental structure, and the values and habits of the people. Melancton Smith argued for example that, "government operates upon the spirit of the people, as well as the spirit of the people operates upon it—and if they are not conformable to each other, the one or the other will prevail."[109]

This belief that the way government and the legal system are designed would affect the character of the citizenry gave rise to one of the Anti-federalists' deepest concerns about the proposed constitution. They feared that the Federalist approach ignored this relationship which they deemed so essential to republican government.[110] Hanson believed that their fears were well founded. He charged that it was the failure of the Federalists to "consider political means for promoting virtue amongst the citizenry that made their proposals both politically and theoretically suspect."

Hanson maintained that the Federalists misunderstood the source of disorder during the era of the Articles of Confederation. They saw it as the result of public participation. Thus, they were moved to adopt an excessively limited view of the role of political involvement in cultivating and sustaining civic virtue among the populace. He concluded:

In limiting popular participation to the selection of leaders, the Federalists consigned the population to a state of lethargy, in which citizens failed to develop a sense of moral and political responsibility that, according to classical republican theory, accompanied civic involvement. Citizens failed to acquire those minimal insights that would have allowed them to choose wise and able leaders. And they failed to learn to love liberty, i.e., to love and pursue the public good in politics. Thus, the Federalists' "realistic" assessment of the decline in virtue in America turned out to be a "gigantic self-fulfilling prophecy" once it found institutional expression in Constitutional arrangements that made scant provision for civic involvement.[111]

It was this skepticism about the possibilities of a virtuous citizenry and the resultant departure from traditional republicanism that was directly antithetical to the Anti-federalist view.

Summary of Anti-federalist Contributions to the Ethical Citizenship Tradition

A review of Anti-federalist literature yields the following major emphases which have continued as constituent elements of the American ethical tradition of citizenship:

1. Focus on the public good.   In tension with Federalist assumptions about the inevitable preoccupation with self-interest stands this Anti-federalist notion that citizens are capable of concern for, and pursuit of, the common good. This ideal is one which we still project through various terms such as *the public interest, the common good, the general good,* and *the common interest.*

Horwitz argued persuasively that both the Federalists and the Anti-federalists shared an adherence to individualistic Lockean ideas. This philosophical perspective, he suggested, tended to move both groups away from traditional republican orientation toward the public good.

It is true that both were concerned for individual happiness, and liberty was a key concept in the language of both camps. However, it does seem clear that the Anti-federalist understanding of both these central terms was primarily oriented toward the political community rather than the individual. Happiness was viewed in the context of shared goals, and liberty was understood as freedom to participate in public affairs.

2. Popular Control of Government.   The Anti-federalist commitment to maximize self-government in the republican tradition remains a central part of the American ethical tradition of citizenship. In spite of a Constitution that gave the citizenry only indirect control over the national government, the sovereignty of the people remains a powerful ideal. In spite of the enormous changes in scale which have occurred in the United States during the last two hundred years, the idea of government *of* the people, and *by* the people, as well as *for* the people, continues as one of the ethical touchstones of American political life.

The Anti-federalist ideal was to be embodied in a small homogeneous republic just one step removed from direct democracy. That vision unquestionably no longer fits the facts of the political community in the United States. The persistent belief in American society that the people must ultimately be sovereign exercises an ongoing tension against tendencies to turn government over to the professional politicians and administrators.

Although today direct representation of popular preferences and demands in the tradition of the Millian delegate seems impossible, the ultimate belief that the people must rule prevents any simple and easy lapse into a totally Burkean trustee perspective. Government is huge and complex; much of the time citizens must rely on the judgment of those who represent them, either elected officials, or career administrators. However, from time to time the populace speaks with the approximation of a single voice and expects their representatives to carry out their wishes.

3. Equality As an Ideal for Society. In tension with the competitive entrepreneurial spirit of the American tradition stands the Anti-federalist emphasis on the importance of limiting class differences. The assumption that citizenship in a republic must be on some roughly equal footing if the public good is to be achieved and maintained continues to influence public policy debate in the United States.

The concomitant belief in the crucial role of the middle class as the essential center of gravity for a republic crops up regularly. When fears about the well-being of the middle stratum and its values emerge they are often linked to concerns about the health of democratic government. The Anti-federalist ideal was not one of a classless society, but certainly one of a society dominated by the equivalent of the agrarian yeoman with sufficient resources to permit political participation, independent judgment, and concern for the greater good of the community.

4. The Importance of Civic Virtue. The Anti-federalist conviction that free government under popular control, and oriented toward the public good, is founded on the moral qualities of the citizenry has continued as a counterpoint to the other American tendency toward a focus on manipulating rules and structures. Preoccupation with passing new laws and rearranging the machinery of government generally evokes an echo from the American Anti-federalist heritage that calls for "better people" in government, or more effective education and training for public service. The idea remains in the ongoing political debate in the United States that if people in government are not virtuous, ethics legislation and structural controls are unlikely to accomplish much of real consequence.

Consistent with this perspective is the opinion which is voiced regularly to the effect that people in government—elected, appointed, or career public servants—are only a reflection of the citizenry as a whole. The assumption that virtuous government reflects a virtuous citizenry is a key Anti-federalist notion.

   5. *Active Participation in Governance by the Citizenry.*   Active participation in the formation of public policy was advocated by the Anti-federalists over the more cautious Federalist approach which severely limited the
role of the citizenry to the electoral process. Even in this, the original Federalist form of the Constitution allowed citizens to elect directly only one
member of the House at the Federal level.

   The Anti-federalists on the other hand, stressed the essential nature of
more active and direct involvement by the people. Only through participation in electoral politics and continual deliberation among themselves, or
with their representatives, could citizens exercise their sovereignty. Otherwise, the upper classes would quickly begin to dominate government and
direct it toward their own interests. Only through active engagement with
the governing process could the people develop as citizens and acquire a
sense of the common good that is the essence of civic virtue. Without participation by the citizenry, republican government would decay into aristocracy.

THE JEFFERSONIAN TRADITION

The significance of Thomas Jefferson for the ethical tradition of American
citizenship is not simply the "historical Jefferson"—the actual man himself.
Nor is it solely his writings, speeches, and actions. Rather it is the larger
tradition of thought, literature, and utterances which emerged from the
man, his deeds, and his literary legacy which is of interest here. It is this
tradition, or as Merrill Peterson termed it, this "Jefferson image," which has
powerfully influenced the American political ethos and, in turn, our views
about the values that ought to inform the citizen role. Peterson defines this
image as "the composite representation of the historic personage and of the
ideas and ideals, policies and sentiments, habitually identified with him."

   This orientation is not primarily concerned with the accuracy of the
way Jefferson is represented in the plethora of speeches and writings about
his conduct and ideas, but with these artifacts of the tradition as "illumina-
tions of the evolving culture and its shaping power." Peterson maintains that
this tradition, or image, is "posterity's configuration of Jefferson," and more
importantly, "it is a sensitive reflector, through several generations, of
America's troubled search for the image of itself."[112]

   Although it is fundamentally this Jeffersonian tradition which ultimately is of significance in the ethical tradition of citizenship in the United
States, it is useful to begin with a brief treatment of the historical seeds from
which it grew. After a review of the main ideas that can be gleaned from

Jefferson's works that are relevant to the citizen role, we will conclude with an assessment of the impact of the tradition.

Philosophical Roots

Jefferson's philosophy of the role of the citizenry was grounded in a doctrine of natural rights which he assumed, as did Locke, to be innate and indefeasible.[113] This doctrine found its most eloquent and best known expression in the second paragraph of the Declaration of Independence:

> We hold these truths to be self-evident that all men are created equal, that they are endowed by their creator with certain unalienable Rights, that among these are Life, Liberty and the pursuit of Happiness. . . . That to secure these rights, Governments are instituted among Men, deriving their just power from the consent of the governed.[114]

Not only do all people share these rights equally, but their maintenance, according to Jefferson, is the only legitimate object of government. Government must be an expression of the will of these individuals exercising their natural rights. Jefferson argued that: "Every man, and every body of men on earth, possess the right of self-government. . . . Individuals exercise it by their single will—collections of men by that of their majority."[115]

In order to prevent government from abrogating these natural rights, power must always be kept responsible to the majority of the people rather than to an elite minority. Jefferson noted the seemingly inherent tendencies in society to assign power to the few, or reserve it for the many:

> Men by their constitutions are naturally divided into two parties. 1. Those who fear and distrust the people, and wish to draw all powers from them into the hands of the higher classes. 2ndly those who identify themselves with the people, have confidence in them, cherish and consider them as the most honest and safe, altho' not the most wise depository of the public interests. In every country these two parties exist, and in every one where they are free to think, speak and write, they will declare themselves.[116]

Jefferson clearly and sharply delineated the ground between the Republicans, whom he supported, and the Federalists whom he identified with elitism.

From his belief in natural rights, Jefferson developed his argument for an active view of citizenship in two directions. He argued both for the educative and developmental benefits of participation for individuals, and for those which will accrue to the political system.

Jefferson's argument for the individual benefits of participation was grounded in a belief that the natural state of man was the social, not the individual state. In this sense, he rejected Locke's fictional state of nature consisting of independent individuals which, according to Peterson, "he neither liked nor used." Jefferson started with man as he found him—as man in society—and maintained that human beings realize their true nature as civilized beings.[117]

Jefferson maintained that an inherent moral instinct led human beings to establish and cultivate fraternal ties. It was, he concluded, a combination of reason and this "moral sense" that restrained the extreme forms of individualism. Virtue that fundamentally consisted of "duty to others," would be obviated by selfishness. Since virtue was considered essential to happiness, preoccupation with individual interests would stand in the way of the "pursuit of happiness."[118] Therefore, the human natural right to pursue happiness required the support of virtue understood as social obligation. Jefferson maintained that happiness was a "public activity" that grew out of "public well-being." Since each individual's happiness depended at least in part on the welfare of society, everyone should have the right to participate in the public realm.

So it seems clear that reason and the moral sense were viewed by Jefferson as crucial prerequisites for constructive participation. Morton White reminded us that ideas about the moral sense were quite common, although somewhat controversial in eighteenth century thought. The main proponents of such a sense, independent of reason, were the Earl of Shaftesbury (Anthony Ashley Cooper), Francis Hutcheson, David Hume, and Adam Smith. Those on the other side who insisted on the primacy of reason and knowledge included Samuel Clarke, William Wallaston, John Balguy, Richard Price, and Thomas Reid.[119]

Jefferson adopted a synthesizing position with respect to this controversy, making room for both reason and the moral sense.[120] His formulation held that the moral sense "indicated" or "intimated" appropriate moral principles to follow in a given situation, but that these principles must be verified by reason. Jefferson's belief in the widespread existence of the moral sense in society, even among the untutored, and of those of lesser intelligence, was the source of his trust in popular sovereignty. Although only a few men were considered able to employ intuitive reason to discover, amplify, and explain self-evident moral truths, all men were endowed with a sense of moral rectitude. If reason was the elite human quality, possessed and cultivated by only a small number of people, then certainly the moral sense could be described as the democratic attribute.

According to White, Jefferson believed "that the Creator has written his precepts so indelibly on our hearts because he did not wish to let the very existence of society depend on what man could achieve by his brain alone, a brain that might have effaced these precepts if they were not deeply rooted in instinct, the moral sense, or conscience." Thus, social cohesion must not be entrusted to the few with well developed rational faculties, but only to the many with an innate sense of right and wrong.[121]

Education for Citizenship

Jefferson was optimistic about the possibility of developing the natural moral inclinations of the people. Although everyone is endowed with moral sense, not all possess it with equal strength. However, all can be taught to exercise it more consistently and effectively, even the "ploughman" with no formal education. And some "gifted" individuals, though not high-born to aristocracy, could be educated to exercise the higher powers of reason "to serve the whole people and guard their liberties by knowing relevant moral principles and historical facts." Indeed the minds of the people *must* be elevated through education and experience in governance since the people, in his view, were "the only safe depositories of government."[122]

Jefferson's approach to education consisted of three divisions including elementary, middle, and higher education. The entire scheme was oriented toward the needs of republican government, and "adapted to the years, the capacity, and the conditions of every one, and directed toward their freedom and happiness."[123] Indeed, "the backbone of Jefferson's republic was a system of public education."[124] Thus, elementary education was focused around the most basic needs of citizens in a republic. It included the "three Rs" and instruction in "the rights and duties of citizens." Jefferson summarized its goals as follows:

> To give every citizen the information he needs for the transaction of his own business; To enable him to calculate for himself, and to express and preserve his ideas, his contracts and accounts, in writing; To improve, by reading, his morals and faculties; To understand his duties to his neighbors and country, and to discharge with competence the functions confided to him by either; To know his rights; to exercise with order and justice those he retains; to choose with discretion the fiduciary of those he delegates; and to notice their conduct with diligence, with candor, and judgment; And, in general, to observe with intelligence and faithfulness all the social relations under which he shall be placed.[125]

He believed that all free children, both male and female, should attend these schools.

Beyond the elementary level the public education system assumed the shape of a pyramid, with only the most able at each stage proceeding on to the next. In this manner Jefferson intended to finally sift out for the most sophisticated learning what he described as *the natural aristocracy*. Although he was opposed to government by an "artificial aristocracy" based on being born to wealth or royalty, he staunchly believed in the importance of cultivating something like a meritocracy.[126] These "natural" aristocrats would emerge from all strata of society and, given the right schooling, provide leadership based on talents and virtue.[127]

However, formal education provided only one kind of training for citizenship. The other was to be found in the kind of learning that is experienced through the process of participating in community affairs. As Mc-Williams suggested, Jefferson's view was in direct opposition to *The Federalist* "for it implied that lesser loyalties and affections should be strengthened and not fragmented." Whereas the Federalists feared the destructive effects of "factions" organized around human "passions," Jefferson saw such associations and affiliations as essential to human development.[128] Society must be directed toward the moral education of the individual through social relations of various kinds, rather than constructing institutional mechanisms to protect government from the destructive impulses inherent in human nature.[129] Participation in the process of governance was understood to be of central importance in this human developmental task.

Participation and Self Government

Not only will individual citizens develop their political and social capacities through participation, but it is also the only way in which a republican form of self-government can be maintained.[130] Jefferson insisted that: "If every individual which composes their mass participates of the ultimate authority, the government will be safe, because the corrupting of the whole mass will exceed any private resources of wealth, and public ones cannot be provided but by levies on the people."[131]

It is worth noting that one of the common justifications heard today for active involvement of the citizenry which Jefferson does not seem to adhere to explicitly concerns the prospect of enhancing public goods and services through citizen input. Apparently he did not want the argument to rest on that point to any extent. He quite readily admitted that a majority frequently makes bad decisions, but argued that this was less injurious than "the self-interested policies of autocrats."[132]

In other words, public services and programs may not always be more effective and efficient in achieving their specified objectives as a result of citizen involvement; in fact they may be worse. However, that was less important in the long run, from Jefferson's point of view, than maintaining and enhancing popular government. Making specific decisions, creating particular agencies of government, allocating resources toward certain ends—these were all important, but only penultimate tasks of government. The ultimate task was to protect liberty, develop the capacities of citizens as much as possible, and uphold the natural rights of the people to govern themselves.

Jefferson was an ardent advocate for active participation of the citizenry in governance, but he acknowledged limitations in the practical implementation of this lofty ideal. In a letter to Abbe Arnoux in 1789 he explained: "We think, in America, that it is necessary to introduce the people into every department of government as far as they are capable of exercising it, and this is the only way to insure a long continued and honest administration of its powers."[133] These words contain both the ideal and the hint that there are qualifications to come. These qualifications are spelled out in this letter and elsewhere.

It should be pointed out that when Jefferson spoke of "the people" he had in mind the agrarian landed gentry. Hofstadter has suggested that this was "the outstanding characteristic of Jefferson's democracy." He maintained that, "it seems hardly enough to say that he thought that a nation of farmers, educated, informed, and blessed with free institutions, was the best suited to a democratic republic...."[134] Hofstadter argued that, in fact, Jefferson believed that popular government would, at best, be improbable in a nation characterized by "large cities, well-developed manufactures and commerce, and a numerous working class." From Jefferson's point of view, the stability and wisdom afforded by proximity to nature, ownership of property, and a liberal education were essential to self-rule. However, given these conditions, Jefferson was "convinced that on their good sense we may rely with the utmost security for the preservation of a due degree of liberty."[135]

Jefferson assumed too, that even in such an agrarian society the mass of people would not be qualified to exercise executive judgment, to legislate, or judge questions of law. However, they were competent to choose executive officers, legislators, and judges. In fact, the citizens in such a society were the only ones qualified to make these decisions.

As concerns the judiciary, not only should the people elect their judges, but they should also participate in the jury system. Jefferson believed that this was an important participatory role. The people might not be qualified to judge questions of law, "but they are very capable of judging questions of fact," which he understood to be the essential role of the jurors.[136]

Jefferson insisted that the way to deal with the problem of scale in a nation the size of the United States was to establish and maintain multiple governments. He maintained on one occasion that:

> Our country is too large to have all its affairs directed by a single government. Public servants at such a distance, and from under the eye of their constituents, must, from the circumstance of distance, be unable to administer and overlook all the details necessary for the good government of the citizens, and the same circumstance, by rendering detection impossible to their constituents, will invite the public agents to corruption, plunder and waste.[137]

What emerged then, as Jefferson developed his theory of self-government, was a multi-level representative system, a *hierarchy of republics*. At the top, with the least participation of the citizenry, was *the general federal republic* that was to deal with "all concerns foreign and federal." Next were the state governments that were to be concerned only with matters pertaining to their geographic area, followed by "county republics with a similar jurisdiction over only those things peculiar to their boundaries."

It was at the lowest level of the hierarchy, where most governmental activity occurred in Jefferson's time, that the most extensive direct participation would occur, that of the *ward republics*. These wards were Jefferson's equivalent of the New England township, which he described as "the wisest invention ever devised by the wit of man for the perfect exercise of self-government and for its preservation." Wards would provide a highly localized arena for selecting a judge and a constable, organizing a militia, providing for peace-keeping patrol, maintaining a school, caring for the poor, building and maintaining public roads, selecting jurors and conducting elections within their area for all higher offices.[138]

The ward republics would then be the locus of most service delivery and other activities that directly impact on the citizenry and also the places where they would exercise the greatest control. Jefferson believed that this direct local participation "by making every citizen an acting member of the government and in the offices nearest and most interesting to him, will attach him by his strongest feelings to the independence of his country and its republican constitution."[139] The political identification of a citizen with the nation would be rooted in and rest upon active citizenship in a proximate community.

Although Jefferson shared many of the Anti-federalists' convictions about the essential nature of the small republic, that point of view did not lead Jefferson to resist the formation of a large nation state with considerable power in the central government, as was true, also, for some Anti-federalists. Rather, he attempted to provide for the small and immediate political community *within* a larger one, as an integral part of it.

McWilliams observed that Jefferson hoped through this local attachment to a small unit of government to cultivate *the ideal of a fraternal citizenry*. As Jefferson understood it, America's fundamental problem was not one of finding the right *principles and values* around which to build a polity; on those he believed there was consensus. Rather the problem was one of "affection;" a need to enhance the *feelings* of belonging to a common political community. The ward republics were to be the mechanisms which Jefferson thought could bring citizens together at the proper scale to accomplish the cultivation of this emotional bond among themselves which could then be extended to the scale of the state and nation.[140]

Jefferson's participatory ideal has not been fulfilled in the ward republics, nor in most local government structures. However, Caldwell observed that "Jefferson's insistence on the free participation of citizens in public affairs has been realized in a way that he could not have foreseen—through the growth of nongovernmental civic organizations."[141] These voluntary associations of the kind that caught the attention of De Tocqueville have served as schools for participatory citizenship, as well as mediating structures between the individual citizen and government.[142]

Thus, Jefferson presented us with a philosophy which calls for as much direct participation as possible, but recognized that little is possible at the upper levels of government. There participation is indirect, involving the election of representatives. From Jefferson's perspective direct, regular, and active participation of the citizenry should take place at the local government level. He assumed that there were essential criteria for determining those who were best qualified to govern. For Jefferson, education was essential, but the ownership of land and agrarian life were also critical prerequisites.

The Republican "Revolution" of 1800

The Federalist perspective dominated the new American government for the first twelve years after the adoption of the Constitution in 1789. Although republicanism provided the common conceptual framework for most of the political factions during these years, the term did not have the same meaning to all. The Federalists adhered to a new republicanism which differed significantly from the more traditional forms. Hanson indicated that the last fifteen years of the eighteenth century may be seen as an internecine struggle between this new republicanism of the Federalists and the older republicanism "to which the Antifederalists, Democratic-Republican Societies, and Jeffersonian Republicans were successive heirs."[143]

Hanson argued that the instigators of the American revolution were committed to a "classical conception of citizenship" rooted in the older tradition of republicanism. This view required virtue understood as a commitment by each individual to value the commonweal over his own selfish interests. Republican citizens were obliged to place specific virtues such as courage, wisdom, and leadership talents in service to the community. In this way, virtue provided the final defense against the most serious threats to the integrity of a republic—invasion and faction.[144] It created cohesive social and political bonds in the face of external challenge, and established limits to domestic conflict.

It is clear that the Federalists valued virtue, as Nigro and Richardson have recently emphasized; the concept is found throughout the *Federalist Papers*.[145] However, according to Hanson, the Federalists understood republican virtue differently. Under the influence of Hume's belief that individuals are dangerously egoistic—driven by passion and self interest—they placed their trust in a virtuous elite and virtue in government understood as "rule-making." That is, political virtue took the form of strictures, procedures, requirements, and structural arrangements designed by a virtuous elite to produce virtuous government.[146]

Hanson's assessment of these dozen years of the Federalist "new science of politics" was that it in fact hastened the decline of civic virtue by failing to provide participatory channels for the people. Widespread disillusionment with the centralizing tendencies of this approach led to the emergence in the 1790s of *an alternative republicanism* with roots similar to those of Anti-federalism and enriched by the diffusion of the French Enlightenment in the United States. Hanson maintained that the philosophical foundations of this movement were laid by Thomas Paine in *The Rights of Man* and generally endorsed by Thomas Jefferson.[147]

Thus, Jefferson's inauguration in 1801 in his own eyes, as well as those of his fellow Republicans, was "a revolution in American government as momentous as the Revolution of 1776." Peterson concluded that the change from the Washington to the Adams administration in 1797 was viewed as only a "succession of Federalist presidents," but Jefferson's assumption of office represented something more momentous—"a transfer of power."[148] Edward Dumbauld, an editor of Jefferson's political writings, argued similarly that Jefferson's victory in 1800 "meant that the Constitution of 1787 was to be used as a vehicle for popular self-government, as an instrument of democracy." Dumbauld opined that if Hamilton had prevailed in the struggle for power, the Constitution might well have been used to move toward monarchy; and concluded that Jefferson rightly called his victory a *second revolution.*[149] Walter Lippman noted the significance of Jefferson's displacement of the Federalists by suggesting that, "It was Jefferson who taught the American people to regard the Constitution as an instrument of democracy."[150] Hanson concluded that in the early nineteenth century the Jeffersonian version of *yeoman republicanism* became the public philosophy of that period.[151]

The most important implication of this shift in the dominant political culture for this review of the ethical tradition of citizenship is that it resulted in a crucial reassertion and reenforcement of the more classical republican citizenship values which had been partially obscured by Federalist ideas. Dumbauld described this resurgence of traditional republican tenets as Jefferson's infusion of the Constitution with "the spirit of the Declaration of Independence" and summarized the new era as follows:

> A new civilization, based on "cherishment of the people," Jefferson believed, was destined to arise in America. The doctrine of Europe (and of statesmen such as Alexander Hamilton) was that the people was "a great beast" and must be restrained by brute force. The Jeffersonian doctrine was "that man was a rational animal, endowed by nature with rights," and could be trusted to maintain law and order by means of a government of limited powers, responsible to the people, and permitting citizens "to think for themselves, and to follow reason as their guide." The philosophy of human brotherhood and enlightenment for which Jefferson stood, the confident faith that America was a virgin land of hope and opportunity, became the dominant and distinctive national tradition.[152]

The Emergence of the Jefferson Image

This treatment of the Jeffersonian tradition opened with a focus not on the historical record of Jefferson, but on the complex set of values, ideas, ideals, principles, beliefs, and attitudes associated with him. It is clear that these cannot be completely separated from Jefferson's conduct as a statesman. Although such an effort exceeds the scope of this book, and is divergent from its central theme, historians have, and should continue to, examine his record to test the consistency of his actions with the views he es-poused. To some extent, Jeffersonian philosophy may be viewed on its own since the power of his image in the American political tradition resides in the fact that he articulated and reasserted philosophical perspectives that transcended the man. It is this ethos as one stream in the ethical tradition of citizenship which is of interest here.

Even though Jefferson loomed large in life, his image took on even more heroic proportions and became more deeply embedded in the Ameri-can political tradition after his death. The fact that his last breath occurred just after midnight on July 4, 1826, precisely on the 50th anniversary of the Declaration of Independence, assumed an almost mystical quality in the minds of Americans at that time. The death of John Adams five hours later on this day for which Americans were prepared to celebrate their first half century of nationhood added to the profundity and fatefulness of the occa-sion. Peterson described the mood and events of those days:

> The charmed death of Thomas Jefferson and of his venerable friend made the Jubilee a solemn monument in American memory and opened a remarkable season of patriotism. . . . Over the next several weeks, from New Orleans to Portland, Americans raised a swelling hymn of praise to Jefferson and Adams. Military stations conferred honors; courts, legislative bodies, and learned soci-eties held commemorative exercises; communities in untold number set aside days of public homage, "the unbought offering of an independent people." Virtually the whole populace of Richmond turned out for the mock funeral procession and Governor John Tyler's eulogy of Jefferson in Capitol Square. Thirty thousand witnessed the services in Baltimore's Howard Park, where Charles Carroll, the last of the Signers of the Declaration, was the guest of all the dignitaries of state and city. On a hot August afternoon Bostonians jammed famed Faneuil Hall, and listened for two and one-half hours to one of the greatest orations of Daniel Webster's career.[153]

Jefferson himself penned the most memorable words heard during these ceremonies only ten days before his death. Declining an invitation to attend the forthcoming Fourth of July celebration in the nation's capital because of his weakened condition, Jefferson summed up his own demo-cratic faith:

> All eyes are opened, or opening, to the rights of man. The general spread of the light of science has already laid open to every view the palpable truth, that the mass of mankind has not been born with saddles on their backs, nor a favored few booted and spurred, ready to ride them legitimately, by the grace of God. These are the grounds of hope for others. For ourselves, let the annual return of this day, forever refresh our recollections of these rights, and an undimin-ished devotion to them.[154]

Peterson viewed the demise of Jefferson, followed almost immediately by that of Adams, as a pivotal moment in the establishment of the Jefferson image as a central element in the American political tradition. It elevated Jefferson's life, words, and ideas to the status of a "fable of the republic" which "brought men into a community of loyalty and belief, and turned the nation's loss into a triumph." Furthermore, according to Peterson, it was a dramatic turning point in the development of American self-consciousness; it encouraged the habit of "looking backward to oracles and landmarks" which "drew the fabled past into contemporary myth." In this American "myth," this interpreted history of the new nation, Peterson insisted that, "No name was more important in this way than Jefferson's. His was the compelling image of the fable."[155]

Summary of Jeffersonian Contributions to the Ethical Tradition of Citizenship

1. Individuals were understood as equal within a social natural state. Jefferson believed that individuals were endowed by natural law with equal political rights, as did John Locke. However, he asserted contrary to the Lockean formulation, that the natural state of human beings is a social one. Jefferson emphasized the importance of the affective bonds of community through associations and affiliations of various kinds for human fulfillment and happiness. The effect of this way of casting the relationship of the individual to the community is to bound the excesses of individualism that would be encouraged by an assumption that the natural state is one of free individuals who artificially construct social relationships for convenience.

2. Jefferson emphasized the importance of civic virtue. He believed that virtue, understood as social obligation, was necessary in order to support the natural social state of human beings. Happiness, in Jefferson's thinking, was not the result of private activity; not a state to be achieved through the individual pursuit of wealth, but a public activity in search of public well-being. This assumption is supportive of active citizenship, whereas the Federalist reliance upon institutional mechanisms and a virtuous elite to produce virtuous government discouraged and limited participation by the citizenry.

3. Jefferson reasserted the classical republican tradition of citizenship. His confidence in the people to govern themselves, rooted in an optimistic view of human nature, provided the basis for his commitment to self-government. Government *must* reflect an expression of the will of the people because they have a natural right to govern themselves; government *may* be able to do so, in fact, because the moral sense is inherent in all, whatever their ancestry or socio-economic status. Moreover, this moral sense may be developed further through education. Thus, the classical republican emphasis on the obligation of the citizen to value the common interest over private individual interests was thought to be feasible because of this positive view of human nature with its innate moral inclinations.

CONCLUSION

Though these examples of idea and experience from the ethical tradition of citizenship in the United States defy any attempt at neat integration into a completely harmonious philosophical perspective, they do embody certain recurring values, beliefs, assumptions, and principles. These common ideas and the experiences that have given them life, existing in a kind of symbiotic relationship, represent an ethical tradition—a stream of normative touch-stones—that have enriched the meaning of American citizenship.

Beyond the legal definitions of citizenship, although more difficult to discern since it is not codified, lies the informal heritage embodied in the experience of forming voluntary associations and westward migration, Puritan thought and community, Anti-federalism, and the Jeffersonian tradition. This is an extraordinarily rich and complex tapestry of thought and conduct, but there seem to be five main ideas which form the backbone of the ethical tradition of citizenship in the United States:

1. The dignity of the individual citizen.   Commonly held assumptions about the possibility of reason and the existence of a moral sense yielded a view of the individual citizen as capable of thoughtful and moral action and, therefore, worthy of trust and respect by fellow citizens, as well as those in authority. Compact, contract, and covenant ideas reflect assumptions that individual citizens are endowed equally with certain rights by natural law and, therefore, entitled to political equality.

2. The consensual nature of authority.   Given beliefs in individual citizens with capacities for reason and moral discernment, and equally endowed with natural rights, it logically follows that collective authority must rest on self-government by consent. Officials who exercise authority ought to do so on behalf of the citizenry, and only so long as they enjoy popular support. Political structures are only conventional arrangements which are subject to modification or replacement, according to popular will. Once consent is given, citizens are obligated to support the authority created until such time as they, acting together as the citizenry, decide to withdraw their consent in favor of other authorities and authoritative arrangements. In order to facilitate the exercise of consent, government should be kept as close to the people as possible. Some centralization is inevitable, but decentralization is desirable wherever possible.

3. A concern for the common good.   Although citizens are individually endowed with certain rights, their natural state is not one of isolated lone individuals, but rather one of natural sociability. Happiness is not to be achieved simply through the protection of individual rights and property, but also through the well-being of society. Therefore, individual citizens are obligated to seek not only their own interests, but also those of the political community. This search for the common good is possible because individual citizens are capable of exercising reason and moral discernment. It is a goal which must be sought by the citizenry, rather than imposed by some omniscient authority—technical, religious, or hereditary—because decisions about the common good must rest on, and be consistent with, popular consent.

4. The importance of civic virtue.   Government based on consensual authority and oriented toward the common good requires not only reason and moral discernment, but civic virtue as well—an inclination, or predisposition, to act on one's rational and moral judgments. Civic virtue is the essential motivation necessary to carry out what one knows to be rational and ethically appropriate. It embodies character traits such as honesty, fairness, and courage which a citizen must possess in order to consistently seek the common good. These personal attributes carry the citizen beyond a preoccupation with mere observance of the letter of the law to a deeper concern for the well being of his or her fellow citizens and the long term good of the community as a whole. Civic virtue can be cultivated and enhanced through governmental arrangements and education of various kinds.

5. The experience of participation in government as not only a right and obligation of citizenship, but also as education for citizenship.   Participation is the most fundamental means for learning how to seek the common good, but it is also crucial in the cultivation of civic virtue. It is through participation in government and voluntary associations that idea and experience come together to form civic habits and skills. It is through participation that a sense of community is engendered and bonds to the whole are created. Participation stimulates "affections" for the political community that give life to political principles such as equality, justice, and freedom. Therefore, participation is an ethical as well as political act. Those in offices of authority must understand that waiting for the people to be "ready" before inviting their participation will not only subvert their rights to participate in self-governance, but stand in the way of their development as citizens. One cannot "get ready" for citizenship any other way.

Having reviewed the various strands and summarized the key ideas in the ethical tradition of citizenship in the United States, in the next chapter we move on to consider how this tradition was obscured and attenuated in the late nineteenth and early twentieth centuries.

REFERENCES

1. *Ethics for Bureaucrats: An Essay on Law and Values* (New York: Marcel Dekker, 1978). While I am critical of Rohr's specific formulation of the American regime values and his view of their most appropriate source, I hasten to declare that, in my judgment, Rohr's contribution in refocusing our search for normative ethics for public administration on this *historical* concept is crucial and of enormous significance. I am convinced that the notion of regime values with its orientation toward historical reflection and research is far more likely to be fruitful in constructing useful and viable normative administrative ethics than further pouring over abstract concepts such as "the public interest" in isolation from the political heritage and culture in which we stand.

2. MARTIN DIAMOND, "Ethics and Politics: The American Way" In *The Moral Foundations of the American Republic,* 2nd ed., ed. Robert H. Horwitz (Charlottesville: University Press of Virginia, 1982), pp. 68–69. Donald Lutz has developed a similar argument more recently in "The United States Constitution as an Incomplete Text" in *Intergovernmental Perspective,* 13 (Spring 1987), 14–17. Lutz insists that the United States Constitution is incomplete without the Declaration of Independence and the state constitutions.

3. Quoted in "Marshall on Constitution: 'Defective From Start'," *Los Angeles Times,* May 7, 1987.

4. I would add the 17th amendment which provides for the direct election of the United States Senate to Marshall's list.

5. JOSEPH CROPSEY, "The United States as Regime and Sources of the American Way of Life" in Horwitz, *Moral Foundations,* pp. 86–87.

6. LOREN P. BETH, *The Development of the American Constitution, 1877–1917* (New York: Harper & Row, 1971), p. xv. The "writer" Beth is quoting is Stanley Bertram Chrimes in his *English Constitutional History* (London: Oxford University Press, 1958).

7. ALEXIS DE TOCQUEVILLE, *Democracy in America.* Volume 2 (New York: Alfred A. Knopf, 1945), p. 115.

8. *Ibid.,* Volume 1, p. 191.

9. *Ibid.,* p. 116.

10. *Ibid.,* pp. 192–193.

11. *Ibid.,* p. 251.

12. The similarity of America to the "state of nature" assumed by Locke and other contractarians was noted by Locke himself in several instances. *See for example, The Second Treatise of Civil Government,* section 49.

13. RALPH BARTON PERRY, *Puritanism and Democracy* (New York: Vanguard Press, 1944), p. 209.

14. ARTHUR M. SCHLESINGER, *Paths to the Present* (New York: MacMillan, 1949), p. 24.

15. *Ibid.,* p. 49.

16. GEORGE D. LANGDON, JR., *Pilgrim Colony* (New Haven: Yale University Press, 1966), pp. 1–2, 12–15.

17. DWIGHT B. HEATH, ed., *A Journal of the Pilgrims at Plymouth* (New York: Corinth Books, 1963), pp. 17–18. This journal provides the earliest known text of the Mayflower Compact.

18. *Ibid.,* pp. 17–18.

19. *Ibid., See* note 5, p. 17.

20. WILMOORE KENDALL AND GEORGE W. CAREY, *The Basic Symbols of the American Political Tradition* (Baton Rouge: Louisiana State University Press, 1970), pp. 30–42, 138.

21. LAWRENCE A. SCAFF, "Citizenship in America: Theories of the Founding" in *The Non-Lockean Roots of American Democratic Thought,* Joyotpaul Chaudhri, ed. (Tucson: University of Arizona Press, 1977), p. 49.

22. *Ibid.,* pp. 51–53.

23. MICHAEL WALZER, *The Revolution of the Saints: A Study in the Origins of Radical Politics* (New York: Atheneum Press, 1970), p. 2.

24. *Ibid.,* p. 14.

25. CHAUDHRI, *The NonLockean Roots,* pp. 50–52.

26. JOHN WISE, "A Vindication of the Government of New England Churches" in Roy Harvey Pearce, ed., *Colonial American Writing* (New York: Rinehart, 1950), pp. 321–322.

27. PERRY, *Puritanism and Democracy* (New York: Vanguard Press, 1944), p. 198.

28. PEARCE, *Colonial American Writing*, p. 324.
29. WALZER, *Revolution*, p. 170.
30. CHAUDHRI, *The NonLockean Roots*, p. 52.
31. WALZER, *Revolution*, p. 170.
32. PEARCE, *Colonial American Writing*, p. 327.
33. CHAUDHRI, *The NonLockean Roots*, p. 52.
34. KENDALL and CAREY, *The Basic Symbols*, p. 31.
35. DON K. PRICE, *America's Unwritten Constitution* (Baton Rouge: Louisiana State University Press, 1983), p. 45
36. PERRY MILLER, *The New England Mind, The Seventeenth Century* (Cambridge: Harvard University Press, 1954), p. 439.
37. GEORGE ALLEN COOK, *John Wise, Early American Democrat* (New York: King's Crown Press, 1952), p. 152.
38. PERRY, *Puritanism and Democracy* p. 197.
39. CHAUDHRI, *The NonLockean Roots*, pp. 51–52, 56, 61.
40. JOHN LOCKE, *Two Treatises of Government.* Peter Laslett, ed. (Cambridge: Cambridge University Press, 1960), pp. 368–369.
41. PEARCE, *Colonial American Writing*, p. 329.
42. Quoted in MILLER, *The New England Mind* (Cambridge: Harvard University Press, 1954), p. 409.
43. PEARCE, *Colonial American Writing*, p. 328.
44. PERRY, *Puritanism and Democracy* (New York: Vanguard Press, 1944), p. 502.
45. CHAUDHRI, *The NonLockean Roots*, p. 62.
46. COOK, *John Wise*, p. 152 observes that the ideas commonly held by Baron Samuel Pufendorf, John Locke, and John Wise had begun to permeate the times.
47. PERRY, *Puritanism and Democracy*, p. 501.
48. MILLER, *The New England Mind*, p. 409.
49. *Ibid.*, p. 398.
50. PERRY, *Puritanism and Democracy*, p. 192.
51. *Ibid.*, p. 192.
52. *Ibid.*, p. 193.
53. *Ibid.*, pp. 194–195.
54. Perry argues that nonseparatist Puritan groups were able to hold fast to the Church of England while adopting a congregational structure of governance by removing themselves physically from direct control by the church hierarchy, thus maintaining a fiction of allegiance. *See* in particular pp. 106–110.
55. CLINTON ROSSITER, *Seedtime of the Republic: The Origin of the American Tradition of Political Liberty* (New York: Harcourt, Brace, 1953), p. 162.
56. *Ibid.*, p. 195.
57. *Ibid.*, pp. 160, 165–168.
58. LARZER ZIFF, *Puritanism in America: New Culture in a New World* (New York: Viking Press, 1973), pp. 104–108.
59. ROSSITER, *Seedtime*, p. 190. Quotations are from *Records of the Colony of Rhode Island* (Providence, 1856–1865).
60. *Ibid.*, p. 192.
61. COOK, *John Wise*, p. 153.
62. *The Anti-Federalist Papers and the Constitutional Convention Debate.* Ralph Ketcham, ed. (New York: New American Library, 1986), p. 31–62.
63. RUSSELL L. HANSON, *The Democratic Imagination in America.* (Princeton: Princeton University Press, 1985), p. 54.
64. *Ibid.*, pp. 55–56, 65. *See also* Herbert Storing, *What the Anti-federalists Were For* (Chicago: University of Chicago Press, 1981), p. 5.
65. *Ibid.*, p. 60. For a summary of traditional republicanism see BENJAMIN R. BARBER, "The Compromised Republic: Public Purposelessness in America: in HORWITZ, *The Moral Foundations*, p. 2.
66. *Ibid.*, p. 62.
67. *Ibid.*, p. 63.

68. *Ibid.*, pp. 64–65.
69. *Ibid.*, p. 73.
70. ALEXANDER HAMILTON, JAMES MADISON, AND JOHN JAY, *The Federalist Papers* (New York: New American Library, 1961), p. 79.
71. HANSON, *The Democratic Imagination*, pp. 71–77. *See also* ROBERT HORWITZ, "John Locke and the Preservation of Liberty: A Perennial Problem of Civic Education" in HORWITZ, *The Moral Foundations*, pp. 132–133; Herbert Storing, *What the Anti-federalists Were For*, chapter 5.
72. *The Antifederalist Papers*, ed. Morton Borden (Michigan State University Press, 1965), pp. xii–xiv. (No place of publication indicated.)
73. HORWITZ, *Moral Foundations*, p. 133.
74. HANSON, *The Democratic Imagination*, p. 74. *See also* STORING, *Wathe the Anti-federalists Were For*, pp. 72–73.
75. Concerning the tensions within the antifederalist camp see STORING, *What the Anti-federalists Were For*, p. 6.
76. KETCHAM, *The Anti-federalists Papers*, p. 20.
77. STORING, *What the Anti-federalists Were For*, p. 72.
78. CECELIA M. KENYON, ed., *The Anti-federalists* (New York: Bobbs-Merrill, 1966), p. xxxviii.
79. KETCHAM, *The Anti-federalists Papers*, pp. 269, 276. According to KETCHAM, "Brutus" was probably Robert Yates, a New York judge who was a delegate to the Federal Convention. Storing's disagreement is cited in Herbert Storing, ed., *The Anti-Federalist* (Chicago: University of Chicago Press, 1985), p. 103.
80. STORING, *The Anti-Federalist*, p. 7, indicates that at the time, "Centinel" was thought to be Judge George Bryan, a prominent Pennsylvania legislator and judge who was also the Anti-federalist leader in that state. However, Judge Bryan's son, Samuel, is now considered the author.
81. *Ibid.*, p. 230. This is a direct refutation of the arguments presented in Federalist nos. 10 and 51. On the Anti-federalist concern that complexity obscured accountability to the people, *see* chapter 7.
82. Quoted in STORING, *The Anti-Federalist*, p. 51.
83. EDMUND BURKE, "Speech to the Electors of Bristol" in B.W. Hill, ed., *Edmund Burke On Government, Politics, and Society* (New York: International Publication Service, 1975), pp. 156–158. John Stuart Mill, "Considerations on Representative Government" in J.M. Robson, ed., *Collected Works for John Stuart Mill*, vol. XIX (Toronto: University of Toronto Press, 1977). For a recent concise discussion of this issue see Amy Gutmann and Dennis Thompson, "The Theory of Legislative Ethics" in Bruce Jennings and Daniel Callahan, eds., *Representation and Responsibility: Exploring Legislative Ethics* (Hastings-on-Hudson, New York: Plenum Press, 1985), pp. 167–195.
84. KETCHAM, *The Anti-federalist Papers*, p. 18.
85. HANSON, *The Democratic Imagination*, p. 75.
86. STORING, *The Anti-Federalists* pp. 17, 43–45.
87. *Ibid.*, p. 84, note 19.
88. *Ibid.*, p. 17.
89. KETCHAM, *The Anti-federalist Papers*, p. 247.
90. MELANCTON SMITH in STORING, *The Anti-Federalist*, p. 336.
91. KETCHAM, *The Anti-federalist Papers*, pp. 50–51.
92. *Ibid.*, p. 18.
93. STORING, *What the Anti-federalists Were For*, p. 17.
94. STORING, *The Anti-Federalist* , p. 114.
95. STORING, *What the Anti-federalists Were For*, p. 20.
96. STORING, *The Federalists,*p. 16.
97. *Sydney*, identified in Borden, *The Antifederalist*, p. 126 as Robert Yates. Quoted in this reference from Storing, *What the Anti-federalists Were For*, p. 18.
98. STORING, *The Anti-Federalist*, pp. 341–342.
99. HANSON, *The Democratic Imagination*, p. 75.
100. STORING, *What the Anti-federalists Were For*, p. 20.

101. *See for example, Brutus* in KETCHAM, *The Anti-federalist Papers*, p. 325 and HORWITZ in HORWITZ, *The Moral Foundations*.
102. STORING, *What the Anti-federalists Were For*, pp. 26–27. *See also* HORWITZ in HORWITZ, *The Moral Foundations*, pp. 132–133 for a discussion of these differences.
103. STORING, *What the Anti-federalists Were For*, pp. 72–76.
104. *Ibid.*, p. 21.
105. *See* the proposals of "A Farmer," not to be confused with "The Federal Farmer," for "seminaries" where the "principles of free government" might be taught, in STORING, *The Anti-Federalist*, p. 271.
106. *Ibid.*
107. STORING, *The Anti-Federalist*, pp. 80–81. The "Federal Farmer" is often thought to be Richard Henry Lee, one of the leading Anti-federalists. Storing sees his authorship as problematic, however. *See* this volume, pp. 23–25.
108. KETCHAM, *The Anti-federalist Papers*, p. 320.
109. STORING, *The Anti-Federalist*, p. 343.
110. HERBERT STORING, ed., *The Complete Anti-Federalist*, Volume 1 (Chicago: University of Chicago Press, 1981), p. 19.
111. HANSON, *The Democratic Imagination*, pp. 75–76.
112. MERRILL D. PETERSON, *The Jefferson Image in the American Mind* (New York: Oxford University Press, 1960), p. vii.
113. GEORGE H. SABINE, *A History of Political Theory* (New York: Holt, Rinehart and Winston, 1961), p. 670.
114. EDWARD DUMBAULD, ed., *The Political Writings of Thomas Jefferson* (New York: Liberal Arts Press, 1955), p. 3.
115. *Ibid.*, p. 83.
116. Letter to Henry Lee, August 10, 1824, quoted in LYNTON K. CALDWELL, *The Administrative Theories of Hamilton & Jefferson* (Chicago: University of Chicago Press, 1944), p. 113.
117. MERRILL D. PETERSON, *Thomas Jefferson and the New Nation. A Biography* (New York: Oxford University Press, 1960), p. 94.
118. Jefferson substituted "pursuit of happiness" as one of the central "unalienable rights" for Locke's inclusion of "property." Jefferson saw property as a civil rather than natural right. Property by his view had instrumental value in the pursuit of happiness, but was not itself a natural right. *See* PETERSON, *Thomas Jefferson*, pp. 94–95 for a discussion on this point.
119. MORTON WHITE, *The Philosophy of the American Revolution* (New York: Oxford University Press, 1978), p. 99.
120. *Ibid.*, p. 100. White argues that Jefferson essentially followed the hybrid doctrine of Jean Jacques Burlamaqui.
121. *Ibid.*, p. 122.
122. *Ibid.*, pp. 137–141. *See also* DUMAS MALONE for a discussion of Jefferson's views on the possibility of improving human nature through education in *Jefferson the Virginian* (Boston: Little, Brown and Co., 1948), p. 179.
123. GILBERT CHINARD, *Thomas Jefferson, The Apostle of Americanism*, 2nd ed. (Ann Arbor: University of Michigan Press, 1939), p. 129.
124. PETERSON, *Thomas Jefferson*, p. 145. Jefferson's educational plan was put forth in "A Bill for the More General Diffusion of Knowledge," introduced into the Virginia Legislature in 1779. The plan was never adopted, however.
125. Quoted in WILLIAM K. BOTTORFF, *Thomas Jefferson* (Boston: Twayne Publishers, 1979), p. 55.
126. PETERSON, *Thomas Jefferson*, pp. 152, 955.
127. EDWARD DUMBAULD, ed., *The Political Writings* (New York: Liberal Arts Press, 1955), p. 91.
128. WILSON CAREY MCWILLIAMS, *The Idea of Fraternity in America* (Berkeley: University of California Press, 1973), p. 212.
129. *Ibid.*, pp. 217–218.
130. Advisory Committee on Intergovernmental Relations, *Citizen Participation in the American Federal System* (Washington, D.C.: United States Government Printing Office, 1979), pp. 25–27.
131. DUMBAULD, *The Political Writings*, p. 92.

132. RICHARD HOFSTADTER, *The American Political Tradition* (New York: Vintage, 1948), p. 33.
133. DUMBAULD, *The Political Writings*, p. 89.
134. HOFSTADTER, *The American*, p. 39.
135. Letter to James Madison, December 20, 1787 in *Thomas Jefferson on Constitutional Issues: Selected Writings, 1787–1825*. Compiled and distributed by the Virginia Commission on Constitutional Government, 1962, p. 5.
136. DUMBAULD, *The Political Writings*, p. 89.
137. Letter to Gideon Granger, August 13, 1800 in *Thomas Jefferson on Constitutional Issues*, pp. 16–17.
138. *Ibid.*, pp. 101, 117.
139. *Ibid.*, p. 117.
140. MCWILLIAMS, *The Idea*, p. 219.
141. CALDWELL, *The Administrative Theories*, 2nd ed. (New York: Holmes & Meier, 1988), p. xiii.
142. ALEXIS DE TOCQUEVILLE, *Democracy in America* (New York: Alfred A. Knopf, 1980). For the concept of "mediating structures *see* PETER L. BERGER and RICHARD JOHN NEUHAUS, *To Empower People: The Role of Mediating Structures in Public Policy* (Washington, D.C.: American Enterprise Institute, 1977).
143. HANSON, *The Democratic Imagination*, p. 54.
144. *Ibid.*, p. 62.
145. WILLIAM D. RICHARDSON AND LLOYD G. NIGRO, "Administrative Ethics and Founding Thought: Constitutional Correctives, Honor, and Education," *Public Administration Review*, 47 (1987), pp. 367–376.
146. HANSON, *The Democratic Imagination*, pp. 73–74. *See* a longer discussion of this point in the section above dealing with the Anti-federalist perspective.
147. *Ibid.*, pp. 76–78.
148. PETERSON, *Thomas Jefferson*, p. 654.
149. DUMBAULD, *The Political Writings*, pp. xxxiii–xxxiv.
150. *Ibid.*, p. xxxiv, note no. 51.
151. HANSON, *The Democratic Imagination*, p. 103.
152. DUMBAULD, *The Political Writings*, pp. xxxiv–xxxv.
153. PETERSON, *The Jefferson Image*, pp. 4–5.
154. Quoted in *Ibid.*, p. 5.
155. *Ibid.*, pp. 5–8.

4

THE TRANSFORMATION OF PUBLIC ADMINISTRATION AND THE ECLIPSE OF CITIZENSHIP

> The citizen, whose chief duty is to participate, is disappearing as an important political actor. The result represents the evaporation not only of a central political status (which means in turn a decline of politics in favor of efficient, instrumental organization) but also the loss of certain key political values which can be sustained in practice only where there is someone to practice them.[1]

In these somber words Robert Pranger described the "eclipse" of citizenship as a participatory public office of the individual in modern democracies.[2] How this eclipse occurred in the United States and its relationship to the emergence of modern professionalized public administration is the focus of this chapter.

The thesis developed here is that the Progressive reform movement of the first two decades of the twentieth century represented a significant shift away from the Populism of the late nineteenth century, with its encouragement of active citizenship, toward an approach to government dominated by a professional corps of public administrators. The argument is similar to that advanced by Robert Bellah and his colleagues in *Habits of the Heart, Individualism and Commitment in American Life.*

Bellah, et al., argued that the Populists, with Thomas Jefferson as their hero, sought reform rooted both in the claims of ordinary citizens to the ability to govern themselves, and in the ideal of face-to-face community—essential values of the ethical tradition of citizenship. They maintained that "Populism was the great democratizer, insisting on the incompleteness of a republic that excluded any of its members from full citizenship."[3] They asserted however, that although the Progressives shared with the Populists certain democratic values, their commitment to science and rationality ultimately dominated their actions and "moved American political discourse away from concern with justice, with its civic republican echoes, toward a focus on progress—a progress defined primarily as material abundance." This result was ironic in view of the Progressives' original espousal of direct democracy, since the reform movement they fostered "shifted the goal of political action away from the realization of a democratic republic and toward the creation of an administrative system that could 'deliver the goods'."[4]

Thus the democratizing influence of the ethical tradition of citizenship, with its encouragement of participation, although evident to a limited extent in the expansion of electoral rights of the citizenry, ultimately was thwarted by the dominance of Progressive values more consistent with those underlying the early legal tradition. Progressive reforms tended to enhance the power of the citizenry at the polls, but stifled active and direct participation in governance by their promotion of government based on efficiency, expertise, and professionalism.

The Progressives may have made *representative* democracy more effective, but in so doing they opted for administrative values which amounted to barriers to more direct *participatory* democracy where it counted most—in the activities of the burgeoning administrative state. In brief, professionalized public administration tended to displace the role of the citizen rather than view itself as an instrument of the citizenry to provide access to governance under the new conditions of modern urban industrial society.

THE LATE NINETEENTH CENTURY: A CHANGING SOCIAL CONTEXT

The beginnings of the fundamental changes in American social conditions which contributed to the shift in reform emphases from those of Populism to those of the Progressive Movement can be discerned in the last two decades of the nineteenth century.[5] Robert H. Wiebe maintained that the crucial transition was from the values of the small town to those of "a new, bureaucratic-minded middle class" which emerged during the urbanization and industrialization of the nation.[6]

As the small towns which provided coherence and stability for the lives of most Americans during the nineteenth century began to be drawn into a national society dominated by mushrooming urban complexes and large corporations, the old ways of conducting business and government proved ineffective. The orderly integration of family, religion, community associations, schools, local business communities, town professionals, and local government was threatened as the towns themselves unavoidably became part of a national economy dominated by large scale business and industrial firms.[7]

In this emerging urban society the kind of individualism that had been at the heart of the American myth, and the informal cooperation of individuals in the relatively intimate relationships of the town, were simply inadequate for the management of life in large cities. Wiebe points out that "The city dweller could never protect his home from fire or rid his street of garbage by the spontaneous voluntarism that had raised cabins along the frontier."[8] The far more complex set of interdependent and often transient relationships that characterized these places, and made their very existence possible, required a new set of values such as regularity, system, and continuity. Individuals could not stand alone and count on their neighbors for voluntary assistance either in times of emergency, or for routine maintenance of the shared environment.

It became necessary for urban government to provide far more formal and elaborate arrangements for such functions as sanitation, fire service, law enforcement, transportation, health services, street maintenance, construction standards, parks, libraries, recreational services, and education than in the towns of the earlier decades of the nineteenth century. In this formalization of the delivery of public services is found the emergence of modern public administration as an occupation to supplant the previously informal self-help activities of citizens. Public administrators replaced the citizenry in many of their functions, but failed to assume the obligations of fiduciary citizenship. The argument summarized in the first chapter of this book, that is to be developed further in succeeding chapters, is that this transition in the performance of these tasks from citizens to paid administrators should have carried with it a fiduciary obligation by administrators to the citizenry. The sovereignty of the people required an administrative identity rooted in the ethical tradition of citizenship.

As happened all too often in the cities, immigrants from the small towns of America found government under the sway of political machines. These unofficial political organizations functioned as *shadow governments*, manipulating the employment of public servants, the allocation of public services, and the interpretation of the law to reward their faithful supporters and punish their enemies.[9] Patronage, nepotism, bribery, and electoral fraud were the forms of corruption which characterized the way these machines worked their will.

The effects of these fundamental changes in the order of society and the relationship of people to their social environment led to confusion, loss of identity, and a sense of impotence in the face of forces beyond the control of the individual. Wiebe observed:

As the network of relations affecting men's lives each year became more tangled and more distended, Americans in a basic sense no longer knew who or where they were. The setting had altered beyond their power to understand it, and within an alien context they had lost themselves. In a democratic society who was master and who servant? In a land of opportunity what was success? In a Christian nation what were the rules and who kept them? The apparent leaders were as much adrift as their followers.[10]

William E. Nelson described the emergence in the late nineteenth century of a "quest for a scientific morality" as a means of coping with this kind of disorientation. It was based on a "simplistic empiricism," a preoccupation with "science" in the form of statistical data.[11] Wiebe remarked upon this same phenomenon which he termed a *quantitative ethic*. He suggested that this ethic "became the hallmark of their crisis in values," and explained it as a reaction to "seeing more and bigger of everything," including trains, corporations, factories, and buildings as the United States urbanized and industrialized. Wiebe concluded that: "For lack of anything that made better sense of their world, people everywhere weighed, counted, and measured it."[12]

This morality of science in the form of quantitative assessment of the world was an expression of the need to regain some sense of control over life in the new society. It gave rise to an approach to governmental reform based on the establishment of leadership in the hands of trained experts. Strange though it may seem at first glance, both Nelson and Wiebe attributed the evolution of this perspective to a yearning for a sense of community self-determination and moral purity in the face of the new alien forces of urban industrial America.[13] Nelson concluded that as the reformers and intellectuals of the late nineteenth century looked backward into the history of the previous hundred years for reference points the communitarian ideal and reliance on aristocratic leadership were identified as two historic preconditions for morality in government.[14]

Since restoration of the isolated communities of the towns seemed impossible, this need for autonomous community life tended to focus primarily on the crucial nature of leadership in national and urban governments. What was required was not leadership by an aristocracy of the wealthy that would use power for its own interests, but an aristocracy of the wise and competent. As Richard T. Ely described it, it was to be "a natural aristocracy . . . which lives for the fulfillment of special service."[15]

This emphasis paved the way for leadership in the hands of an aristocracy of competence in applying the "scientific" ethic to public affairs. Since administration was beginning to assume greater and greater significance in the process of government, the attention of the reformers then quite naturally focused on public administrators as the instruments of their reform aspirations and civil service reform as their goal.[16] Nelson concluded:

Thus, by the end of the nineteenth century the administrative process was coming to be understood, in accordance with the scientific ideal of reformers, as one that required experts who made decisions and otherwise performed their tasks in accordance with autonomous, abstract standards.[17]

The bureaucratic ideas which became dominant in the reform movement by the end of the nineteenth century superficially appeared to restore the traditional values of the village. Virtues such as frugality, promptness, foresight, and efficiency seemed to be shared by town culture and bureaucracy. As Wiebe observed, "the morals of the farm town had moved to the industrial city" and had been transformed in the process. Efficiency, which had been associated in the minds of Americans with "know-how," "Yankee ingenuity," or the "better mousetrap," now referred not to specific individual solutions to everyday problems, but rather to "an approach to a fluid social process," a systematization of work evaluated by quantitative measures.[18] Individual genius was replaced by an impersonal relationship between input and output.

Thus the scene was well set for the emergence of the Progressive movement by the end of the nineteenth century. These shifts in social and economic conditions, and the ideas which became prominent among reformers of that era in response to the changes, established the general perspective which would be worked out in the reform of government in the twentieth century under the guidance and sponsorship of the Progressives. This perspective was embodied in an eclectic political theory drawn from a variety of sources including both reformers and scholars such as Herbert Croly, Walter Weyl, Frederick Howe, Jane Addams, Albert Shaw, Benjamin De Witt, and Franklin Giddings. According to Wiebe, "the new political theory borrowed its most revolutionary qualities from bureaucratic thought":

> Trained, professional servants would staff a government broadly and continuously involved in society's operations. In order to meet problems as they arose, these officials should hold flexible mandates, ones that perforce would blur the conventional distinctions among executive, legislature, and judiciary.[19]

This political theory provided the basic rationale for the Progressive agenda and the development of the American administrative state.

THE PROGRESSIVE MOVEMENT AND THE TRANSFORMATION OF PUBLIC ADMINISTRATION

By the second decade of the twentieth century a consensus for reform clearly existed throughout the nation, but reform leadership had shifted from the farmers and residents of the small towns to middle and upper class urbanites.[20] The Progressive movement which emerged from this consensus included a rather eclectic agglomeration of Americans. There appear to have been several different strains of Progressives including business leaders, humanitarians—both religious and secular—politicians, and scholars. Mann argued that it was actually several different movements loosely related by similar goals. He identified three tendencies of this collection of movements: efforts to remove corruption from government, a struggle to democratize the structure and machinery of government, and advocacy for more involvement of the government to relieve social and economic distress.[21]

The earliest and most significant concrete expressions of Progressivism were to be found at the level of local government, particularly in the large cities of the East and Midwest.[22] Wiebe attributed the particular values manifested by the Progressives to the anxiety experienced by ambitious upwardly mobile middle class residents of these expanding cities. He explained that in the towns power was personal, but:

> When they moved into a broader arena, however, they soon found that they could neither see, know, nor even know about the people upon whom they had to depend. The legal framework changed; new groups, some abiding by quite different values, complicated the pattern; and relationships often followed an inner logic. The system was so impersonal, so vast, seemingly without beginning or end.[23]

At the heart of their unease was a perception that a "patchwork government" was no longer adequate to deal with the complexity and range of problems posed by these changes as expertly and economically as they believed necessary.[24]

In the uncertainty of this new social and political environment these middle class urbanites sought stability, not that of the small face-to-face community as had the nineteenth century reformers, but stability to be found in bureaucratic structures and procedures. They sought the reassurance and control created by hierarchical systems; government by professional expertise, efficiency, and orderly rules. Wiebe asserted that "The heart of progressivism was the ambition of the new middle class to fulfill its destiny through bureaucratic means." He observed that rather than engaging in a defense of the old communities, "Most of them lived and worked in the midst of modern society and accepting its major thrust drew both their inspiration and their programs from its peculiar traits."[25]

These Progressive reform efforts at the municipal level were characterized by a pursuit of the first two of the three tendencies mentioned above—the abolition of corruption and the establishment of more democratic forms of municipal government.[26] The strategy adopted by the Progressives was one of representing the enemy as the "devilishly effective" System supported by an alliance of political bosses and wealthy businessmen. Of course, they then offered themselves as opponents of the System who would destroy it "and, by implication, substitute a natural, individualistic democracy." As Wiebe pointed out, the irony of this way of representing the reform struggle was that it was the Progressives who were the systematizers and "their opponents the slovenly, albeit sometimes democratic, governors."[27]

Experimentation by local governments began to produce innovations intended to increase efficiency by placing government on a more business-like footing. The commission plan of city government, first developed in Galveston, Texas as an efficient means of managing reconstruction after a disastrous tidal wave in 1900, was adopted by a number of other cities within a few years. The city manager plan was first instituted in Staunton, Virginia in 1908 and was subsequently adopted by Sumter, South Carolina in 1911. The National Municipal League, which had been organized in 1894, created an education and information service to provide technical assistance to cities, as well as model charters and new options for municipal organization. This national association also had local counterparts in the forms of citizens unions, good government associations, reform leagues, and civic clubs.

One notable example of these associations at the municipal level was The Civic Federation of Chicago, founded in 1894 by William T. Stead, a Christian humanitarian, and a coalition of business and labor leaders in reaction to the depression of 1893. It was organized under a council of one hundred members and thirty-four ward presidents. Daniel Levine described its basic mission as follows:

> Honesty, system, and economy were to be achieved through publicity. Arouse the public conscience and virtue would triumph. If publicity alone were not enough, personnel, organization, or laws could be changed and evil would vanish. Thus better aldermen, a new charter, or a new franchise law could cure Chicago's ills. The Federation envisioned a good life which was not very different from life as it already was. All aldermen would be honest, election fraud would disappear, government would be simple and cheap, and public-service franchises would be granted only in return for a fair payment to the city.[28]

In short, the Federation sought clean and efficient government. However, as Levine observed, "By the end of the century, many reformers asked not only that government be honest and efficient, but also more directly responsive to the popular will."[29] Although the Federation was committed to the elimination of fraudulent elections, and corruption of government by machines and corporations, it was hardly devoted to the cultivation of active participatory citizenship.

For example, the Federation opposed the initiative and referendum that had been adopted in a number of states prior to their emergence as issues in Illinois in 1910. Specific reasons for its opposition to a combined proposal for adopting these measures included that "It strikes at *representative* and *efficient* popular control"; "It is not progress, but a return to 'town *meeting'* and 'mob rule,' the rock on which early popular government was wrecked," and "It takes responsibility from the elected legislators and gives it to unofficial irresponsible minorities."[30] (Emphasis added.)

Underlying these criticisms was a rather low estimation of the competence of the people to participate directly in governance. Levine maintained that the Federation "believed that the common run of humanity was not capable of governing itself." He continued: "In opposing the initiative and referendum, the Federation insisted that direct, popular control could lead only to disaster, that the 'mob' needed to be controlled, and that a more capable elite, presumably of wealth, had to lead in order to protect the people from their own foolishness."[31]

The Civic Federation of Chicago may have been more conservative than other Progressive reform associations, since the initiative and referendum were generally supported by Progressives. The reason for this tendency can be explained as the result of its upper class leadership. Although the Progressives are generally thought to have been of middle class origin, there was significant involvement by business people. This was the case in Chicago where the leaders of the Federation were clearly wealthy corporation directors, bankers, and businessmen. They participated in reform, not out of a sense of *noblesse oblige*, but "from pure economic self-interest."[32]

PROGRESSIVE ELECTORAL REFORM

Even though the Federation may have represented the right wing of the movement, the values which influenced the Federation were not significantly different from those held by the Progressive movement generally. Although more "direct democracy" was one of the espoused goals of the Progressives, suspicions of direct popular rule were widely held throughout the movement. Landon Warner maintained that,

> Although progressive leaders represented the "people"—the exploited small businessman, office worker, laborer, immigrant, and farmer—against the "interests"—the powerful business corporations that dominated political as well as economic life—these reformers had less faith in the "people" than most would admit. There was a strong strain of elitism in the assertion of their own leadership and their dependence on the expert. They were committed to social planning and bureaucratic effort.[33]

Ardent advocacy of representative government, rather than more direct participation by the citizenry, made it possible for the Progressives to present themselves as democrats while, at the same time, promoting reform designed to place control in the hands of "apolitical" professional administrators.

Ekirch pointed out that while they were making changes in the electoral process such as the short ballot and secret voting, Progressives at the state level were managing to secure state constitutional amendments which tended to centralize power in the hands of governors and administrators.[34] Supportive of this line of argument, he called attention to what he described as "an evident contradiction between the Progressives' confidence in extending direct democracy and their willingness to centralize political authority and interpose independent regulatory commissions between the people and their elected representatives."[35]

Through the efforts of the Progressives, American voters gained the direct primary, the direct election of the United States Senate, shorter ballots, secret voting, woman suffrage; and many, if not all, secured the referendum, the recall, and the initiative. These were not insignificant achievements, but most of them do not amount to "direct" democracy. Rather they provide direct election for *indirect* representative democracy. Although all of these innovations were termed "direct" democracy by the Progressives, under close examination it seems clear that only two—the initiative and the referendum—can accurately be understood as "direct" exercises of citizenship. Even these were never adopted at the national level, nor were they instituted by all of the states.

All of the other electoral reforms, while unquestionably improving the representativeness of representative democracy, did not provide for "direct" participation in the process of governance. Laudable and long overdue as it was, woman suffrage only allowed women to participate in the selection of representatives; important and also long overdue was the direct election of the United States Senate; finally, after more than a century, permitting American voters to vote for someone to represent them in the upper house of the Congress. The short ballot made voting for representatives less confusing, less cumbersome and more efficient; secret voting assured voters of the freedom to vote for representatives without fear of intimidation or reprisal; direct primaries gave citizens the right to participate directly in the selection of party nominees for representative electoral offices; and the recall gave the voters power to change their minds about their choice of representatives. All these measures amounted to enhancements of representative government, not direct democracy.

The most significant electoral reform achievements of the Progressives did contribute to the effectiveness of representative democracy and, in so doing, did amount to movement toward democratization in the short run. Linked to a different view of the public administrative role, they might also have been steps toward democratization in the long run. Joined with an understanding of public administrators as supporters and encouragers of active citizenship rather than with certain "scientific" professionals possessing only arcane knowledge, these enhancements of representative democracy could have been developed as stepping stones in the long march toward a more direct participatory democracy in the United States, but they were not.

PROGRESSIVE ADMINISTRATIVE REFORM

Even though advocacy for electoral reforms was couched in the language of democracy, the changes proposed were constrained by the underlying adherence of Progressives to their core values—impersonality, independence, and expertise.[36] These reforms were essentially a means for removing entrenched political machines which they opposed. Their ultimate end was the transfer of power to a professional administrative elite under "wise" and "enlightened" public leadership in order to achieve more scientific and, therefore, more efficient government.

It was the mutual commitment to this goal that made it possible for humanitarians and business leaders to join their efforts in the reform movement. Humanitarians wanted better public services and a more orderly and decent political and social environment, while businessmen sought "more dependable and predictable relations with city government." Efficiency of the kind delivered by bureaucratized government conducted by professional, technically skilled public administrators served the purposes of both camps.[37] McConnell indicated that science and management techniques were their hope and that "confidence in impersonal technique took on an almost millennial tone."[38] Haber described the preoccupation with efficiency during these years as a "craze" that "hit like a flash flood."[39]

Ekirch indicated that an increased emphasis on efficiency and the systematic training of public employees also served another of the Progressives' purposes. It "proved useful . . . to many of the Progressives who were trying to create a reform program without stirring the social conscience or revolutionary feelings of the masses." The key to the Progressive agenda was to create change toward greater stability and order without rejecting democratic values. According to Ekirch, "Planning and social control via state regulation, in place of laissez faire, could be justified in terms of scientific principles and good public administration."[40] "Good public administration," of course, meant *efficient* administration produced by trained administrators employing supposedly "scientific techniques." Samuel Haber observed that: "Efficiency provides a standpoint from which those who declared allegiance to democracy could resist the levelling tendencies of the principle of equality."[41]

Among the most potent instruments of Progressive administrative reform were the municipal research bureaus that were established in some of the larger cities just after the turn of the century. These were intended to replace the *spoils system* of the urban political machines with civil service systems based on merit in the form of technical competence, and systematic accounting and budgeting systems intended to prevent corruption and waste. These were nonprofit associations organized independently of government, and typically funded by wealthy business leaders who, according to some scholars, were concerned about putting government on a more "businesslike" footing.[42]

The New York Bureau of Municipal Research, the most ambitious of these efforts, was organized in 1906 and became a model for other cities. Ekirch described it as "an example of the growing use of trained experts in public administration and of the application of the principles of political science to the needs of local government."[43] The New York Bureau and the proposals of Robert Moses in particular, will serve here to exemplify the administrative reform efforts typical of the Progressive Movement at the local level.

Robert Caro vividly depicted the atmosphere of reformist zeal and idealism at the New York Bureau in its early years through his biography of Robert Moses.[44] In Moses' proposals for personnel management reform in New York City one can clearly discern the Progressive commitment to rationality in the form of orderly categorization, science understood as quantifiable measures, and fairness expressed as standardized treatment. The corrupt influence of the Tammany Hall machine was to be replaced by a system which Caro describes as being "of a purity, a strength and a scope that was almost more religious than governmental."[45]

Moses' proposal called first for a complete standardization of salaries "so that employees doing the same type of work would be getting the same pay even if they were working in different departments." He insisted on "only one standard or promotion in public life: 'open competition,' how hard and well a man worked and how he performed on examinations." The results of these examinations would be posted publicly, and "report cards would be open to public inspection so that every city employee would know the basis whereon he and his competitors were judged." This led logically to a declaration that "Seniority would become unimportant; not experience but ability would be crucial."[46]

Moses' penchant for taxonomic order was revealed in his proposal to divide all government service into sixteen categories: "*executive, legislative, judicial, professional, subprofessional, educational, investigational, inspectional, clerical, custodial, street cleaning, fire, police, institutional, skilled trades,* and *labor.*" He then advocated dividing each category into specific jobs, and then each job should be "scientifically analyzed" to identify its specific functions and responsibilities.

Robert Moses' commitment to "science," understood as quantitative measurement, could then be seen in his belief that the functions and responsibilities of each job, of which there were dozens for most jobs, "could be given a precise mathematical weight corresponding to its importance in the over-all job." Caro reported that Moses assumed that "the success of the employee in each function and responsibility could be given a precise mathematical grade" that could be "added according to weight and combined in service records for each employee." These mathematical grades would be recorded cumulatively, and these grades alone used for determining salary increases and promotions.[47]

Caro observed that Moses' recommendations were "the proposal of a fanatic." He concluded that "John Calvin specifying permissible arrangements for women's hair in sixteenth-century Geneva was not more thorough than was Bob Moses enumerating the 'functions' and 'responsibilities' of New York's civil servants." Caro emphasized Moses' obsessive belief that everything must be subjected to mathematical scores: "No aspect of conduct on the job was too small to be graded. Even personality must be reduced to number. 'Personality,' Moses said, "includes those intangible elements the existence of which do not readily admit of proof, but nevertheless . . . each employee *must* be rated on personality."[48]

The "human element" was a problem for Moses; it was always getting in the way of "the mathematical perfection of his system" and his strategy was to seek to suppress it. So strong was his concern to prevent political manipulation by Tammany that his commitment to "scientific" objectivity was absolute. He believed that it was necessary "to have a definite, almost a mechanical, program of adjustments in order to avoid personal and political pressure." However, examiners—those who worked most closely and routinely with the system—were always "mucking up" its objectivity. Caro said, "They were always becoming sympathetic to individuals and talking about the 'human factor.' According to Moses, "an examiner who . . . always wishes to take the 'human factor' into consideration is a *dangerous* man to associate with such work."[49](Emphasis added.)

Moses' supreme confidence in professional technical expertise was summed up by Caro:

> Shining through all Moses' statements was confidence, a faith that his system would work, a belief that the personalities of tens of thousands of human beings could be reduced to mathematical grades, that promotions and raises could be determined by a science precise enough to give every one of those human beings the exact rewards he deserved. Asked once if it might not prove difficult to divide a job like that of janitor into different levels based on different functions and responsibilities, Moses replied flatly that it would not be difficult at all. To the expert, he said, such differences are "clearly discernible."[50]

Perhaps Caro was right—perhaps Moses was a fanatic. However, for better *and* for worse, he did clearly reflect the motivating values and principles which typified the Progressives, though as an extreme case. The commitment to rationalizing public administration, the concern for making it more "scientific" through the use of numbers, the emphasis on standardizing everything from personnel systems to budget procedures to delivery of public services as a means of achieving fairness ("without fear or favor"), were all aspects of the Progressive approach to reforming the administration of government.

Even in the case of Progressives of the humanitarian strain such as Jane Addams, there was a similar, although less severe, preoccupation with being "scientific" although it sometimes appeared to mean only employing the trappings of science to make a point. Addams was heavily influenced by the new science of sociology which led her to approach social ills, not primarily in terms of individual and group psychology, but rather as a problem in readjusting the "social machinery." The goal was to eliminate conflict in order to achieve a "higher type of social unity." Levine argued that, "This does not mean that she was willing to forego human sympathy in favor of a cold scientism, but simply that normal impulses of compassion must be systematized to become more effective."

Addams believed that the first step in this process of manipulating social mechanisms was "the accumulation of data." Although these data were hardly objective and impartial since they were always selected to support a point, and "the conclusions were in hand before the investigation was begun," Jane Addams believed that data collection could eventually lead to a new science. Furthermore, since charity and social reform were to proceed "on the basis of carefully compiled data," Addams concluded by employing the scientific methods of sociology that such work "could be best administered by professionally trained workers, whose training supplemented but did not submerge normal human emotions."[51]

The fundamental problem, of course, was that this naive faith of the Progressives in science and numbers created a moral vacuum in their efforts to purify American government. It reflected the logical development of the late nineteenth century hope for a morality of science under the assumption that somehow the pursuit of quantitative methods in organizing and ordering society would produce a good society. The ethical realm was not to be abandoned, but fulfilled through the scientific analysis of society.

The difficulty with these assumptions was that "the good" was not reducible to numbers, nor was "the good society." Numbers without ethical principles do not define social values. Enhancement of efficiency in government was the espoused core principle of the Progressives, but efficiency is an *instrumental* value, not a *terminal* value; it does not specify an end, but only means.[52] Thus the question lingered over the movement—"Efficiency for what?" Jeffrey Sedgwick noted that the lack of goals for administrative reform was one of the major barriers to effective reform under the Progressives. They provided support for the development of scientific management, but they had difficulties specifying objectives and the measurements of success.[53]

McConnell similarly observed that the Progressives ultimately foundered on their lack of positive goals for society. Their utilitarian formula— "the greatest good of the greatest number in the long run"—was intended to subject value judgments to the test of numbers, but the basic questions were not answered by numbers:

> What was "the greatest good of the greatest number in the long run?" How should it be recognized? Who should determine "the highest use?" Antipathy to private power was no guide to the exercise of public power. Worst of all, a definition of positive goals did not automatically derive from the denial of private goals. The one was not the opposite of the other; virtue was not enough.[54]

The ethic of science and numbers proved futile in addressing the crucial questions concerning the values which should inform the discretion of administrators who were being given greater and greater power.

ACTIVE CITIZENSHIP AND PROGRESSIVE REFORM

The focus on representative democracy by the Progressives, combined with the administrative values they supported, may have advanced democratization in the short run, but this dual orientation created impediments to more active citizenship in the long run. While taking steps toward more effective representative democracy, these reformers encouraged the establishment of a relatively depoliticized, technically oriented, and more powerful professional bureaucracy that thwarted the long term trend toward greater democratization. Their faith in administrative expertise simultaneously obviated the need for active citizens and eroded the effective power of political representation. Citizens might well have gained more control over the selection of their political representatives, but the efficacy of those representatives was weakened by the expansion of professionalized and technically oriented administration. The result, according to McConnell, was that even in places where some degree of popular control of the political process was achieved, "nothing was left to politics; quietism, good government, businesslike management, administration were all that remained."[55] Corrupt politics may have been separated largely from the administration of government, but so were citizens and their elected representatives. Marver Bernstein suggested that the Progressives had "an abiding faith in regulation, expertness; and the capacity of the American government to make rational decisions provided experts in the administrative agencies could remain free from partisan political considerations."[56] This kind of thinking tended to isolate the new administrative policymakers from popular control, either directly through citizen participation, or indirectly through their representatives. Haber concluded that: "The Progressives who greeted efficiency with enthusiasm were often those who proposed to let the people rule through a program in which the bulk of the people, most of the time, ruled hardly at all."[57]

In fact, truly direct democratic participation of the citizenry seemed unnecessary if one assumed, as the Progressives tended to do, that everyone, given the proper education, would want a society that was essentially efficient and technically functional. This anticipated consensus for an urban technocracy would reflect "a new urban unity, the Progressive version of the old community ideal." Nostalgia for the "friendly village" was replaced by visions of "the professionally serviced city" which would be a "paradise of new-middle-class rationality." Wiebe suggested that this assumption was the basis for a "new bureaucratic vision" which "accepted the impersonal flux of the city and anticipated its perfect systematization."[58]

The distancing of the American citizenry from its government induced by the emphasis on professionalized, scientific, apolitical administration, on the one hand, and representative democracy, on the other, was compounded by the national political philosophy of at least a major segment of Progressivism which was articulated by Herbert Croly.

HERBERT CROLY: THE NATIONAL PROGRESSIVE PHILOSOPHER

The multifarious nature of the nineteenth century roots of the Progressive reform movement have been discussed previously. However, late in the first decade of the twentieth century the political philosophy of the movement began to take on a more coherent form through the work of Herbert Croly. Link and Catton described Croly's work as the "most significant formulation of progressive political theory" and Croly himself as being "the chief philosopher of progressivism."[59] Kennedy attributed to Croly the less inclusive, but nevertheless highly significant, role of "chief intellectual spokesman for an important variety of Progressive thought."[60]

Croly's thought made a particularly impactful contribution to the movement at the national level as a major source for Theodore Roosevelt's "New Nationalism" in 1912. Ekirch described Croly's *The Promise of American Life* as "the most systematic expression of the Rooseveltian philosophy" and "a significant statement of the Progressive program and philosophy."[61]

The Promise of American Life, published in 1909, began by challenging the continuing viability of American assumptions of national destiny. In it Croly argued passionately for the establishment of a national purpose to replace simple fatalistic reliance on the maintenance of a "set of political institutions" and fulfillment of American destiny "by the vigorous individual pursuit of private ends." Individual freedom, which had led to a "morally and socially undesirable distribution of wealth" had to give way to "a large measure of individual subordination and self-denial."[62]

Croly called for strong national action to deal with the concentration of wealth and widespread corruption which he believed had resulted from this profligate individualism. However, that would require subordination of the individual to "the demand of a dominant and constructive national purpose." At times Croly's advocacy for the priority of national purpose over individual freedom assumed rather stringent tones calling for "stern discipline" and "schooling" that might require "severe coercive measures."[63] His understanding of national purpose and interest tended toward a benevolent, but powerful paternalism in which the state would teach men "how they must feel, what they must think, and what they must do, in order that they must live together amicably and profitably."[64]

Consistent with this general perspective which he termed *national democracy*, Croly also called for limits on popular protest; they must "conform to certain conditions." Protest must always be bounded by obedience to the law and must "never be made the excuse for personal injustice or national disloyalty." Protest against the injury of private interests by national policy "must be able to show either that such injuries are unnecessary, or else [that] they involve harm to an essential public interest."[65]

Herbert Croly's Progressive political philosophy represented a radical departure from the Constitutional federal system with its reserved powers for the states. National purpose was to become heavily dominant over individual and local purposes. Croly clearly saw the states as failures due to their chaotic and inefficient approach to governance. His proposals for reforming state governments moved in the direction of greater centralization of authority under strong governors. In this more powerful state, executives would actually determine what legislation would be introduced for consideration by the legislatures; state legislative bodies would not have power to independently initiate and deliberate upon legislative proposals. Governors, then, would convene as a "House of Governors" to plan and coordinate legislative action nationally. The principle of checks and balances and separation of powers at the state level was, in Croly's view, unnecessary and the source of great inefficiency.[66]

Throughout his treatment of reform of the states, Croly's guiding principle was the achievement of greater efficiency in administration. This led him in the direction of replacing the federal system with a hierarchically oriented governmental structure, with the states being subordinate to the national government. He did not carry these tendencies to the logical extreme of proposing a completely monocentric state, but his inclination is certainly evident.

Also, although Croly claimed to be seeking Jeffersonian ideals through the use of Hamiltonian means, he admitted repeatedly his strong preference for the philosophy of Hamilton.[67] He acknowledged that Hamilton's thought was not sufficiently democratic, but he believed that he was somehow wedding the noble, but insubstantial popular sentiments of Jefferson to the sound operational mind of Hamilton. However, after lip service was paid to Jefferson it seems clear that the essence of the Jeffersonian perspective embodied in the Declaration of Independence was specifically abandoned in Croly's proposals.[68] Croly saw Jeffersonian notions of equal rights as inadequate to prevent unequal accumulations of great wealth, and as providing the power to corrupt government. Since all people were not equally endowed with ability, the provision of equal rights simply allowed those who could achieve more to do so without any consideration of how they used their acquired status and resources.[69] Croly argued instead that the national public interest must be advanced by "positive and aggressive action." "The nation," he asserted, "has to have a will and a policy as well as the individual; and this policy can no longer be confined to the merely negative task of keeping individual rights from becoming in any way privileged."

It seems reasonable to conclude that, as Kennedy suggested, although Croly claimed to be presiding over a marriage of Hamilton to Jefferson, to many of his critics it appears that the former inevitably overwhelmed the latter "and the two elements are ultimately incompatible."[70] Croly's commitment to Hamiltonian rather than Jeffersonian values is manifested in his advocacy of determination of rights by the state:

> The arduous and responsible political task which a nation in its collective capacity must seek to perform is that of selecting among the various prevailing ways of exercising individual rights those which contribute to national perpetuity and integrity. Such selection implies some interference with the natural course of popular action; and that interference is always costly and may be harmful either to the individual or the social interest must be admitted.[71]

One can discern quite clearly in this reasoning about rights, a concept of the state; not as something created by individuals to preserve their individual rights and liberties, but as an entity with an interest and will of its own that transcends those of individual citizens or a majority of individual citizens, and, at times, may conflict with them. The state also has a right to "perpetuity and integrity" which precedes the rights of citizens.

In fact, Croly's references to the American state evidenced an almost religious fervor and his language assumes a sacred aura. He speaks repeatedly in a mystical fashion of the "American Promise," presumably using the upper case "P" to suggest something of transcendent character. In one passage he proclaimed, "The American idea is no longer to be propagated merely by multiplying the children of the West and by granting ignorant aliens permission to vote. Like all *sacred causes*, it must be propagated by the *Word, which is the Sword*." (Emphasis added.) The precise meaning of this language is obscure, but its tone is that of the religious zealot.[72] Haber characterized Croly's work as at some points sounding "like Friedrich Nietzsche presiding as a YMCA discussion leader."[73]

Belief in the priority of the rights of the state as well as in the existence of a will and interest of its own, logically led to Croly's conclusion that whenever the citizenry and the state are in conflict the state must prevail. These assumptions and political notions were intended to be diametrically opposed to Jeffersonian perspectives which sought to establish individual rights grounded in natural law in order to prevent the state with its great power from riding roughshod over the citizenry. From a Jeffersonian social contract point of view, Croly's argument amounted to a dangerous reification of the state, which indeed did reflect Hamiltonian thought, but precious little of the American political mainstream which had existed since Jefferson's presidential administration.

However, as Croly saw it, the restoration and preservation of democracy in the United States required such a shift in political values. With his concern for abolishing private privilege through accumulated wealth and his commitment to efficient government, the Hamiltonian approach seemed necessary and appropriate. At the heart of the problem with twentieth century American government, he believed, was an inordinate fear among Jeffersonians of strong governmental leadership. Croly assumed, to the contrary, that placing great power in the hands of "men of special ability, training, and eminence" was the way to produce "responsible and efficient government."

Croly accused Jefferson of an inconsistent belief in the goodness of human nature, on the one hand, and a "cordial distrust of the man of exceptional competence, training, or independence as a public official," on the other. He charged Jefferson with making "faith in the people equivalent to a profound suspicion of responsible official leadership" because of his belief that, "Exceptional power merely offered exceptional opportunities for abuse." He described this distrust of government as "the sign by which the demoralizing influence of the Jeffersonian democratic creed is most plainly to be traced."

Thus Croly praised Theodore Roosevelt since "his influence and work have tended to emancipate American democracy from its Jeffersonian bondage." He admired Roosevelt's confidence "in an efficient national organization as the necessary agent of national interest and purpose." With enthusiasm he expressed his appreciation for Roosevelt's abandonment of "that part of the traditional democratic creed which tends to regard the assumption by the government of responsibility, and its endowment with power adequate to the responsibility as inherently dangerous and undemocratic."[74]

Croly criticized democracy of the Jeffersonian variety, but nevertheless affirmed his faith in democracy throughout the book. This apparent contradiction is explained when one looks carefully at the kind of democracy he advocated—a kind of nationalistic democracy. As John William Ward explained in his introduction to *The Promise of American Life*, Croly shifted the center of reference for his political theory from the "self to society, from the spontaneous, unfettered, undisciplined individual to the disciplined, controlled, trained individual."[75]

It is important to note in passing that although Croly's political philosophy was more fully elaborated and articulated than that of most other Progressives, and hewed to a harder line in its argument, it is possible to find similar views of the state held by others identified with the movement, such as the humanitarian Jane Addams. Daniel Levine described Addams concept of the state as "possessing some sort of a transcendent existence." He continued, "The State was a mystical entity above and beyond the institutions and individuals which composed it . . . It embodied the collective will and the collective conscience." Levine explained that "there were few aspects of life toward which Jane Addams did not feel government had a prime responsibility . . . In return, each individual had responsibilities to the State, that is, to society." He concluded: "These duties forbade every individual, every family, and every group from concentrating on its own well-being."[76] Croly developed more pointedly and consistently this kind of elevated view of the state as a central cornerstone of Progressive philosophy.

Since he viewed individuals as needing cultivation before they could be trusted with governance, Croly "did not accept a populistic, majoritarian notion of democracy." Croly believed that because popular and national interests would conflict to some degree, and since he believed the national interest to be of fundamental importance, majority rule was in his view therefore lacking in moral authority. Croly preferred the concept of national sovereignty to that of popular sovereignty. In flat opposition to Lockean and Jeffersonian notions about the sovereignty of the individual who enters into a social contract to form the state, Croly maintained that,

> The people are not Sovereign as individuals. They are not Sovereign in reason and morals even when united into a majority. They become Sovereign only in so far as they succeed in reaching and expressing a collective purpose. But there is no royal and unimpeachable road to the attainment of such a collective will; and the best means a democratic people can take in order to assert its Sovereign authority with full moral effect is to seek fullness and consistency of national life. They are Sovereign in so far as they are united in spirit and in purpose; and they are united in so far as they are loyal to one another, to their joint past, and to the Promise of their future.

Laying the groundwork for a substantial break with prevailing traditions of democracy in the United States, Croly continued:

> The Promise of their future may sometimes demand the partial renunciation of their past, and the partial sacrifice of certain present interests . . . Sacrifices of tradition and interest can only be demanded in case they contribute to the national purpose—to the gradual creation of a higher type of individual and associated life. Hence it is that an effective increase in national coherence looks in the direction of the democratic consummation—of the morally and intellectually authoritative expression of the Sovereign popular will.[77]

Croly's references to a *national will* and a *collective will* as the *democratic consummation* suggest a view of democracy that is so subordinated to his almost mystical, or even religious, concept of the state that it amounts to a process of redefinitionism that all but destroys the substance of the concept of democracy. What emerges from Croly's thought is, to be sure, government *for* the people, but certainly neither *of*, nor *by* the people—at least not of or by many of the people. Rather it seems to amount to a benevolent paternalistic social order in which an elite composed of "men of special ability, training, and eminence" form policy and administer the government efficiently for a "disciplined, controlled, trained" citizenry who offer their loyal support, with only a highly constrained right to protest governmental actions.

Herbert Croly's political philosophy provided an articulate, elaborated and supportive rationale for the Progressive reform movement. It carried the Progressive emphasis on representative democracy to its logical conclusion. Citizens should not only not attempt to be directly involved in governance, but they should not even assume the right to instruct those who represent them; neither those whom they select by ballot, those who hold political appointments, nor those who occupy permanent positions in the bureaucracy. Croly's vision amounted to the resolution of the abiding tension in American political thought between *delegate* and *trustee* concepts of representation, in favor of the Burkean trustee who would exercise wise judgment on behalf of what he or she deemed to be in the constituents' best interests. Elected officials, appointees, and administrators of exceptional ability, and untroubled by the sway of individual and group interests, would use their professional expertise in the scientific development and implementation of policy.

This professional expert judgment would, of course, be directed toward the development and maintenance of efficient government in the national interest. Unfettered by the clamor of diverse local interests, American political and administrative leadership at all levels would focus their efforts toward clarifying and carrying out the national will. This concentration of purpose and effort would channel the nation's efforts consistently and productively rather than dissipate them in internal contention and attempts to respond to diverse preferences and demands.

These ideas were quite consistent with the core Progressive values of efficiency in government through the application of scientific techniques and professional expertise. Croly's integration of these principles into a national framework with a moral, or even quasi-religious, commitment to a national collective will extended and reenforced Progressivism's previous local and state orientations. In so doing, Croly's philosophy contributed to the attenuation of direct democracy and the further removal of governance from access by the citizenry. It was, indeed, a step toward Hamiltonianism, and a step away from the ideals embodied in the ethical tradition of citizenship as it has been described herein.

THE EFFECTS OF THE PROGRESSIVE PHILOSOPHY

As Jeffery Sedgwick observed, this nationalistic thrust of the Progressives, combined with their emphasis on professionalism in government, reflected a strong centralizing tendency. He noted that,

> In this formulation there was an assumption that a viable national community had evolved in the United States that was able to speak for itself directly

through the election of a President. No longer was it assumed that a conception of the public interest must of necessity be built up from a clash of different local and state interests subject to the restrictions of the national Constitution. Rather, the executive branch was charged with efficiently implementing the public's will as articulated in presidential elections.[78]

What this amounted to, according to William Schambra, was community without the state, local, and private institutions that the Anti-Federalists had seen as the basis for community. Schambra interpreted this as the Progressives' way of avoiding the "price of provincialism for community" since the "great community" would be created by a powerful national government, and especially by a powerful and progressive President who would use his office to "preach selfless devotion to common good."[79]

However, John Dewey, himself a Progressive, asserted in the waning years of the Progressive era that the modernization of America through transportation and technology had, indeed, created a "great society" at the national scale, but that the "great community" had not been achieved. He concluded that the local communities in the United States had been invaded and practically destroyed by the larger national society through the network of transportation and communication which had emerged by that time. The "great society" involved national interdependence which produced both positive and negative "indirect consequences" for third parties (spillovers, externalities), including local communities. However, it was the yet to be created "great community" that Dewey believed would make it possible for publics to form and exercise democratic influence on national public policy to regulate the consequences of interdependence. The missing ingredient was the shared signs and symbols that are essential to community life. They had not yet been created at the national level. This Dewey understood as the democratic public's fundamental "problem." The consequence, of course, was that the citizenry tended to lose control over government as centralization occurred without an embracing "great community."[80]

Further exacerbating this centralizing trend was the simultaneous emphasis on professionalism in public administration. According to Samuel Beer, there is "an inherent tendency for professional knowledge to promote governmental centralization." This is a result of the general and theoretical nature of professional knowledge which professionals attempt to apply to similar problems wherever and whenever they occur. He explained:

> What the professional brings to government is not just knowledge of how to cope with a particular problem at a certain time and place, but rather a preparation to deal with all such problems anywhere, anytime. His professional equipment directs him to work through and enlist the initiative of the widest possible jurisdiction.[81]

Beer further observed that when professionals with similar training begin to work with each other across jurisdictional boundaries and levels of government they bring a common stock of knowledge and theory to the task. This "shared knowledge" approach provides the basis for harmony and cooperation which tends to "offset the Madisonian checks and balances that might otherwise arise from intergovernmental differentiation."[82]

The result, as Sedgwick saw it, was that dialogue within local and state multipurpose communities, addressing a variety of human needs, and struggling to achieve the common good or public interest, was supplanted by "a fragmentation among different functions, each professionalized and each, as a result, tending toward homogenization and centralization."[83] Thus, the combined emphasis on a national political community and professionalization of public administration amounted to an intensely centralizing strategy. This contributed to the emergence of a public administration largely disconnected from the citizenry and reoriented away from responsiveness to local communities.

It should be clear that there is no intention to suggest here that Herbert Croly and Progressives who held similar views were malicious, unintelligent, or inhumane. In fact, their support for national action and professionalization of public administration appears to have grown out of genuine concern for better governmental response to pressing human needs. Even those in the business community who saw the Progressive agenda in self-serving terms as good for business development no doubt included many with an ultimately benevolent and paternalistic concern for the economic well-being of American society.

However, one may very well accuse them of a lack of understanding of the importance of the citizenship role. In seeking to accomplish efficiency in government, root out corruption, and regulate the inordinate power of large corporations, they resorted to strategies which significantly undermined the effectiveness of the citizen in the American democracy and obscured the obligations of the citizenry for their government. One might well respond that in seeking a more active national government the Progressives were merely doing what had to be done to cope with the realities of a modern industrial society which had expanded to national scale. Also, it might be argued that a professional public service was also unavoidable if government at all levels was to be able to respond to service delivery needs that were inherent in a prosperous modern state. And needless to say, it would be difficult to argue that these general strategies of energizing the national government and professionalizing public administration were inappropriate.

In retrospect, it seems apparent that both these strategies were pursued in the absence of a high priority for optimizing direct participation of the citizenry in the process. The argument here is that, indeed, the emerging complexity and interdependence of American society in the early twentieth century could not, and should not have been ignored for some nostalgic adherence to the agrarian and small town democracy of a former era; that in coming to grips with the new era there was a failure to *struggle* to maintain as much efficacy for the citizen as possible.

John Diggins suggested that the leading Progressive historians, Beard and Parrington, failed to lead Americans back to their own history to find a usable past for dealing with the twentieth century. He maintained that,

> At this juncture classical political ideas would have offered an alternative . . . and had the Progressive scholars embraced these ideas they might have been able to look backward with hope and forward with visions of the great promise of civic virtue. But the idea of political virtue ceased to have relevance and meaning in America . . .[84]

Diggins suggested that Dewey might have played a significant role in this process, since he shared many of the values of classical politics, but his rejection of history cut him off from it.[85] Thus the failure of Progressive intellectuals to root their reforms in civic values led to the displacement by science of public virtue and the classical political tradition.[86]

Although Progressive reforms were typically advanced under the banner of a citizenship movement with journals such as *The Efficient Citizen*,[87] the long-term result was not one of enhancing the control and participation of the citizenry.[88] It was rather the strengthening of an emerging class of technically oriented administrators who were committed to the development of a scientific approach to public administration, as suggested by Wilson and others.[89] What those reformers failed to foresee was the impossibility of maintaining the subordination of "expert," "professional" administrators to the politicians in a modern industrial state. The power of technical expertise and specialized knowledge, the complexity of the problems to be faced, and the scale of government have tended to crowd out both the citizenry and their would-be representatives.[90]

Public administration was launched upon a course which devalued citizenship because of an inadequate definition of professionalism. Its commitment to political neutrality, a truncated pseudo-science, and a limited concept of efficiency deprived it of a normative foundation in the ethical tradition of citizenship, which is the appropriate source for public administration professional values. Rather than finding its point of reference in the democratic values of active citizenship, it oriented itself to a mechanical and myopic understanding of efficiency, an overly narrow view of science compounded by a naive optimism about the extent to which public administration could become scientific, and a bent toward centralization that failed to recognize the diversity of American society, and the importance of adapting government to that diversity.

MARY PARKER FOLLETT: A DIFFERENT VOICE

The ethical tradition of citizenship, though eclipsed, was not entirely without significant expression. American public administration was not completely bereft of alternative perspectives to that of the Progressives. During the peak of the Progressive era in 1918, Mary Parker Follett, drawing heavily upon her experience with community center work in Boston, published *The New State: Group Organization The Solution of Popular Government*.[91] Elliot Fox and Lyndall Urwick indicated that this book was popular with a generation that had become "disenchanted with the traditional democratic devices" that had been corrupted by political machines and wealthy industrialists. They report that it was reviewed both nationally and internationally in scholarly journals, and brought Follett widespread recognition. Its popularity is evidenced by the fact that it went through four printings, the last in 1923.[92]

In *The New State*, Follett's commitment to reforming government toward greater democracy is clear and pervasive. In the introduction to the book she charged that "Direct democracy as at present is a mere phantom of democracy" and proclaimed that "The immediate problem of political science is to discover the method of self-government."[93] However, it is equally obvious that Follett rejected the methods and approach of the Progressive movement in achieving reform. She admonished the Progressives for wanting "voters, not men" and went on to assert that "It makes little difference whether we follow the boss or follow the good government associations, this is all herd life—'following the lead'—democracy means a wholly different kind of existence."[94]

Follett repeatedly hammered away at these criticisms of the Progressives to whom she attributed the best of motives, but to whom she also ascribed inappropriate methods and undemocratic results. She identified three faulty methods of the Progressives: (1) "change in the forms of government" (charters, etc.), (2) "the nomination of 'good' men to office," and (3) "exhortation to induce 'the people' to elect them." While granting that good government associations represented an advance beyond party organizations, she saw their focus on electoral politics and a few "good men" as similarly misguided.

Follett attacked the tendency of these organizations to seek better government by revising the structure of government. To these efforts she stated, "We can never reform American politics from above, by reform associations, by charters and schemes of government."[95] Follett even included as targets of her biting wit the "sacred cows" of Progressives and their good government associations: the referendum, recall, and initiative. She believed the Progressive reformers failed to see that these potentially useful devices would, in fact, be useless without more basic cultivation of the citizenry. Follett insisted that these new mechanisms for expressing the popular will were based on a fallacious assumption. They "assume that we have a will to express; but our great need at present is not to get a chance to express our wonderful ideas, but to get some wonderful ideas to express." The prior task, according to Follett, was to create true public will by first developing "a people" with a shared will created through discussion and debate in a variety of groups.[96]

The most acerbic criticism was reserved for the Progressives' focus on political leaders. According to Follett, they naively seemed to believe that all they needed to do was find "three or four 'good men' and then once a year hypnotize the electorate to 'do their duty' . . . and then all would go well." Her criticism for this assumption was unrestrained:

> What a futile and childish idea which leaves out of account the whole body of citizenship! It is only through this main body of citizenship that we can have a decent government and a sound social life . . . The wide-spread fallacy that good officials make a good city is one which lies at the root of much of our thinking and insidiously works to ruin our best plans, our most serious efforts. This extraordinary belief in officials, this faith in the panacea of a change of characters, must go. If our present mechanical government is to turn into a living, breathing, pulsing life, it must be composed of an entire citizenship educated and responsible.[97]

In this attack on the presumptions of the Progressives concerning the priority of political leadership, it is possible to discern the outlines of Follett's prescriptive proposals. They focused on citizenship development at the grassroots as the first and most fundamental task of democratic reform. Therefore, Follett's normative position represented a frontal attack on Progressivism which was full of talk about citizenship and "direct democracy," while its preoccupation was with the machinery and elite leadership of government.

Although it is unclear why *The New State* seems to have made so little impact on the reform movement, it may well have been that the Progressive tide, with staunch support from the business community, was so strong and well established by the time of its publication, that Follett's approach was simply overwhelmed. It would have required a considerable shift in the whole reform strategy and probably would not have had as much appeal for the business community as that of the Progressives. Nevertheless, her prescriptive argument reflects the continuing presence of the tradition of direct participatory democracy with its elevation of the rights and obligations of citizenship.

In an introduction by Lord Haldane added to the third printing in 1920, it was pointed out that the crux of Follett's argument presented the view that neither monistic, nor pluralistic views of the state seemed adequate. The state should not be "a self-subsisting entity into which all sover-

eign power is really gathered up and exercised outside the central government only by permission or delegation."[98] Nor should the state consist
merely of an aggregation of groups organized to achieve and protect individual interests which engage in conflict, negotiation, and bargaining among
themselves. Thus Follett rejected both the pluralist approach, with its orientation of interest group theory, and the rational model of central coordina-
tion by the state.

Rather, the state should be composed of groups consisting of individuals who "live and think only in communion with others of our kind," who
"evolve the collective will which, in its fullest and most imperative form,
gives rise *as its outcome* to sovereignty."(Emphasis added.) Haldane explains
Follett's position as one that rejected the notion of the individual being
understood as "atomistic"—as isolated from others by his or her own need to
protect self-interest, hence affiliating with groups primarily for that purpose. Instead Follett argued that: "Relations to his fellow men are of the
essence of his life, and they are ever in active process of development";
people are "always to some extent engaged in developing these relations." In
turn, the subordinate groups in which people have their primary relationships are constantly struggling to "bring themselves into relation with each
other."[99]

Follett understood each group experience to be contributing only
partially to the full development of human life. Even as a citizen, one of the
most complex and comprehensive roles, she believed one must become
involved in many different kinds of group life in order to fully develop one's
humanity. Sometimes one may be "a workman and also a shareholder; a
clerk, and the representative of my fellow citizens on a local authority; a
lawyer and a fellow of a college or a professor." Through these differentiated
group experiences one gets an education in opposing viewpoints and may,
indeed, actually contribute to opposing views. In the process one develops a
larger outlook on society and the political community in which opposing
perspectives may be accommodated.[100]

In this process of seeking to enlarge the net of relationships, the general will, which is the basis for the sovereignty of the state, is built up from
below rather than imposed from above. Haldane explained that according to
Follett, the "sovereign state is nothing apart from the citizens who compose
it, and whose assent to its objects and its organization it embodies."[101] The
state becomes an instrument for the expression of human development
through expanding relationships, rather than a means of identifying some
transcendent "national purpose" produced by "the best and the brightest"
to which individuals must conform, possibly by coercion. Almost as if she
were offering a direct rebuttal to Herbert Croly, Follett insisted that "Loyalty
to a collective will which we have not created, and of which we are, therefore,
not an integral part, is slavery."[102] Haldane explained Follett's perspective as
follows:

> Sovereignty is a relative notion. The individual is sovereign over himself in so far as he can develop, control and unify his manifold nature. The group is sovereign in so far as its members in unity direct themselves in the expression of the common purposes they are evolving. A state is sovereign only in so far as it does the same thing, and it gives rise to the power of a great group unified by common ends. It is the expression of elements of identity in purpose.[103]

This general vision of the state advocated by Follett, growing out of a view of human beings as social creatures, represented a sharp contrast to that of the Progressive philosophy advanced by Croly.

Follett looked not to a benevolent elite, but to neighborhood organization and education. Simply tinkering with voting arrangements would not create true democracy, as opposed to the pretense of democracy, such as she believed to exist in 1918. Only by intelligent discussion among individuals in a variety of group forms could common purpose be evolved. In that process the individual would become a citizen who is "always potentially more than he knows himself to be." That is because "he is no passive element in an assemblage," but a member of a living group through which his personality is developed, and an integrated public opinion can be formed.[104] This participation would both create and form the citizenry and make possible the emergence of *publics*, in the sense described by John Dewey.[105]

In commenting on Follett's work, Haldane suggested that Follett held a broader view of efficiency than that espoused by the Progressives—one that places efficiency at the service of democracy, rather than vice versa. In this understanding of efficient government, professional administrative experts do not remove themselves from the citizenry to apply some sort of arcane scientific knowledge to the operation of government in order to achieve efficiency. Rather, neighborhood groups are organized to assess the needs of the people of a given area, and then the expertise of the people is *combined* with that of the government. Haldane indicated that this occurs so that:

> the highest skill and experience can be applied to meeting the needs disclosed, and to bind the people and the technically skilled groups together in such a way that the people can tell the specialists what they want done, and the specialists can point out how to do it, submitting plans, programmes, and policies to the people for their approval. *To put it another way, the plan is an attempt to bring efficiency to democracy.* (Emphasis added.)[106]

This more efficient democracy, then, enhances the short term specific accomplishments of government, but more importantly for the long term, it creates solidarity between technical experts and citizens. This kind of mutual commitment and collaboration not only make the accomplishment of particular tasks more productive, but they serve more profound purposes as well. The working relationship which Haldane described defines the role of the public administrator as one of assisting the citizenry, establishes the sovereignty of citizens, and contributes to their self-education.[107]

Follett's vision of direct democracy in the United States proceeded not only from a denial of the efficacy of Progressivism; her critique went much deeper. It was based on a fundamental rejection of representative democracy itself. She asserted that representative government with its political parties and dependence upon majority rule, had failed and was just so much "deadwood."[108] Her central bone of contention was that representative democracy ignored the individual. Follett maintained that no government could survive or be effective that did *not* rest on the individual. Therefore, direct democracy which would recognize and develop the individual was to be sought.

Follett did not perceive individualism in the liberal social contract sense by which individuals enter into a community after they have reached full maturity, and are motivated by the need for protection of their private interests;[109] rather Follett based her proposals on an understanding of how individuals emerge and develop in society through group participation. She rejected both the notion that individuals precede society and take initiative to form it, and the idea that individuals are mere products of society:

> We cannot put the individual on one side and society on the other, we must understand the complete interrelation of the two. Each has no value, no existence without the other. The individual is created by the social process and is daily nourished by that process. There is no such thing as a self-made man.[110]

Thus, individuals are created out of the interaction between people and their society and they, in turn, create and form the society. This interplay of individual and society is an ongoing circular process of mutual development.

Individuality, then, involves finding one's place in the whole. This concept consists of two key ideas: that of each one having "a place," that is a unique contribution and impact on society; and that of "the whole" within which one contributes and exercises influence. Follett was careful to point out that this in no way should be taken to suggest that the individual is confined to some predetermined class, function or role; she rules out the mechanical analogy of the machine and its parts as too static and passive. Rather, the relationship between individual and society is unpredictable, creative, and evolving. Follett summed up her view of individuality by explaining that "individuality is a matter primarily neither of apartness nor of difference, but of each finding his own activity in the whole." She continued:

> Every distinct act of the ego is an affirmation of that amount of separateness which makes for perfect union. Every affirmation of the ego establishes my relation with all the rest of the universe. It is one and the same act which establishes my individuality and gives me a place in society. Thus an individual is one who is being created *by* society, whose daily breath is drawn *from* society, whose life is spent *for* society . . . It is eternally due us that the whole should feed

and nourish and sustain us at every moment, but it cannot do this unless at every moment we are creating it. This perfect interplay is life ... The spirit of the whole is incarnate in every part.[111]

Follett goes on from this view of the individual in society to affirm the importance of communities and groups. Since our interests are never purely individual, but are always interests rooted in, and dependent upon, a community or group, they are always "inextricably interwoven." She maintained that recognition of this social nature of our individual interests should help people realize that though such apparently altruistic and benevolent actions as social welfare legislation may not appear to benefit everyone directly, they are for the good of all if they strengthen the community upon which all depend.

Follett concludes, therefore, that, "Every decision of the future is to be based not on my needs or yours, nor on a compromise between them or an addition of them, but on the recognition of the community between us." Thus she dismissed both utilitarianism and interest group politics as outmoded expressions of the "old individualism" which produces a "crowd-state" of isolated individuals rather than a "group-state" which would give rise to true individuals, group individuals."[112]

Direct democracy consistent with this view of the individual and the community must also eschew another concept of the "old individualism"— that of the natural rights of a particularistic individual. Follett insisted that since no such isolated individual exists, the fictions of natural rights and social contracts no longer provide a meaningful basis for democracy.[113] They obscure the psycho-social interdependence of the individual and the community which provides the basis for democratic government, as well as its imperative.

It should be emphasized here that by this negation of natural rights theory Follett did not intend to deny the existence of individual rights, but only the notion that these rights are attached to a freestanding individual apart from some society. Indeed, individual rights are essential for the healthy development of both the individual and the group. They are provided and maintained by some society or community from which the individual receives his or her very existence.

The implication of Follett's rejection of both the Progressive approach to democratic reform, and the old individualism which informed it, is that effort must be invested primarily in the development of the citizenry rather than in the tinkering with the government machinery, or in the seeking of elite leadership. According to Follett, direct democracy must be based on the organization of the citizenry into small groups. It is essential that citizens hold membership in many different kinds of groups (e.g., occupational, religious, professional, social), however the most crucial group for linking all group loyalties and interests to government is the geographically based group. This group should be organized at the neighborhood level and must add to the bond of geographic location the "consciousness of real union" in a community.

Follett envisioned regular meetings of neighbors to discuss neighborhood and civic problems rather than ad hoc sessions to deal with specific issues. In these meetings neighbors would not only discuss problems, but engage in a broader learning process through the sharing of experience, participation in community artistic expression, and in taking more responsibility for the general life of the neighborhood. The latter would include the establishment of regular connections between the neighborhood, city, state, and national governments.

These neighborhood meetings were to be the "new method in politics."[114] The creation and maintenance of this kind of citizen infrastructure would not simply be a way of empowering neighborhoods so they could *get* certain things; Follett was not advocating the creation of more interest groups. Rather these groups would have a broader community, state, and even national perspective. They were intended to "bring about a different mental life." She explained that "The question in neighborhood organization is—Is our object to get a new playground or to create methods by which playgrounds will become part of the neighborhood consciousness, methods which will above all educate for further concerted effort?"[115]

Follett insisted that this kind of localized group democracy would provide the basis for evolving a true public opinion, a public will at all levels of government. She argued that simply fighting the abuses of government by the machine bosses and wealthy industrialists was only "tilting at windmills" and should be abandoned for the more fundamental task of building "(1) an *active* citizenship, (2) a *responsible* citizenship, (3) a *creative* citizenship—a citizenship building its own world, creating its own political and social structure, constructing its own life forever." Follett noted in passing that the power of machines like Tammany was rooted in a similar kind of grassroots cultivation of the citizenry, but for its own self-serving purposes.[116]

Follett understood this development of citizenship as the central moral responsibility of the state as "the great moral leader." She believed the *supreme function* of the state to be *moral ordering*. However, Follett did not mean this in the sense of autocratically imposing some official moral doctrine or ideology upon the citizenry. Rather, she defined morality as "The fulfillment of relation by man to man, since it is impossible to conceive an isolated man: the father and mother appear in our mind and with the three the whole infinite series."[117] That is, the relatedness exemplified by the family indicates that human beings cannot exist alone, but must exist in interdependence. These are the necessary conditions for the emergence of mature individuals. The state bears a moral obligation to recognize this fundamental phenomenon of human existence and support its development.

Follett then addressed how it is that the state acquires the moral power and authority to fulfill this role of moral leader. Her response was that it does so only through its citizens as they become increasingly aware through group relationships of their connectedness with the entire nation. The state accumulates moral authority from the bottom up as citizens turn their hands to creating the state:

> Democracy does not exist unless each man is doing his part fully every minute, unless every one is taking his share in building the state-to-be . . . A creative citizenship must be made the force of American life, a trained, responsible citizenship always in control creating always its own life.[118]

She described this perspective as "a new ethics and a new politics founded on citizenship as an activity to be exercised every moment of the time." It is from this active involvement of the citizenry in the affairs of the state, *and* the recognition of their essential role by the leadership of the state, that the state acquires moral legitimacy and, therefore, moral authority.

Consequently, citizenship training is essentially moral training rooted in the relationships of people in modern societies oriented toward seeking a common will and purpose. It is achieved not by exhortation, but "by creating those forms within which good citizenship can operate, by making it possible to acquire the habit of good citizenship by the practice of good citizenship."[119] She summarized this argument as follows:

> The training for the new democracy must be from the cradle—through nursery, school and play, and on and on through every activity of our life. Citizenship is not to be learned in good government classes or current events courses or lessons in civics. It is to be acquired only through those modes of living and acting which shall teach us how to grow the social consciousness. This should be the object of all our supervised recreation, of all our family life, of our club life, of our civic life . . . What we want to teach is interdependence, that efficiency waits on discipline, that discipline is obedience to the whole of which I am a part.[120]

CONCLUSION

The early decades of the twentieth century were a *crucial* era—truly a crossing point in the formation of the ethical identity of the public administrative role in American society. The rise of the administrative state in response to modernization, including both the urbanization and industrialization of the United States, moved the public administrator increasingly into the seat of power and prominence in government. The Progressive movement for the reform of government at all levels during this time of transition was the key force in defining the core values that public administrators should serve, what essential functions they should perform, and what their priorities should be.

Some approximation of classical democratic values might well have been adopted as those to be served, representation and implementation of citizen preferences might have been the primary functions to be performed, and development of citizenship responsibility and competence might have been established as the professional priorities of American public administrators. If this road had been taken, one more clearly rooted in the ethical tradition of citizenship in the United States, *something like* the perspective advanced by Mary Parker Follett might have shaped the ways in which public administrators viewed themselves, their work and the citizenry.

Of course, there is much that can be criticized in Follett's normative proposal: it is rather vague and rhetorical, it is more than a little naive in its assumptions about the possibilities of creating ongoing groups in each neighborhood, and its hope for the achievement of a *general will* generated from the bottom up seems to assume an accommodating kind of human being that does not exist, at least not in sufficiently great numbers. Moreover, a serious deficiency for a theory of public administration was her failure to address in any detail the growing presence of the administrative state in its relation to the groups she advocated.

Nevertheless, the point is not that Follett had *the* specific plan for a more ethically oriented democratic public administration, but that she articulated values, principles, and general perspectives on government which were rooted squarely in the tradition of ethical citizenship which had been evolving in the United States through the nineteenth and early twentieth centuries. These included the following:

1. The state was understood by Follett to be an artifact of the political community—the creation and recreation of the citizenry—not some transcendent form to be preserved eternally, to which people should conform themselves. This creative process was rooted in human development through a variety of group relationships, if not based on a contract or a covenant. She believed the state to be a moral instrument for the fulfillment of human relationships through this creative political process.

2. Since Follett understood the state as an instrument of human development, she valued the sovereignty of the citizenry and sought methods for upholding and enhancing the priority of popular rule at all levels of government.

3. She viewed citizenship as having the characteristics of an office, although she never described it in those terms. Follett strongly affirmed individuality, but always in the context of interdependence in a community. Therefore, she supported a concept of individuality which conceived of both rights and obligations in relationship to human development through community. The citizen was responsible for not acting simply on the basis of self-interest, but also with regard to the well-being of the community.

4. Although she did not project in any detail the working relationship between citizens and public administrators, she clearly saw an appropriate role for

each, but with administrative judgment subordinated to that of citizens. Administrators were to be servants of the public will working closely with the citizenry to discern the wishes of the people and offering their technical expertise as *part* of the policy formation process.

Follett's view did not become a dominant influence on the development of American public administration in the ensuing decades of the twentieth century, however. The public administrative role continued to be conceived as one based on science, carried out with neutrality, and essentially expressing itself in terms of expert judgment apart from citizen participation, until the post World War II era. Since the challenge to the "classical" model of public administration in the 1940s and 50s, both the ethical dimensions of public administration and the appropriate participation of the citizenry in the administrative process have received increasing attention.

The next chapter proposes a normative perspective on both the citizenship and public administrative roles in the United States, which reestablishes an integration of the two by grounding both in the ethical tradition of citizenship.

REFERENCES

1. ROBERT I. PRANGER, *The Eclipse of Citizenship: Power and Participation in Contemporary Politics* (New York: Holt, Rinehart & Winston, 1980), p. 3.
2. *See* Pranger, *The Eclipse,* pp. 25–26 on citizenship as "an official status" and the citizen as "an office-holder."
3. ROBERT N. BELLAH and others, *Habits of the Heart, Individualism and Commitment in American Life* (Berkeley: University of California Press, 1985), p. 259.
4. *Ibid.,* pp. 261–262.
5. ARTHUR MANN, ed., *The Progressive Era, Liberal Renaissance or Liberal Failure?* (New York: Holt, Rinehart, & Winston, 1963), p. 1.
6. ROBERT H. WIEBE, *The Search for Order, 1877–1920* (New York: Hill and Wang, 1967), p. vii.
7. *Ibid.,* p. 12.
8. *Ibid.,* p. 14.
9. While it may be true that, as some revisionist historians such as Samuel P. Hays maintain, machines provided greater access to government services for ordinary people than was the case under the professionalized government created by the Progressives, I am not prepared to assume that these are the only two options. Making a case for the machines based on comparative ability to consume public services ignores the fundamental question of democratic rights and popular control of the government itself. One received benefits from machines only as long as one supported the machines' positions and politicians. *See* Samuel P. Hays, "The Politics of Reform in Municipal Government in the Progressive Era," in David M. Kennedy, ed., *Progressivism: The Critical Issues.* (Boston: Little, Brown and Co., 1971), pp. 87–108.
10. *Ibid.,* pp. 42–43.
11. WILLIAM E. NELSON, *The Roots of American Bureaucracy, 1830–1900* (Cambridge: Harvard University Press, 1982), pp. 82–86.
12. Wiebe, *The Search,* pp. 42–43.
13. Nelson, *The Roots,* pp. 82–88, 91; Wiebe, *The Search,* pp. 52–56.
14. Nelson, *The Roots,* p. 89.
15. Quoted in *Ibid.,* pp. 90—91.
16. *Ibid.,* p. 91.

17. *Ibid.,* p. 125.
18. Wiebe, *The Search,* pp. 146–147.
19. *Ibid.,* p. 160.
20. There is an ongoing debate amongst scholars about whether the Progressive movement was the work of the middle class in the cities, or of upper class business interests. For a sense of this debate, see the various chapters in David M. Kennedy, ed., *Progressivism: The Critical Issues* (Boston: Little, Brown and Co., 1971). Space and focus constraints do not permit an examination of these arguments in any detail in this text, but a reasonable position would seem to be one that would include both the middle and upper classes as active components of the movement. It seems clear that while a good bit of the active leadership and work of the movement was in the hands of the middle class, a significant amount of the financial support came from wealthy business leaders such as Andrew Carnegie and John D. Rockefeller. *See* the chapter by Grantham in the Kennedy volume cited above for a "mixed" view of this kind.
21. Mann, *The Progressives,* p. 2. See a similar analysis in Arthur S. Link and William B. Catton, *American Epoch, A History of the United States Since the 1890s* (New York: Alfred A. Knopf, 1955), pp. 68–69.
22. Wiebe, *The Search,* p. 166. *See also* Samuel Haber, *Efficiency and Uplift: Scientific Management in the Progressive Era, 1890–1920* (Chicago: University of Chicago Press, 1964), pp. 103–115.
23. *Ibid.,* pp. 164–165.
24. *Ibid.,* p. 167.
25. *Ibid.,* pp. 165–166.
26. Link and Catton, *American Epoch,* pp. 83–86.
27. Wiebe, *The Search,* p. 167.
28. DANIEL LEVINE, *Varieties of Reform Thought* (Madison: The State Historical Society of Wisconsin, 1964), p. 59.
29. *Ibid.,* p. 55.
30. *Ibid.,* p. 56.
31. *Ibid.,* pp. 56–67.
32. *Ibid.,* pp. 60–61.
33. H. LANDON WARNER, ed., *Reforming American Life in the Progressive Era* (New York: Jerome S. Ozer, 1971), p. 5.
34. ARTHUR A. EKIRCH, JR., *Progressivism in America: A Study of the Era from Theodore Roosevelt to Woodrow Wilson* (New York: New Viewpoints, 1974), p. 113.
35. *Ibid.,* p. 117.
36. GRANT MCCONNELL, "Private and Public Power" in Kennedy, *Progressivism,* p. 124.
37. *Ibid.,* p. 7.
38. McConnell, op. cit., p. 124.
39. Haber, *Efficiency,* pp. 51–52. On p. 64 Haber cites several books that reflect the preoccupation with efficiency even in the religious realm: George Arthur Andrews, *Efficient Religion* (New York: George H. Doran, 1912); Clarence Augustus Barbour, ed., *Making Religion Efficient* (New York: Association Press, 1912).
40. Ekirch, *Progressivism,* p. 107.
41. Quoted in *Ibid.*
42. *See* Hays in Kennedy, *Progressivism,* pp. 91–92 where he indicates that the New York bureau was financed largely through the efforts of John D. Rockefeller and Andrew Carnegie, the Philadelphia bureau by an investment banker, the Chicago bureau by a group of wealthy Chicagoans, the Dayton bureau by John H. Patterson of the National Cash Register Company. George Eastman was the driving force behind the Rochester bureau.
43. Ekirch, *Progressivism,* pp. 101–103.
44. ROBERT CARO, *The Powerbroker: Robert Moses and the Fall of New York* (New York: Vintage Books), 1974.
45. *Ibid.,* p. 75.
46. *Ibid.*
47. *Ibid.*
48. *Ibid.* The intensity of Moses' commitment to quantification was evident in his insistence

on quantifying personality after acknowledging that personality "includes those *intangible* elements the *existence of which do not readily admit of proof.*" (Emphasis added.) Thus, he advocated quantifying something that, in actuality, could not be demonstrated to exist!

49. *Ibid.,* p. 76.
50. *Ibid.*
51. Levine, *Varieties,* pp. 24–25.
52. *See* Milton Rokeach, *Beliefs, Attitudes, and Values* (San Francisco: Jossey-Bass, 1970), for this distinction.
53. JEFFREY LEIGH SEDGWICK, "Of Centennials and Bicentennials: Reflections on the Foundations of American Public Administration," *Administration & Society,* 19, (1987), 298.
54. Kennedy, *Progressivism,* pp. 126–127.
55. *Ibid.,* p. 127.
56. Quoted in Ekirch, *Progressivism,* p. 117.
57. Haber, *Efficiency,* p. xii.
58. Wiebe, *The Search,* p. 170.
59. Link and Catton, *American Epoch,* p. 79.
60. Kennedy, *Progressivism,* p. 31.
61. Ekirch, *Progressivism,* p. 157.
62. HERBERT CROLY, *The Promise of American Life* (Indianapolis: Bobbs-Merrill, 1965), p. 21–22.
63. *Ibid.,* pp. 153, 282.
64. *Ibid.,* p. 284.
65. *Ibid.,* pp. 285–286.
66. *Ibid., See* full discussion of these ideas in Chapter XI, "State Institutional Reform," pp. 315–350.
67. *See* Croly p. 29: "I shall not disguise the fact that, on the whole, my own preferences are on the side of Hamilton rather than of Jefferson. He was the sound thinker, the constructive statesman, the candid and honorable, if erring, gentleman; while Jefferson was the amiable enthusiast, who understood his fellow-countrymen better and trusted them more than his rival, but who was incapable either of uniting with his fine phrases a habit of candid and honorable private dealing or of embodying those phrases in a set of efficient institutions."
68. *See* Croly's discussion of Jefferson and Hamilton on p. 153.
69. *Ibid.,* pp. 187–189.
70. Kennedy, *Progressivism,* p. 31.
71. Croly, *The Promise,* p. 190.
72. *Ibid.,* p. 21.
73. Haber, *Efficiency,* p. 86. Haber refers specifically to Croly's later work, *Progressive Democracy* (New York: Macmillan, 1914), which had become even more fervent and moralistic in tone.
74. Croly, *The Promise,* pp. 169–170.
75. *Ibid.,* p. xxi.
76. Levine, *Varieties,* pp. 28–29.
77. Croly, *The Promise,* pp. 280–281.
78 Sedgwick, "Of Centennials," p. 299.
79. Quoted in Sedgwick, "Of Centennials," p. 299.
80. JOHN DEWEY, *The Public and Its Problems* (New York: Swallow Press, 1927).
81. Quoted in Sedgwick, "Of Centennials," p. 300.
82. Quoted in *Ibid.*
83. *Ibid.*
84. JOHN P. DIGGINS, *The Lost Soul of American Politics: Virtue, Self-Interest, and the Foundations of Liberalism* (Chicago: University of Chicago Press, 1984), p. 130.
85. *Ibid.,* p. 162.
86. *Ibid.,* p. 156.
87. LAWRENCE JOSEPH O'TOOLE, "The Concept of Participation in the Literature of American Public Administration: A Study of the Orthodoxy of Reform" (unpublished doctoral dissertation, Syracuse University, 1975), pp. 207–218.
88. SAMUEL P. HAYS, "The Politics of Reform in Municipal Government in the Progressive Era," *Pacific Northwest Quarterly,* 55 (1964), 157–169.

88.   SAMUEL P. HAYS, "The Politics of Reform in Municipal Government in the Progressive Era," *Pacific Northwest Quarterly,* 55 (1964), 157–169.
89.   WOODROW WILSON, "The Study of Administration," *Political Science Quarterly* 2 (1887) 197–222.
90.   *See* Haber's discussion of this point in *Efficiency,* pp. 103–116.
91.   Follett, Mary Parker, *The New State,* Peter Smith Publisher, Inc.: 1965, Gloucester, MA.
92.   ELLIOT M. FOX AND LYNDALL URWICK, eds., *Dynamic Administration, The Collected Papers of Mary Parker Follett* (New York: Hippocrene Books, 1973), p. xv.
93.   Follet, *The New State,* pp. 5–11.
94.   *Ibid.,* p. 6.
95.   *Ibid.,* p. 202.
96.   *Ibid.,* pp. 176–177, 218–220.
97.   *Ibid.,* p. 168.
98.   Introduction by Viscount Haldane in *Ibid.,* pp. vi–xi.
99.   *Ibid.,* pp. viii–ix.
100.   *Ibid.,* p. x.
101.   *Ibid.*
102.   Follett, *Ibid.,* p. 59.
103.   Haldane in *Ibid.,* p. viii.
103.   Haldane in *Ibid.,* p. viii.
104.   *Ibid.,* p. xiv.
105.   Dewey, *The Public.*
106.   Haldane in Follett, *The New State,* p. xv.
107.   *Ibid.,* pp. xviii–xxv.
108.   Follett, *The New State,* p. xv.
109.   *Ibid.,* pp. 61, 75.
110.   *Ibid.,* pp. 61–62.
111.   *Ibid.,* pp. 67–68.
112.   *Ibid.,* pp. 75, 79–81, 295.
113.   *Ibid.,* pp. 137, 142, 169.
114.   *Ibid.,* pp. 204–205, 207.
115.   *Ibid.,* p. 208.
116.   *Ibid.,* p. 222.
117.   *Ibid.,* p. 333.
118.   *Ibid.,* p. 335.
119.   *Ibid.,* p. 339.
120.   *Ibid.,* p. 363.

5

THE CITIZEN ADMINISTRATOR: THE PUBLIC ADMINISTRATOR AS VIRTUOUS CITIZEN

If, as was argued in chapter one, the tradition of ethical citizenship can be understood as providing a viable normative foundation for the public administrator, the next steps in developing such a perspective are to first sketch out a normative outline for ethical citizenship consistent with the ethical tradition discussed in the third chapter, and then to draw out its implications for the public administrative role.

In the language of Dennis Thompson, "An ideal in citizenship theory pictures a desirable state of affairs which is not yet realized."[1] He insists that such ideals need not be realized to be justified because they may function as "myths" that are "value-impregnated beliefs and notions that men hold, that they live by or live for." Thus, in proposing an ideal we are holding up for ourselves a form of citizenship which has been realized, heretofore, only partially and imperfectly, that we may aspire to fulfill both in our roles as citizens and as citizen administrators.

ESSENTIAL ELEMENTS IN THE ETHICAL TRADITION OF CITIZENSHIP

The following four points are the most important in suggesting the broad brushstrokes of such an ideal of citizenship:

The Polity as a Social Construct of the Citizenry

Whether it is conceptualized in terms of a contract, a covenant, or a group process, the belief that the polity is only a useful artifact of the people, rather than a transcendent phenomenon which somehow stands above and beyond human wish and will, is a key component in the ethical tradition of citizenship in the United States. Although it is quite true that there are significant philosophical differences among these three concepts, they all share in common the assumption of the instrumental nature of the polity. In all three, the political system is understood as both a creature of the citizenry and a social construct established for human ends, even though the particular ends assumed are somewhat different in each case. Each has represented a way of affirming the importance of subordinating the polity to the citizenry and asserting its right and responsibility for the creation and continual recreation of the polity.

The general idea of the social contract has shaped the ethical tradition of citizenship in this way more fundamentally than simple adherence to the specific tenets of Lockean theory. In fact, one might reasonably argue that the contract idea has had a life of its own at a popular political level largely detached from its fully elaborated philosophical theory. In spite of the individualistic philosophical assumptions in Locke's formulation and the logical, practical problems of taking its assumptions about a state of nature too literally, the *metaphor* of a social contract has had, and still does have, considerable symbolic power that is suggestive of how we relate to one another in a political community. Although it is true that we are all naturally born into existing societies, political communities are artifacts of those societies; they are created and maintained by a plethora of agreements among individuals and their communities which resemble contracts.

James Kettner, in his historical study of American citizenship, reminded us that although our British roots were oriented toward *subjectship*, with hierarchical ranks possessing differential rights and privileges, Americans built their concept of the role more upon the notion that "the tie between the individual and community was contractual and volitional, not natural and perpetual."[2] Citizenship in a republic ought to be uniform for all; it ought to rest on consent; it ought to confer equal rights; and it ought to be without invidious gradation.

A similar concept from another strain in the American tradition is that of the *covenant* which was central to the Puritan experience. More conditional, immediate, and subject to change than the notion of a social contract, the covenant was viewed as the living expression of the human capacity for self-government. Citizens were thought to be capable of exercising reason in approaching each other as "natural equals," and in working out arrangements for establishing order and protecting liberty. Citizens were viewed as the architects and builders of the political community who possessed the competence to reconstruct it at any time, and reserved the right to do so.[3]

The idea of covenant was more community oriented than the individualistic concept of the contract. A covenant was always an expression of a preexisting community within which an individual found meaning, identity, and purpose. In the case of the Puritans this was, of course, a religious community.

A third concept which affirmed the idea of the polity as a creation of the citizenry was Mary Parker Follett's belief in the group process as the source of significant political initiative. She believed that citizens acting as individuals, but acting together, created the structures, procedures and norms of governance. She held strongly to the importance of individuality, but argued that one becomes an individual only through interacting with others in a search for the common good. Individuals create the state, but they do so by engaging each other in an exchange of ideas that becomes more than a compromise, or contractual agreement. Rather, something new is sought and achieved which enhances the community and develops the individuality of its members. Thus, human development occurs as a concomitant of the group political process.

The common element in all three of these concepts is that the establishment of the polity is the work of the people themselves, in which all are participants. The contingent nature, the temporariness and malleability, of the political structures is also contained in all three to varying degrees.

A PRIMARY POLITICAL BOND THAT IS HORIZONTAL RATHER THAN VERTICAL

The social contract, covenant, and group process ideas all imply that a citizen's fundamental orientation is, as Pranger (1968) argued, "laterally or horizontally to his fellow citizens."[4] The citizen "orients himself spacially with horizontal, nonhierarchical referents." In this relationship, "citizenship becomes a kind of group dynamics involving friends and equals, a spontaneous 'field' of the polites where collaborators create a common union." Similarly Walzer, with specific reference to social contract theory, maintained that we need to remember: "the citizen is bound not to authorities at all, but to his fellow citizens . . ."[5]

This line of argument leads ultimately to a horizontal theory of authority rooted in the consent, preferences, demands, and perceived common good of individual citizens. The elaboration of such a theory is no easy task; it is fraught with problems concerning divergent interests, the appropriate exercise of coercion, the distribution of power, and the links, if any, between horizontal and vertical authority. However difficult such a project may appear, it is clearly one worth addressing. We have become much too inspired with awe when we turn toward those whom we have elected to represent us and work on our behalf. The trappings of office and the coercive power of bureaucratic organizations distract us from our major task as citizens, which is to engage each other in an effort to discern our common needs.

One of the consequences of redirecting our attention to our fellow citizens rather than allowing ourselves to be entranced by an official hierarchy may be a greater willingness to express opposition to particular corrupt or unjust governments. If citizens are the creators of the state through something like a contract, covenant, or group process among equals to protect and maintain the common good, then the thought of replacing one government with another may seem less threatening. In caring for the common good, citizens may be led either to support, or to oppose, a corrupt government which happens to be in place at any given time.

PARTICIPATION IN THE PROCESS OF CONSTRUCTING THE POLITY AS A CENTRAL OBLIGATION OF CITIZENSHIP

The key here is not so much the quantity of participation as it is the type and quality. Charles Evans Hughes once argued: "The responsibilities of citizenship, then, embrace all those acts or possible acts, all those habits or attitudes, which express the totality of one's possible contributions to the formation of public opinion and to the maintenance of proper standards of civic conduct."[6] He was quite explicit in indicating that participation must not be restricted to voting, the use of electoral machinery or involvement in political campaigns.

The maintenance of the democratic political process of constructing and reconstructing the polity in all its manifestations, and at all levels of government, requires the cultivation of a political community in which ideas are exchanged. Perceptions are shared concerning the nature of problems, preferences are mutually expressed for the use of public resources, and proposals are entertained for changes in the machinery of government.

Individual rights and liberties cannot be adequately protected, nor can mutual obligations be upheld, without this kind of volitional participation in the nurturing and development of the "social bargain" upon which government is constructed. Pranger argued that the politics of participation "accentuates the individual citizen's responsibility for the freedom of all. . . ."[7] It is the manner in which a subjective commitment to the citizenship obligation of the polity is created and maintained.

Citizenship as a Public Office

Although in the liberal tradition private citizens have no official roles and are left to pursue their own particular interests, there is another stream of thought which counters the limitations of this perspective.[8] Meiklejohn suggested that "We are, in fact, legislators and judges ultimately of the exercise of power wherever it occurs. In this we are, to paraphrase Jefferson, all public agents, just as we are all private individuals, too."[9]

The responsibility of the citizen is not that of a participant in the market—engaging in a competitive struggle for maximum personal political benefits—but rather the responsibility of occupying a public office. Citizenship as the public office of the individual member of the polity carries with it an obligation to consider the well-being of the polity as a whole. When a citizen proposes new policies, advocates changes in procedures, calls for a different allocation of public resources, or participates in the selection of representative officials, the obligations of the office require one to consider not only how he or she will profit, but how the "commons" will be impacted.

Samuel Walker McCall, a former governor of Massachusetts, asserted in his Dodge Course lectures at Yale, that as "an equal partner in the work of governing the individual has no right to vote for what appears to be his own private interest if it also appears to be against the good of the State." He continued: "His vote should be an expression of his judgment rather than his interest, and it should be his aim to express his sense of the common interests."[10] In a similar vein, Walzer maintained that the ideal of citizenship rests on "a sense of the whole over and above their sense of themselves as particular persons."[11]

This line of argument should not be understood as an expectation that citizens must become selfless and totally altruistic in their conduct. However, it does imply that citizens have a responsibility to identify *both* their own personal interests *and* those of the political community within which they bear contractual obligation for self-governance. Pranger explained that "incumbent upon the good member, the virtuous citizen, is the ability to make political decisions which at once protect his own integrity and take cognizance of the integrity of others."[12]

Yankelovich captured this balance very well in his call for the abandonment of the *ethic of self-fulfillment* and the adoption of an *ethic of commitment.*[13] The former emphasizes exclusively the satisfaction of one's inner impulses and desires, while the latter encourages collaborative, mutually fulfilling interactions. Yankelovich argued that in times of economic constraint, that he terms "the great reversal," we must cultivate the social bonds among family, neighbors, and fellow citizens. We must recognize that individuals achieve fulfillment, not in unconstrained autonomy, but in community.

This dual obligation of citizenship has its roots deep in the civic humanism tradition of Anglo-American thought. J.G.A. Pocock described the citizen in this tradition as one who "having entered the political process in pursuit of his particular good, now found himself joining with others to direct the actions of all in pursuit of the good of all."[14] He continued with the explanation that "the attainment of his private good was not lost but must take a lower priority."

These four aspects of citizenship represent the essential normative components of an adequate definition of the role rooted in the ethical tradition of American citizenship. Furthermore, they suggest the points at which citizens and public administrators share a common ethical identity.

THE PUBLIC ADMINISTRATOR AS CITIZEN

The notion of citizenship as a basic point of orientation for public adminis-tration is not completely new. It seems significant that the two oldest schools of public administration, Syracuse and the University of Southern Califor-nia (USC), both began as schools of citizenship: The Maxwell School of Citizenship and Public Affairs, and the University of Southern California School of Citizenship and Public Administration, respectively. Citizenship courses were offered at the Maxwell School from the outset, and USC's earliest days were characterized by heavy involvement of the citizenry in the life of the school.[15] However, somewhere between then and now the profes-sionalism of the administrator with its attendant concern for administrative science and techniques has come to dominate the field.

Therefore, it is appropriate to attempt to restore and further explicate the ethical identity implied by the names of these pioneering schools by identifying the obligations of the public administrator as first and foremost those of citizenship. The administrator of the public's business is not primar-ily a technician, not most essentially a specialist in some policy arena, nor simply an employee of a public organization; the most fundamental role of the public administrator is that of *citizen*. Public administrators are best understood as *citizen administrators*. They are, according to Walzer, "citizens in lieu of the rest of us; the common good is, so to speak, their specialty."[16] Herbert Spiro summed it up rather well:

> Moreover, the bureaucrat is also a citizen. By virtue of assuming his delegated, specific, additional responsibility and accountability qua bureaucrat, he does not surrender his original, general, responsibility qua citizen. *His situation as a citizen, and that of his fellow citizens, must be the main center of our attention.* (Empha-sis added.)[17]

The ethical identity of the public administrator then, should be that of the citizen who is employed *as* one of us to work *for* us; a kind of professional citizen ordained to do that work which we in a complex large-scale political community are unable to undertake ourselves. Administrators are to be those "especially responsible citizens" who are fiduciaries for the citizenry as a whole.

As discussed in chapter four, the bifurcation of the citizen and admin-istrative roles has taken place in large part because of the politics administra-tion dichotomy that was sought by the Progressive reformers of the early twentieth century. If administrators are to be removed from the realm of politics, they must be deprived largely of the citizenship role while acting as employees of government. If bureaucrats are to be viewed only as instrumen-tal experts, accountable to elected officials for substantive direction, the rights and obligations of citizenship must be set aside while enacting that role. From this perspective the citizen role is a political one that must not be allowed to comingle with the administrative role.

However, Waldo observed that if we reject this dichotomy and conclude, as most scholars in public administration seem to have done that the separation of politics from administration is impossible, we are faced with a problem of legitimacy. He raised the critical questions:

> How can nonneutral public administration be justified in, and adapted to, the Constitutional system? Whence should an administrator get norms for official decision-making and official-related personal conduct, so far as these are neither given to him by Constitutionally derived sources (or these sources conflict!) nor flow "inexorably" from technical-scientific sources? Regardless of provenience, how can such norms be justified?[18]

The answer offered here is that the legitimacy of the public administrator is to be derived from his or her prior role as a citizen.

If we move in this direction, an ethic for public administrators needs to be consistent with, and flow from either the four points outlined above, or some type of outline specifying the obligations of the citizen role. The citizenry in their equal and mutual obligation to protect and maintain the common good must be the center of political gravity. The responsibility to help in creating and maintaining the political community as suggested by the covenant, the group process of citizenship, and the social contract metaphor, must be central to a public administrative ethic. Expertise and technical specialization should always be placed into this larger context. Obligation to elected officials must be seen as conditional, and derived from their role as representatives of the citizenry also; as fellow constructors of the polity.

Furthermore, an ethic for citizen administrators should hold them responsible for a horizontal orientation to authority which looks *both* to the politician *and* to the citizenry for direction. Mary Parker Follett's notion of *power with* rather than *power over* suggests the style of conduct which would be appropriate for this view of the administrative role.[19] "Power with" involves a collaborative *integrating of desires* among participants in a decision making process, instead of a quest for dominance by some. It grows out of *circular behavior* in which participants have a genuine opportunity to influence each other. In a dynamic iterative process, administrators should receive legislative direction from elected officials who are responsible for aggregating the wishes of their fellow citizens in the form of broad policies; bureaucrats then return to the citizenry for guidance in implementation; and, on other occasions, return to the politicians with recommendations from the citizenry for revisions and for new policies. Information, judgment, and advice flow back and forth around the circle of political authority.

At times this horizontal view of these relationships may require the administrator to resist or oppose elected officials who misperceive the common good, or intentionally subvert it. As Ostrom argued:

> The public servant in a democratic society is not a neutral and obedient servant to his Master's command. He will refuse to obey unlawful efforts to exploit the commonwealth or to use the coercive capabilities of the state to impair the rights of persons, but he will use reason and peaceful persuasion in taking such stands. Each public servant in the American system of democratic administration bears first the burden of being a citizen in a constitutional republic; and citizenship in a constitutional republic depends upon a willingness to bear the cost for enforcing the rules of constitutional law against those who exercise the prerogatives of government.[20]

It also follows that the public administrator should be held ethically responsible for encouraging participation of the citizenry in the process of planning and providing public goods and services. Participation may or may not be *useful* or *satisfying* to the administrator, but it is essential to the creation and maintenance of a self-governing political community. The administrator should be obligated to inform the citizenry, provide the best expertise in conducting participation opportunities, and take what is produced seriously. The public office of the citizenry should be respected and upheld by the derivative offices of both "administrator" and "elected official."

This definition of the ethical obligations and identity of the public administrative role is highly congruent with the coproduction strategies which are emerging both in the literature and in actual practice.[21] These approaches assume that public services cannot be effectively delivered without some minimal level of cooperation from the citizenry. The encouragement of active collaboration between people and their government is increasingly being viewed as a way of reducing the costs of everything from public sanitation to library service. If citizens take responsibility for moving their trash cans to the curb or sweeping the sidewalks in front of their businesses, the costs for trash disposal and maintaining clean streets will be less. Or, in the case of libraries, shrinking budgets may be offset by volunteer labor to assist in checking out books.

A view of the public administrator's role grounded in citizenship provides a rationale for coproduction which is sounder and likely to be more enduring than justifications which are founded on expedient responses to current fiscal crises. A recognition of the importance of involving citizens in the delivery of law enforcement, education, public health, park construction, and a host of other public services should grow out of an understanding of democratic political community, and the role of citizens within it, not out of desperation over revenue reductions and shrinking budgets. Whether there is fiscal retrenchment or not, the social construction of the polity is enhanced by this kind of collaboration and sharing of responsibility. The public administrator's obligation is fulfilled through encouraging, enabling, and supporting the involvement of the citizenry in coproduction rather than in attempting to maintain total control.

The citizen administrator role definition is also consistent with flexible and decentralized approaches to public services such as those being advocated and adopted by some local governments.[22] Neighborhood budgets, block clubs, benefit-assessment districts and other such mechanisms can become the administrator's tools for encouraging his or her fellow citizens to share the responsibilities and the rights of governance.

An administrator who understands the prior obligations of citizenship in maintaining the democratic political community will value the active participation of his or her fellow citizens. A citizen administrator will seek to enhance collaborative efforts and restructure the machinery of government to fit the preferences and needs of diverse communities. This kind of administrator will understand that the socially constructed polity must assume forms which vary more or less from time to time, neighborhood to neighborhood, city to city, and state to state. It is an ongoing creative process that is never finished.

Deriving the ethical foundations of the public administrative role from the citizenship role is a strategically important step in strengthening and expanding the significance of citizenship in the United States. The pervasiveness of public administration, together with its resources and position in government, offer considerable leverage. If public administrators begin to understand themselves most fundamentally as citizens and see that they have an obligation to enhance the role of their fellow citizens in government, words may ultimately become deeds, and a resocialization process of decades may begin.

PROFESSION AND PRACTICE IN PUBLIC ADMINISTRATION

What are the implications of these proposals for the professionalism of public administrators? That depends on what is meant by the term *professionalism*. It is not very fruitful to begin with the construction of an ideal type of professionalism to which we compare ourselves. It is better to first examine the phenomena that have been associated with professionalism in public administration, and then to consider the value base that is inherent in those phenomena. We need to ask whether those values are consistent with the core values of citizenship in a democratic society. If not, we need to ask what shape professionalism should assume in order to be consistent with those values. We should consider whether the concept of professionalism is appropriate and useful for public administration, or whether it might better be replaced by some other concept, such as MacIntyre's idea of a *practice* which might better serve as a framework within which the public administrative role may be defined.

Beginning in that fashion, if we mean something akin to the drive for neutrality, order, efficiency, control, standardization, and quantification that characterized the Progressive era of public administration and much of our history since, there are serious problems, indeed. These values tended to sever the public administrative role from its citizenship roots, set public administration apart as persons with specialized technical knowledge and skill, and, in so doing, subvert active citizenship. Single-minded attempts at furthering this kind of professionalism among public administrators cannot but continue to erode the ethical dimensions of citizenship.

Efficiency, technical expertise, rational approaches to problem solving, and specialized knowledge are not to be eschewed; they do have important *instrumental* value. However, they must not provide the fundamental norms for the identity of the public administrator. The pursuit of these instrumental values must be guided by, and subordinated to substantive values. Otherwise, we reenforce the role of the politically passive citizen who views government as provider of public services, and the role of the professional administrator who views the citizen as consumer.

It was this "consumer" image of the citizenry, with its deprivation of political responsibility for government, that emerged as one of the central concerns of the bicentennial conference of the Center for the Study of Federalism. In commenting on the deliberations at that conference, Daniel Elazar observed:

> Particularly in a republic and most particularly in a democratic republic, those who share in the polity cannot be less than citizens if the polity itself is to survive in its chosen form. Consumers, at most, pick and choose among goods offered them by others, in whose offering they have no real share. How different such a course is from that of citizens who must share in determining the activities of the government as well as in utilizing its products.[23]

Again, it is not that the expertise of public administrators as providers of public goods and services should be shunned or dismissed. Rather, it is that expertise and the capacity for achieving efficient operations of the bureaucracy must not provide the fundamental norms for the public administrator's relationship to the citizenry. As Norton Long argued, we must not "substitute a market with consumers for a polity with citizens."[24] This is precisely the risk in identifying professionalism in public administration with technical expertise and efficiency.[25]

Rosenbloom cautioned against adopting "the traditional goals of professionalized public administration in the United States" for similar reasons. He identified this tradition of professionalism in the late nineteenth and twentieth centuries with values that were derived from Wilson's famous essay, the scientific management school, and the movement for scientific principles of public administration.[26] He argued that these values were efficiency, economy, and effectiveness—"the trinity for the professional bureaucrat." Rosenbloom further maintained that at some point, "orthodox public administration" adopted "the greatest good of the greatest number" as its definition of the public interest because this principle was most consistent with its professional values.

According to Rosenbloom, however laudable these values and this principle may be when applied conditionally, when employed *unconditionally* they present a threat to the rights of the citizenry. Rosenbloom correctly insisted that this perspective is at odds with the values and principles of the United States Constitution which "places no premium on efficiency, economy, or even effectiveness in a programmatic sense." Rather the Constitution places limits on majoritarianism and sets a high value on liberty, individual freedom, and "moderately representative government." He concluded that "constitutional values simply do not mesh well with the values of professionalized public administration." Consistent with the argument developed here, one might add that nor do the values of the broad ethical tradition of citizenship in the United States.

What is the source of this conflict or tension? It is the lack of a normative base for the public administrative role which would properly condition the influence of that trinity of values which Rosenbloom attributes to traditional professionalism in public administration. These are *penultimate* values for democratic government which must always be measured against the more *ultimate* values associated with citizenship. In a democratic state, efficiency must never be allowed to displace the right and obligation of the citizenry to debate issues and influence formation of the polity and its public policy. Effectiveness of particular programs and policies should always be viewed in terms of positive and negative impact on the ability of citizens to secure and maintain self-governance. Economy should never be the justification for actions that threaten the common good. The application of "the greatest good of the greatest number" should never be allowed to jeopardize the constitutional guarantees of a minority.

An understanding of professionalism in public administration that is appropriate for a democratic society should be one that is grounded in what is described in the first chapter as a high ethical view of citizenship. Public administrators should identify themselves first with the citizenry in their sharing of authority, in their right and obligation to participate in the affairs of the political community. They should begin to develop the meaning of professionalism in public administration from this normative base. However, they should not do so for the self-serving instrumental reasons that are so typical of "professional" activities in many fields. The problems of poor professional image and indiscriminate attacks upon the public services by unscrupulous politicians to which Jack Rabin has alluded must not be ignored.[27] But, these are insufficient justifications "to move ahead on the subject of professionalism." These are expedient reasons that will be so perceived by the people, and are problems that are only symptomatic of the extent to which we have a deeper problem regarding the legitimacy of the public administrative role.

Why then should public administrators be concerned with professionalism, and why should they begin from the perspective of citizenship? The answer to the first question is that public administrators should not be concerned about professionalism as such, but rather that their focus should be primarily on the problem of legitimacy. That does suggest that they should be clear about what they "profess" or "avow publicly."[28] They need to be accountable for the core values that guide the exercise of their role. They will achieve that, not by measuring themselves against the plethora of generic definitions of professionalism, nor by working their way down the "laundry lists" of professional attributes, but by clarifying the source of their authority; to what end should that authority be exercised, and by what status as well.

Public administrators and scholars of public administration should begin their redefinition of the public administrative role from an understanding of citizenship because that is where the clarification of the role in a democratic society leads. The source of their authority is the citizenry. Public administrators are employed to exercise that authority on their behalf. They do so as one of citizenry; they can never divest themselves of their own status as members of the political community with obligations for its well-being. A search for a redefined public administrative role requires an exploration of what it means to be a citizen administrator.

The Concept of *Practice*

After considering the considerable negative baggage with which the term *profession* is burdened, perhaps it would be wiser to simply set it aside as too tainted with undesirable and inappropriate meanings to be worth attempting to rehabilitate for our purposes. *Profession*, unfortunately, has gained the connotation of self-protection and self-aggrandizement. It tends to produce images of paternalistic expertise that are not appropriate for public administration in a democratic society.

A better option seems to be the concept of *practice*, advanced by Alasdair MacIntyre.[29] It is a generally equivalent, though more inclusive, concept which might serve better as a framework within which the normative ethics of the public administrative role can be defined. *Practice* is a larger framework that can include the citizen's role rather than separate public administrators from citizens. *Practice* provides a broader concept which permits escape from often petty, and generally class-conscious debates over which occupations are properly understood as professions. It includes professions as well as many other human activities.

Although his conceptualization needs revision and development, this general perspective is useful as a beginning point for scholars and practitioners involved in the development of normative administrative ethics. To consider the usefulness of this theoretical framework, the following concepts are briefly defined: practice, internal goods, external goods, and virtue.

MacIntyre focuses on *practices* rather than *professions* in dealing with the ethics of groups of people involved in common activities. *Practices* are forms of activity that possess the following characteristics:

1. They exhibit coherence and complexity.
2. They are socially established.
3. They are carried out through human cooperation.
4. They involve technical skills that are exercised within evolving traditions of values and principles.
5. They are organized to achieve certain standards of excellence.
6. Certain internal goods are produced in the pursuit of excellence.
7. Engaging in the activity increases human power to achieve the standards of excellence and internal goods.
8. Engaging in the activity systematically extends human conceptions of its internal goods.

MacIntyre explains that the skillful throwing of a football is not a practice, but "the game of football is, and so is chess. Bricklaying is not a practice; architecture is. Planting turnips is not a practice; farming is. So are the enquiries of physics, chemistry, and biology, and so is the work of the historian, and so are painting and music." He concludes that "the range of practices is wide," including "arts, sciences, games, politics in the Aristotelian sense' and "the making and sustaining of family life."

This notion of "practice" is particularly appropriate as a conceptual perspective for understanding ethical problems inherent in organizational hierarchies. It suggests that the work of public administration needs to be understood in terms that transcend employment in a particular public organization. Organizations are unequivocally the *setting* for administrative practice, but the practice must have norms of its own. That is the best reason for the adoption of a code of ethics by the American Society for Public Administration (ASPA).

More broadly, the eight characteristics of practices represent a normative framework that might be used profitably to guide reflection about the ethical development of the public administrative role. They suggest a working agenda and establish some tentative boundaries for inquiry. This concept calls attention to normative dimensions of public administrative activity that need greater clarity, particularly concerning the fourth, fifth, and sixth characteristics.

Internal Goods of a Practice

The concept of internal goods is essential to understanding the nature of practices. These are goods that can be realized only through participating in a particular practice, or one very similar. For example, only through pursuing the practice of painting is one able to cultivate the finest sense of color, tone, texture, perspective, line, and proportion, as well as the skill to employ the relationships among these artistic elements in the pursuit of aesthetic excellence that can enrich the lives of others.

These goods that are internal to practices cannot be purchased, stolen, or acquired through persuasion. They must be gained by engaging in a practice and submitting to its standards of excellence until one is able to go beyond them. It is in the nature of internal goods that although they are produced out of competition to excel, "their achievement is a good for the whole community."[30] The ethical norms for a practice of public administration, therefore, must grow out of an understanding of its internal goods.

Can public administration be understood as a practice? As we consider the viability of conceiving of public administration in this way, *internal good* is clearly one of the central concepts on which normative thinking must focus. Although the field has achieved neither precision nor clarity of its internal goods, public administration practitioners are aware of these in a general way. Administrators refer to such normative concepts as the *public interest, popular sovereignty, accountability, social order, social justice, citizenship development, political equality, efficiency,* and *liberty* as goods that they are attempting to achieve.

What appears to be needed is further discussion and reflection on the meaning of these concepts and priorities among them. There is a need to consider *how* certain values should be understood as supportive of public administration practice and *how* they may subvert it. The practice may require maintaining a certain balance between social order and social justice, while organizational goals may well favor social order for the sake of organizational stability, predictability, survival, and control. Without some clarity about those goods that are internal to the practice of public administration in a democratic society, public administration practitioners remain vulnerable to organizational definitions of what is good, and are at the mercy of arbitrary organizational authority.

No intelligible way exists to distinguish the work of *public* administration from that of *business* administration without identifying the internal goods that are the unique ends of each. Without clarity concerning the goods toward which the practice is directed, it is impossible to identify the virtues that public administration practitioners should be expected to embody.

External Goods of a Practice

External goods are those that can be achieved in many ways other than engaging in a particular practice. They are genuine goods in that they are necessary to some extent for the support of members of the practice, but they do not contribute directly to the development of a practice. Typical of these external goods, such as money, prestige, status, position and power, is that they always become the property of some individual, and, the more one person has in a fixed sum situation, the less there is for others. Consequently, external goods are often objects of competition in which there are winners and losers. This is essentially different from the value accrued through the achievement of internal goods that is shared by the community of practice and the larger community as well.

External goods may become the dominant concerns of either organiza-tions or individual practitioners.[31] It is important at this juncture to remem-ber that organizations should not be confused with practices, yet do coexist in an interdependent relationship. Practices typically require support by organizations, and organizations are in turn, often dependent on practices for their very existence. Considerable evidence shows that organizations do *tend* to corrupt the practices that they support as a result of their focus on external goods.[32] In the competitive struggle for the scarce resources neces-sary for survival, organizations "are involved in acquiring money and other material goods; they are structured in terms of power and status, and they distribute money, power and status as rewards." Organizations have goals oriented toward achieving and maintaining these external goods; practices should not allow these to have priority over internal goods.

Practices should be primarily oriented toward their internal goods, the tradition that has evolved from the quest for those goods, and a relationship among those currently seeking such goods.[33] However, most practices are dependent upon organizations for resources and work settings. Conse-quently, the internal goods of a practice are at risk in an organizational environment dominated by the external goods inherent in organizational survival and growth. A precarious relationship exists; the practice of organi-zational management can support or corrupt the integrity of practices that function under their purview.[34]

Virtues and Practices

Finally, the concept of virtue is to be considered. Virtue, along with the internal goods of public administrative practice, is one of the two points on which fundamental normative thinking must focus. Virtue has been an important word in ethical thought throughout most of western philosophi-cal history; it is rooted in Aristotelian thought.[35] When the language of moral philosophy in recent decades is considered, a substantial break is evident in the long and lively intellectual history of the concept of virtue.[36] Neverthe-less, a revival of interest in virtue has occurred during the last fifteen years.[37]

During this recent period, the works of four scholars, in addition to MacIntyre, exemplify the revival of interest in virtue as a significant concept in moral philosophy: Stuart Hampshire, James D. Wallace, R.E. Ewin, and William Frankena.[38] All five reflect a generally Aristotelian perspective, at least in some basic respects. For example, all understand virtues as inclinations or dispositions to act, not just to think or feel in a certain way. They are traits of character, more or less reliable tendencies to conduct oneself in a generally consistent fashion under similar conditions. Virtues are not innate and must be cultivated. In the work of all four scholars, virtues appear to involve cognitive activity. Virtuous conduct does not amount to merely conditioned reflex behavior; it is not just unthinking habitual response to stimuli, even though the term *habit* is sometimes used to characterize virtues, even by Aristotle. One might say that reason is employed in addressing particular situations, but with a certain preestablished attitude and a conditioned will.

MacIntyre contributes an additional dimension of meaning to the concept of virtue. He understands virtues as the character traits that make it possible for one to engage effectively in a practice by seeking to excel in achieving its internal goods while keeping the external goods of its organizational setting in a position of lesser importance. For example, if beneficence for the citizenry is one of the internal goods of public administration, benevolence on the part of public administrators is an essential virtue. If justice is also an important internal good for public administration practice, then fairmindedness is a necessary attribute for administrators.

Scholars and practitioners of public administration need to determine which human attributes are most likely to advance the internal goods that are defined as essential to the practice and protect them from organizational pressures, to the extent that is possible. For example, attributes associated with effective administration and management in the business world, such as competitiveness and profit orientation, may be unsuited to, or less appropriate to, the interests of a democratic political society. Similarly, virtues such as concern for efficiency which advance organizational goals may not create openness to popular sovereignty if given more than secondary importance. The virtues of the public administrator must be consistent with agreed on internal goods of the practice of public administration.

THE PRACTICE OF PUBLIC ADMINISTRATION

In defining the practice of public administration it is necessary to identify and understand its internal goods and virtues. That is the prior task that must be engaged before particular issues can be addressed adequately or general rules of conduct can be prescribed. At the outset of this discussion, it is important to address the instrumental orientation of the field. Public administration is an instrumental practice, but only in a particular sense. Its reason for being is to create and sustain institutional and other frameworks within which other practices such as public health, planning, accounting, law enforcement, and education may flourish.

The justification for supporting other practices is that they provide goods which a democratic citizenry has determined either directly, or through its representatives, to be in its collective interest. Therefore, public administration should not be understood as instrumental in the sense of the *classical paradigm* with its assumptions about the separation of politics from administration, but in the sense of instrumental to a democratic polity.

The practice of public administration involves more than the simple subordination of the administrative role to that of the politician, and the dominance of functional rationality as the only legitimate style of thought for the administrator. The role of the public administrator as a fiduciary for the citizenry gives rise to certain internal goods and virtues associated with carrying out the trust inherent in that role. In fact, the argument being developed herein implies that the *ultimate* obligation of the practitioner of public administration is to uphold and protect the practice of citizenship, while his or her *penultimate* obligation is to support and preserve the particular institutions mandated by the citizenry.[39] This means that the virtuous administrator should exemplify the character traits of the virtuous citizen. Let us consider next how those virtues of democratic citizenship in the American tradition might be understood.

THE VIRTUOUS CITIZEN

What is implied by the term *virtuous citizen?* First, it is important to delineate the boundaries of this question and therefore, its answer. Describing the essential character traits of the virtuous citizen is a far narrower and more limited task than that of specifying those of the virtuous person, unless one assumes that the terms are synonymous. One might argue in a generally Aristotelian fashion, for example, that since human beings are essentially political creatures, to be a virtuous citizen is the essence of being a virtuous person.

However, that is not an assumption that underlies this book. Such an assumption might be defensible in a traditional society that has an homogeneous value system that binds religion, philosophy, politics, aesthetics, society, culture, and family life into a coherent integrated whole. But in modern society there is nothing approximating that degree of coherence and integration of life. Modern people live out their lives through an aggregation of social roles, each imposing a set of obligations to be met, and each invested with a set of interests to be fulfilled.

These roles are linked together by a more or less stable and consistent personal identity, and integrated into a more or less coherent and meaningful whole experience of life. Both the degree of stability, and the extent to which life seems coherent and meaningful vary from time to time; one's personal identity in modern societies is always fluid and problematic. The metaphor that captures this modern person is the "juggler" who sometimes keeps all the balls in a state of dynamic equilibrium, but from time to time wavers precariously on the edge of chaos as a new ball is thrown in, or one is removed, or one is dropped, or attention wanes, or the stress of the whole thing begins to erode the necessary balance.[40] And of course, it is not unusual for the modern "juggler" to lose balance completely as the constantly managed array of roles becomes too much to handle.

The role of *citizen* in modern society is experienced as just one among many competing roles which must be maintained to a greater or lesser degree. Consequently, the definition of *virtuous citizen* is rather limited in scope, presumably fitting into a larger complex of roles, each with appropriate virtues, that are meshed in varying degrees with each other and, in turn, more or less integrated with some overarching set of personal values and attendant virtues.

CIVIC VIRTUE AS *SELF-INTEREST RIGHTLY UNDERSTOOD*

When we focus specifically on the citizen role in modern society, we might expect that the virtue(s) necessary for its maintenance and enactment will be different from those of traditional societies and classical Greek thought. Vetterli and Bryner developed an argument along these lines concerning the meaning of civic virtue adhered to by the founders of the American republic. They maintained that in late eighteenth century America the essential virtue for the citizen was *civic*, or *public* virtue. They argued that this was not the classical understanding of virtue, or even civic virtue. Rather, it was a modern version that represented a "fusion of *personal* and *public* virtue—a modern *republican* virtue—that represented an amalgam of some elements of traditional civic virtue and of personal virtue, which was impregnated with biblical moral theology."[41]

This republican version of civic virtue was less severe than the classical form from which it was derived.[42] Whereas the classical understanding of virtue assumed the primacy of the state and the subordination of the individual to the state, the modern American perspective made room for self-interest. Rather than combining the interests of the individual citizen with the interests of the state, this perspective accepted the kind of individualism that was prevalent in the new world.

There was no general expectation in late eighteenth century America that individual interests should be totally subordinated to those of the state. The prevailing political consensus assumed that individual citizens had natural and civil rights that were to be respected by government. The state was understood generally to be the creature, not the creator of the political community—nor of the individual citizens who constituted it by an act of free choice. Both Lockean social contract theory and the Puritan covenantal tradition informed and undergirded this assumption.[43]

Civic virtue of the modern sort involved free individuals who from time to time *voluntarily* demonstrated a willingness to forego their self-interests for the common good. This kind of virtue involved a "willingness to sacrifice individual concerns for the benefit of society as a whole." But Vetterli and Bryner explained that "this was seen as a concern for the common well-being, not an all-consuming and unqualified acquiescence to the political regime." Instead, it amounted to personal restraint in the face of a general expectation that "people would voluntarily temper their demands and pursuits enough so liberty could flourish."[44]

De Tocqueville described this modern American understanding of civic virtue as "self-interest rightly understood."[45] He observed that Americans "almost always manage to combine their own advantage with that of their fellow citizens," but that moralists in America "do not profess that men ought to sacrifice themselves for their fellow creatures *because* it is noble to make such sacrifices." Rather, "they boldly aver that such sacrifices are as necessary to him who imposes them upon himself as to him for whose sake they are made."[46]

According to de Tocqueville, it was the pervasive equality of people in the United States, a key attribute of American society, which inclined "every member of the community to be wrapped up in himself." This tendency, rooted in the social conditions of the new world, made self-interest unavoidable, and "more than ever the principal if not the sole spring of men's actions." De Tocqueville maintained that Americans had discovered that "in their country and their age, man is brought home to himself by an irresistible force; and, losing all hope of stopping that force, . . . turn all . . . thoughts to the direction of it." The result is that ever practical Americans ceased denying self-interest, or attempting to suppress it in favor of total dedication to the state. They accepted the idea that "every man may follow his own interest, but . . . endeavor to prove that it is the interest of every man to be virtuous."[47]

De Tocqueville points out that although enlightened self-interest is not a "lofty" principle, it is "clear and sure." It does not aspire to the highest of human ideals, but it is suited "to the wants of men of our time," since it conforms admirably to "human weaknesses." With respect to Americans Tocqueville argued, "I regard it as their chief remaining security against themselves." Self-interest rightly understood is not the kind of heroic ideal espoused by aristocratic societies, but a modest, effective, workable ideal; one appropriate to an egalitarian democratic society. It is as mundane as democracy itself. Self-interest rightly understood:

> produces no great acts of self-sacrifice, but it suggests daily small acts of self-denial. By itself it cannot suffice to make a man virtuous; but it disciplines

a number of persons in habits of regularity, temperance, moderation, foresight, self-command; and if it does not lead men straight to virtue by the will, it gradually draws them in that direction by their habits. If the principle of interest rightly understood were to sway the whole moral world, extraordinary virtues would doubtless be more rare; but I think that gross depravity would then also be less common. The principle of interest rightly understood perhaps prevents men from rising far above the level of mankind, but a great number of other men, who were falling far below it, are caught and restrained by it. Observe some few individuals, they are lowered by it; survey mankind, they are raised.[48]

In short, the principle of self-interest rightly understood *is* the principle of civic virtue for a democratic society based on equality—a clear example being the United States.

The genius of this redefinition of civic virtue for an egalitarian society was, according to de Tocqueville, that this same social characteristic of equality also drove Americans to form associations. Equal individuals found it necessary to combine into groups in order to muster the power and other resources needed to accomplish their social and political goals.[49] The result was that self-interested individual citizens were constantly confronted with their dependence on the community. Under these circumstances *enlightened* self-interest became not only possible, but an obviously essential quality of character. Without it groups could not function effectively, and without them self-interest was likely to remain unfulfilled and frustrated. Each required the other. Self-interest rightly understood meant then, understanding the origins of one's self in community and accepting one's resultant obligations to it.

Implicit in this relationship between the new form of civic virtue and associational life is another difference from classical civic virtue. The older perspective assumed that the state was to be the initiator, source, and cultivator of public virtue. However, in the American context it was assumed only that the state could be structured to evoke an already existing inclination to serve the common good.[50] The cultivation of civic virtue was thought to be the province of the various institutions generally associated with the private spheres of life. Enlightened self-interest was taught directly and indirectly in the process of creating and maintaining these associations. Principal among them was the church, but also included the family, schools, neighborhood, and other associations. The interactions of these various forms of association "provided a political, economic, and social ecology that could support an extraordinary freedom and at the same time experience a spontaneous moral restraint."[51]

Vetterli and Bryner argued that these social institutions assumed the role of inculcating and nurturing "values of concern for others, respect for law and social order;" they inherited the primary responsibility for giving shape and content to "the values and beliefs essential to social life." These mediating institutions provided the supportive matrix for the "civil religion" from which the new civic virtue was derived. These institutions which we generally associate with private life, "not the state, made the community; they, not the political institutions, gave the people the allegiance and the positive emotional response to coalesce the Republic."[52]

It is clear that de Tocqueville viewed the role of educational institutions as playing a particularly crucial role in cultivating civic virtue as self-interest rightly understood:

> I do not think that the system of self-interest as it is professed in America is in all its parts self-evident, but it contains a great number of truths so evident that men, if they are only educated, cannot fail to see them. Educate, then, at any rate, for the age of implicit self-sacrifice and instinctive virtues is already flitting far away from us, and the time is fast approaching when freedom, public peace, and social order itself will not be able to exist without education.[53]

The adjective *enlightened,* as well as the qualifiers *rightly understood,* suggest the importance of the cognitive dimensions of this kind of civic virtue. Citizens must *understand* their self-interest in terms of the broader interests of the community. They must not only be possessed of predispositions to serve the common good, but they must also be able to comprehend it. They must have knowledge about the community and their interdependence with it; they must be able to reason their way toward discernment of this mutuality in particular situations.

The realization that civic virtue defined as *self-interest rightly understood* was a requisite of associational life, in turn, formed the basis for understanding the relationship between this view of civic virtue and republican government. A crucial implication of this reliance upon private institutions was that virtue must be inculcated *first* in the individual citizen through associational life if it was to be possible to create and sustain republican government.

It was generally believed that this new civic virtue instilled in each citizen was necessary for the survival of a republican government as one form of association. Gordon Wood has summarized prevailing thought of that era on this point as follows:

> In a monarchy each man's desire to do what was right in his own eyes could be restrained by fear or force. In a republic, however, each man must somehow be persuaded to submerge his personal wants into the greater good of the whole. This willingness of the individual to sacrifice his private interests for the good of the community—such patriotism or love of country—the eighteenth century termed *public virtue.* A republic was such a delicate polity precisely because it demanded an extraordinary moral character in the people. Every state in which the people participated needed a degree of virtue; but a republic which rested solely on the people absolutely required it. . . . The eighteenth century

mind was thoroughly convinced that a popularly based government "cannot be supported without *Virtue*." Only with a public-spirited, self-sacrificing people could the authority of a popularly elected ruler be obeyed, but "more by the virtue or the people, than by the terror of his power."[54]

CIVIC VIRTUE AND COMMUNITY

Any doctrine that flies under the flag of self-interest, even "enlightened," or "rightly understood," deserves scrutiny with the most jaundiced eye by those who are concerned about the common good. With some development, this modern view of civic virtue as "self-interest rightly understood" may serve a democratic community quite well. At the outset it is important to consider the possibility that there may be more to the actual meaning of self-interest than mere selfishness. As Michael Novack observed, there are latent communitarian dimensions to self-interest:

> To most persons, their families mean more than their own interests; they frequently subordinate the latter to the former. Their communities are also important to them. In the human breast, commitments to benevolence, fellow-feeling, and sympathy are strong. Moreover, humans have the capacity to see themselves as others see them, and to hold themselves to standards which transcend their own selfish inclinations. Thus the "self" in self-interest is complex, at once familial and communitarian as well as individual, other-regarding as well as self-regarding, cooperative as well as independent, and self-judging as well as self-loving . . .[55]

There is some support in recent psychological research literature, not only for the possibility of a more complex form of individualism, but for its current existence in some places in the United States, and more extensively in other societies. Edward Sampson, after a review of research on the subject by psychologists during the last fifteen years, argued for the existence of two major mutually exclusive forms of individualism: *self-contained individualism* and *ensembled individualism*.[56]

The self-contained form, that emphasizes the separateness of each person from all others and from the group, is the one generally associated with American society. It is both praised and criticized for its key attributes, including a *firm boundary* between the self and others, a sense of internalized *personal control* over one's conduct rather than external control by groups or society, and an *exclusionary* concept of the self that assumes that other selves do not belong within one's self-definition.

On the other hand, according to Sampson, ensembled individualism manifests *fluid boundaries* between the self and others, a sense of *control by a field* that includes influence by other selves and groups, and an *inclusive* concept of the self that views the self as partially constituted by other selves. This form of individualism is typical of the Japanese, Chinese, Islamic, and

Hindu cultures, among others, and seems to include both modern and so-called "primitive" social contexts. However, contrary to the general assumption about American society, there is substantial evidence for the existence of a kind of ensembled individualism that is indigenous to the United States. Research in the United States on lower social classes, studies of some urban communities, and feminist research show the presence of a form of individualism that manifests the ensembled attributes.

Sampson's ensembled individualism seems to fit well with the concept of self-interest rightly understood and to provide support for the kind of ethical conduct that it dictates. Sampson argued that self-contained individualism functions socially through contractual, exchange relationships, while ensembled individualism functions socially through noncontractual, mutually obligatory communal relationships. Both can produce socially responsible behavior, but in the noncontractual, communal form "responsibility does not issue from a firmly bounded self acting on the basis of self-interest, but rather precisely because one is not so defined." Presumably, in the case of ensembled individualism responsibility issues from something like the motivation of self-interest rightly understood that views self-interest within a larger social context.

Sampson argued that "when socially responsible behavior must issue from an indigenous psychology of self-contained individualism, over time, increasingly strong external rule will be required in order to contain the excesses that self-interested behavior produces." The pursuit of simple self-interest by self-contained individuals tends to disintegrate society unless it is contained by rules and sanctions designed to bound self-interest. Thus, it appears that the ensembled form of individualism is more consistent with democratic government and supportive of a self-governing citizenry. To the extent that strong external rule must be exerted on the citizenry, it is less self-determining and more subordinated to some hierarchy of authority. Consequently, since forms of individualism appear to be socially created, "The task is to move toward the affirmation of the ensembled form and to encourage those kinds of social structures and arrangements that make its advent more likely."[57]

Gary Orren, after reviewing the recent research literature on the dominant models in both economics and political science, also strongly challenged the prevailing assumptions about the inevitability of simple self-interest.[58] Upon examining voting patterns he concluded that "Efforts to explain U.S. voting patterns in terms of economic self-interest have failed consistently." Instead he observed that " 'Solidary' factors (group psychological identifications, especially partisanship) and 'purposive' goals (policy issues) are far more influential, analysts have found." Orren insisted that the "impoverished language and premises of self-interest" cannot express and explain powerful human feelings such as compassion, loyalty, affection, and duty that influence people's conduct in important matters.

While Orren's review of research called into question the dominant notions of self-interest as the key motivation in politics and economic activity, Steven Kelman's examination of research from various disciplines offered positive support for the presence of altruism in political behavior.[59] He concluded that self-interest explains the behavior of people on some issues, but certainly not all, and not on those of greatest importance. Citizens are motivated significantly by the wish to select good policy that reflects concern for others rather than just oneself.

Enlightened self-interest then, appears to be plausible as a form of civic virtue, but only when its latent "other regarding" aspects are firmly and explicitly cultivated through community experience and supported by a theory of community. Such a theory must recognize the reality of individuals and the legitimacy of their rights claims, as well as the ultimate dependence of individuals upon a network of associations and the obligations incurred thereby.

During the founding era this kind of theory was provided largely by Puritan theology. The concept of the covenant embodied the essential balance between individuals and the community. It reflected the experience of Puritan communities and, in turn, provided supportive conceptual justification for that experience.[60] Unhinged from these, or similar, ideas and experiences, self-interest seems likely to be anything but "enlightened," and, in all probability, destined to erode rather quickly in the direction of calculating self-aggrandizement.

If it is assumed that we are stuck with the kind of modern individuals described earlier in this paper, then self-interest seems as inescapable now as it did to de Tocqueville. The task is not to banish it, but to bound and humble it, through education in the broad sense—through the experience of association supported by theoretical understanding of the nature of community. The underlying assumption here was captured by Rossiter in the proposition that, "If man was a composite of good and evil, of ennobling excellences and degrading imperfections, then one of the chief ends of community, an anonymous Virginian advised, was 'to separate his virtues from his vices,' to help him purposefully to pursue his better nature."[61] Therefore, it behooves us to turn our minds earnestly to an understanding of community adequate for modern times, and our hands to the cultivation and sustenance of associational life.

The basic strands of a theory can be found in the communitarian literature. This section will include a brief sketch of *one* approach to a theory of community developed by Clark Cochran, drawing heavily upon the political philosophy of Yves Simon.[62]

Cochran advanced a critique of "autonomous individualism and its liberal origins" by arguing that there is no necessary opposition between individualism and community—a perspective bearing strong similarity to Sampson's concept of ensembled individualism. Both individual autonomy and community are necessary for the full development of human character. The moral autonomy of the individual is possible only after education and nurturing by some community through family, friends, teachers, and fellowship within a particular social and cultural context.[63]

Cochran suggested that if the chief end of democratic government is taken to be the common good, then it is only within a theory of political community that a defensible notion of the common good can be developed. He then outlined a "theory of communal pluralism" that is compatible with the conditions of modern society: urbanization, industrialization, mobility, and transformed educational, occupational and social structures.[64]

These facts of the modern world tend to attenuate the "warm personal relations" that are typically associated with the vision of small community. Thus, it is necessary to understand community in terms that include these affective dimensions, but are *less* defined by characteristics that were more typical of the villages and towns of traditional societies of the past. Cochran defined community as "the *experience* of solidarity in social relations, when men are mutually aware of the common ties that bind them in work, pursuit of the truth, intimate experience, and love."[65] He acknowledged that community may develop evil objects, with the Charles Manson clan offered as an example.

Cochran then introduced the concept of *communion* to suggest the kind of community that is desirable because it promotes full human character development. Communion "suggests the solidarity which promotes freedom and displays belonging, cohesion, trust and sympathy in connection with good objects." He adopted terms from C.S. Lewis in indicating that communion is rooted in *gift love*, not *need love*.[66]

The full development of human character can occur only within communities of this kind. Character includes two elements: the *center*, and the *masks*. The *center* consists of the set of moral qualities that comprise personal identity. These are the virtues that establish the continuity of the self through the varying circumstances of life. The *masks* are the complex set of social roles assumed by a person in modern society, as presented earlier by the juggler metaphor. These masks are the way fragments of the self are projected to meet the varying interests and obligations associated with these often conflicting and competing roles.

Character is harmonious and well-developed to the extent that the center and the masks are integrated. Cochran explained that, "To live from the center of character is not to reject masks but to choose those which are appropriate and to remember that they should express character, not supplant it."[67] Responsibility is that element of character that maintains a link between the inner life of the individual and the complex social life of the modern world.

Character is fully developed only through the experience of community because that is the means by which effective education occurs concerning the appropriate relationship between the self and its social roles. It is at this point that the relationship between community and civic virtue as self-interest rightly understood emerges.

Self-interest becomes "rightly understood," and, therefore, worthy of being considered virtuous, only when the interdependence between the individual and his or her various communities is clearly discerned and understood. That comprehension occurs only in the experience of community, and is manifest in the form of character. Character, as the integration of self and social roles, is crucial for producing conduct consistent with this comprehension of interdependence. Therefore, community, through its character building function is the essential means for achieving civic virtue.

CIVIC VIRTUE AND THE COMMON GOOD

The remaining step in outlining a theory of civic virtue is to indicate more specifically how enlightened self-interest is to be structured in relation to the common good. Cochran identified three kinds of goods: individual goods, personal goods, and the common good.[68] *Individual goods* are material goods such as health, income, occupation, and property. These are generally the equivalent of one's "interests." *Personal goods* are such goods as "rationality, integrity, freedom, virtue and relation to God."[69] Although the individual goods of various citizens may diverge, or become objects of divisive competition, this cannot be so for personal goods:

> These have an objective, transcendent focus. Persons do not come into conflict in their ends, for the goal of full human development and autonomy is the same for each. The full development of one does not detract from the full development of others. The goods, however, which are possible means to such development very often are mutually incompatible.[70]

It might be said that while individual goods are private in nature, personal goods are essentially public.

The development of character involves the enhancement of one's personal goods. Cochran argued that personal goods are of higher value than individual goods, since individual goods are essentially means to personal goods, which, in turn, are the particular qualities that are essential for character development.[71]

The *common good* must, by definition, be a good shared by all members of a community, "thus, not a good external to men." Individual goods can never be considered as the common good. However, particular individual goods may be used to achieve personal goods which, in turn, contribute to the development of character. Character building is the goal of human fulfillment.

Since the experience of community is the source of character development, Cochran concluded that the common good should "be identified with the *life* of the community itself, not with any particular goal or policy." He was quite clear that the common good is *not the community itself,* since that is external to individual human beings and can become a source of oppression.

Cochran insisted that "only by viewing the common good as the life of a community can a correct ethical account be given of the relation between the common good (or the public interest) and individual goods (or interests)." He continued:

> Only the common life, experience, and action of a community is ultimately both common and distributable to each individual. Particular goods or policies—such as public safety, schools, libraries, public roads—may be for the common good, or a requirement of the common good. But they cannot constitute *the* common good.They promote good because they make possible and enhance the personal goods of the members of the community. A rich communal life is requisite to the full development of individuality . . . Thus, if the common good refers to the set of communal relationships among the members of the community, a policy will be adjudged "in the common good" if it protects, strengthens, improves, or extends these relationships. Policy in the common good preserves what community already exists, attempts to make it better wherever possible, and strives to extend it to those not yet or only imperfectly included. For example, civil rights legislation is justified not only on the basis of justice, but also for its contribution to bringing minority groups more fully into the life of the community.[72]

Civic virtue as self-interest rightly understood involves an understanding of these essential relationships among individual goods, personal goods, and the common good, the ability to put them into proper perspective in any given situation, and the inclination to act in ways that reflect the priorities among them. Earlier in this chapter it was argued that when treating the normative dimensions of the role of citizen, it is appropriate to think of that role as the "public office" of the individual member of a democratic political community. The most essential quality required for the public office of citizenship is civic virtue defined in this way.[73] Recalling MacIntyre's perspective and terminology, the common good understood as the experience of community life is the primary internal good of citizenship. It is protected from the competing external goods of individuals (money, status, power,etc.) by civic virtue defined as self-interest rightly understood.

THE VIRTUOUS ADMINISTRATOR

The virtuous administrator *is* the citizen administrator. The citizen administrator *is* the virtuous citizen . . . and more. He or she is also employed by the citizenry to function on its behalf in pursuing the common good through the political community. This involves the production or provision of certain *particular* common goods such as the building of roads, the enforcement of law and order, the delivery of water, the conduct of public education, and the maintenance of public health.

Providing and producing these particular common goods is the *penulti-mate* obligation of the citizen administrator. His or her *ultimate* obligation is to deliver these goods in ways that enhance *the* common good of community life through which character and civic virtue are formed. That is, the administrator's most fundamental responsibility is to encourage and sup-port existing communities, and to give priority to policies, programs, rules, procedures and methods that will be conducive to the emergence of new communities. For example, economic development, enforcing the law, building expressways, educating the young, and maintaining the public health should be planned and carried out with a view toward reducing interference with existing communities, and moreover, with careful consid-eration of how they may enhance such communities and encourage the development of new ones.

Communities characterized as communions "cannot be built directly." They cannot be created through some plan generated by public administra-tors or any outside source. They are the by-products of "common work in pursuit of a group's goals and purposes or of those around which prospec-tive members have coalesced."[74] The appropriate role for government in relation to these communities is to provide a supportive environment in which they may flourish. For example, the stimulation and support for community provided through sensitive and well-conceived common work in the form of "coproduction" strategies is a more appropriate justification for such schemes than cost reduction.

With this general approach the body politic becomes a "community of communities;" an "association made up of thousands of different small and large communions and groups." It sees as its goal the achievement of a pluralism of such communities. The political community viewed in this way seeks "to conserve existing small communions and foster political and social conditions necessary for the creation and growth of new communions."[75]

If government is to be understood as a community of communities, the key concept linking the citizen administrator to the various communities within a jurisdiction is authority. The administrator as fiduciary of the citizenry is charged with exercising authority on behalf of the political community and its citizens. In so doing, the citizen administrator is obli-gated to function as a "witness for the common good." The implication is that the administrator will "build on what the community is, but will always call the community to become something it has not yet become."[76] The citizen administrator is obligated to respect existing communities, but also to attempt to broaden their perspective to include the diversity of communi-ties that typifies a healthy political community.

The citizen administrator can exercise authority in this way only through *indirect administration*.[77] This means that to the extent possible, "the administration of policy should make use of existing communions and their authorities in order to strengthen communion throughout the society."[78] Implied in this notion is a subordination of administrative expertise to community leadership and authorities, rather than the assertion of superiority to lay citizens based on technical knowledge and skill.

Cochran suggested that achieving this approach has been a serious problem. After discussing the importance of voluntary associations in community building, consistent with the argument developed in the previous chapter, he observed: "Yet recent tendencies toward centralizing, professionalizing, and bureaucratizing public programs have tended to weaken the independent and participatory character of voluntary associations in the United States."[79]

Essential to this indirect administration and the subordination of administrative technical expertise is a revised understanding of authority along the lines suggested by Carl Friedrich and Yves Simon.[80] Friedrich defined authority as "the capacity to issue communications permitting reasoned elaboration in terms of the values, beliefs, and interests of the political community to which they apply." *Capacity* suggests the *potential* for such elaboration and the recognition among the citizenry, whether or not it is ever actually undertaken. It "refers to a set of values which the person possessing authority shares with his followers." These shared values are the link between governmental authority and community. Community provides a foundation for authority. Authority, explained Cochran, exists to relate particular judgments to the basic values of a community.

Simon carried this general way of understanding authority and community a step further. He maintained that authority is not linked just to the immediate and specific values of a community, but ultimately to the common good, understood as the experience of life in the community. He argued that the binding power of authority "is derived from its moral cogency, its relation to the common good." The efficaciousness of authority grows out of its ability to "elicit a distinctively ethical motive for obedience."

In the course of discussing the functions and justifications of authority, Simon provided a further argument that can be used to legitimate the role of the public administrator, although he does not refer specifically to that role. Simon suggested that if the virtue of all individual citizens cannot be counted on to always cover all essential aspects of the common good, then authoritative direction might be necessary.

It is conceivable that this direction might be provided by a committee of citizens, thus requiring no distinct governing personnel, although in some cases such arrangements will be required.[81] The perspective developed in this book has assumed that the conditions of modern society require such personnel, including politicians and administrators. If this is true, the provision of administrative authority is legitimate whenever scale and complexity make it impossible for the citizenry to exercise authority directly.

A further condition implied by Simon is that administration is legitimate to the extent that it acts to support the common good by resisting the natural human tendencies of particular individual citizens to neglect the common good. An administrator has the responsibility of upholding the shared values of the community, not through force, coercion, or administrative fiat, but through reasoning with his or her fellow citizens about the common good.

It seems logical to suggest, then, in the language of MacIntyre, that the central internal good of the practice of public administration is the common good defined as the experience of community life. The primary virtue necessary to protect that internal good from the external goods of the organizational settings in which public administration is practiced is self-interest rightly understood, also the paramount virtue of citizenship.

Since public administrators are not only citizens, but *fiduciary* citizens as well, the practice of public administration calls for the heightened importance of three other virtues. Administrators share these with the citizenry, but they are particularly important for the support of the trustee functions of the administrative role. These are the virtues of public spiritedness, prudence, and substantive rationality. The virtuous citizen administrator should excel in these character traits in addition to self-interest rightly understood.

Public spiritedness, according to Irving Kristol, is often confused with holding "passionate opinions about the public good" and working "furiously to translate these opinions into reality."[82] These are the attributes of the advocate for a particular cause. Public spiritedness means "curbing one's passion and moderating one's opinions in order to achieve a large consensus that will ensure domestic tranquility;" it is "a form of self-control, an exercise in *self*-government." (Emphasis added.) Thus it is clearly one of the constituent virtues of self-interest rightly understood since it involves the restraint of limited self-interest.

Public spiritedness, an essential virtue for all citizens, rises to central importance for the public administrator as fiduciary citizen. In the practice of public administration this virtue is an inclination or predisposition to behave in ways that value and respect the rights and obligations of the citizenry.[83] The citizen administrator needs to embody this predisposition to see the public as having rights to be as involved as often and as much as possible in governance, whether that complicates the administrative task or not; whether that creates inefficiencies or not; whether or not that suits the preferences of the administrator.

The literature on citizen participation reflects four major bases for justifying its employment in the formation and implementation of public policy: *citizen rights to participate in a democracy, citizenship development through participation, the probability of producing better policies through participation, and the contribution of participation as a form of system feedback to maintaining stability in the governmental system.*[84] Public administrators, reflecting an instrumental view of the citizen's role, have tended to focus on the latter two justifications. The result has been weak support, or outright resistance to public involvement since it is not at all clear that participation *necessarily* produces better policies. Justification based on the maintenance of stability also tends to lead to a minimalist approach by administrators—just enough participation to keep the people from getting too upset.

From the perspective of popular sovereignty and democratic government, it seems clear that the primary consideration must be subordination of administrative concerns for efficiency, or even effectiveness, to popular will. In order to carry out the fiduciary responsibilities of the public administrator it becomes necessary to act from public spiritedness—to develop a predisposition to restrain one's expertise and efficiency. The administrator must learn to turn to the people for consultation, deliberation, and as Reich terms it, *civic discovery*, because it is their right to participate whether the result is better policy or stability in government.

Public spiritedness also implies an administrative inclination to contribute to the process of citizenship development by encouraging the public to offer their ideas, information, creativity, and energy to the development and implementation of public policy. It is through the give and take of public deliberation that citizenship development occurs. It is through the struggles for both substantive resolution of public issues and the integration of values with technical expertise that citizens and citizen administrators grow in their capacity to exercise their responsibility for continually recreating the polity.

What is intended here is more than just a willingness to allow public participation, but rather the citizen administrator role requires an earnest, enthusiastic, and proactive stance in relationship to public involvement. This is the difference between administrators who make a halfhearted token effort and then find their skepticism confirmed when few citizens show up to participate, and those who see a lack of public response to a participation opportunity as a problem to be solved through their initiative and ingenuity.

Finally, public spiritedness implies a primary bond of loyalty to the citizenry that transcends loyalty to a particular department, administrative superiors, or to political officials. It involves the inclination to inform one's fellow citizens of past conduct, proposed actions, problems, and current programs which are perceived to be detrimental to the common good. Citizen administrators will, of course, attempt to deal with these concerns responsibly, respecting established procedures, but should ultimately place their knowledge and insight before the people if necessary.

Prudence is also a critically important virtue for the public administrative role. Since this concept seems to have acquired negative connotations of preoccupation with self-interest in some contemporary discourse, both popular and philosophical, it is important to point out that this is a relatively recent phenomenon. Through most of the western philosophical tradition, prudence has been understood quite differently and regarded with greater esteem. For Aristotle, prudence (*phronesis*) was an essential human quality for moral conduct, as was true also in the thought of St. Thomas Aquinas as he appropriated and incorporated Aristotelian concepts into his Christian theology. In both these cases prudence meant *practical wisdom* the ability to achieve good ends through the use of good means. Prudential judgment was understood as the deliberative process necessary to move from principle to specific action in a concrete situation.

Elizabeth Minnick saw judgment of this kind as central among the civic virtues.[85] It is the ability to relate principles to particulars "without reducing those particulars to simple instances." It is "neither deduction nor induction" since it does not involve deriving rules from principles, nor does it turn particulars into mere illustrations of a principle. Instead it is a process in which principle is illuminated—understood better—by being brought to a specific situation, or conversely, a process in which insight is gained into the meaning of a particular person, problem, or situation when it is connected to a principle.

Experience is the third element in this process of judgment that mediates between principle and particular. It provides a practical context for deciding how best to act in order to preserve both the principle and the specific case. Minnick described this act of judgment as "almost a leap" of mind that can be explained, but never proved since "there is no rational necessity behind it." We recognize good practical judgment as a reasonable course of action for acknowledging both principle and concrete situation, but not as an ineluctable conclusion.

Understood in this sense one might very reasonably argue that prudence is one of the most essential virtues for public administrators. The public administrator often finds it necessary to move from a general description of socially desired ends to specific means of achieving those ends. The practical wisdom to perceive fitting and supportive techniques for specified values is a key virtue linking technical expertise with the citizenship role. Prudent administrative judgment keeps technique in its proper relationship to the wishes of the citizenry. It inclines one to weigh techniques carefully with an eye to the full range of values they encourage and discourage, rather than only selecting those means that produce efficiency. Prudence is the means for maintaining what Chester Newland called "the symbiotic character of effective citizenship (civic duty) and professional expertise (responsible public service) in constitutional democracy."[86]

Yves Simon had the importance of this kind of judgment in mind in his observation that when experts are placed in positions of authority they are "likely to act upon society in more than instrumental fashion." He insisted that, "An instrument must be light; as a result of technology, the expert has become an instrument so heavy as often to get out of control." His conclusion was that "leadership belongs to prudence, not to expertness; rather than the bearer of a technical ability, a leader is supposed to be a man of virtue, a man of human experience, a man who knows men. . . ."[87] Simon pressed this point by arguing further that "violence is done to the nature of public life whenever government is in the hands of an expert rather than in those of a prudent man" because "government by experts is government by outsiders."

This way of framing the problem is highly illuminating for the central thesis of this book. Simon's language points up the fact that when the public administrative role is defined primarily in terms of expertise it necessarily implies one who is an "outsider," one who acts on the basis of values and principles other than those that emerge from the internal goods and virtues of a democratic polity. The expert comes to governance with a particular practice organized around its own internal goods and virtues. Therefore, to the extent that governance de facto passes into the hands of administrative experts in the modern administrative state, it passes into the hands of outsiders. Thus in order to maintain the integrity of the polity in the administrative state the public administrative outsider must be converted into an insider; technical expertise must be made compatible with, and supportive of, the practice of citizenship. The inclination to approach public problems prudently involves employing wise judgment in linking technique with democracy.

Substantive rationality is a third crucial virtue for the citizen administrator. This has to do with the inclination to reason about the ends of governmental action and its inherent value assumptions, as well as to engage in instrumental rationality—the most efficient means of carrying out such action. Instrumental rationality has dominated the definition of the public administrative role since the Progressive era advocated the latter in order to separate the administrator from political influence. As has been argued previously, the cultivated predisposition to reason in this way has tended to undermine democratic government since public administrators have exercised increasing discretion in proposing and implementing public policy.

The assumption that only politicians accountable to the citizenry would engage in substantive rationality, while administrators would simply carry out their decisions dutifully, has been proved fallacious in the modern administrative state. In fact, it seems clear that due to the technical complexity of many contemporary governmental problems, public administrators are unavoidably involved in substantive reasoning as they consider recommendations about policy options and during the process of developing the detailed implementation rules and regulations. An attempt to define the public administrative role purely in terms of instrumental reasoning can only amount to deception of oneself and the public. Pretensions to administrative reasoning exclusively about technique can only lead to covert or unacknowledged reasoning of a substantive nature.

Even beyond the conditions of the modern administrative state it may be argued also that to separate substantive rationality from any form of human conduct is impossible, and any efforts to do so can only distort and do violence to the humanity of those involved. For example, Alberto Guerreiro Ramos insisted that any theory of human associated life must be based on substantive reasoning about the meaning and purposes of human action.[88] He argued that a truly social science cannot copy the physical sciences in their attempt to separate facts from values. Ramos was led to conclude then, that since public administration is rooted in a theory of human association in organizations, it must orient itself by the use of substantive rationality.

What is intended is not the notion of public administrator as philosopher king who contemplates the value implications of governmental action in lofty isolation and arrives at a rational judgment alone. Instead it is the inclination to engage in both personal and group reasoning about the ends of public decisions and conduct. The citizen administrator is a practitioner who understands his or her responsibility to be personally clear about the values and ethical dimensions of administrative action, but moreover to engage in what Reich called "civic discovery."[89] This means that the public administrator is neither a net benefit maximizer through the use of technical analysis tools, nor an interest group mediator (both of which assume administrative value neutrality), but one who supports, encourages, and participates in the process of social learning about public values. When a problem emerges the public administrator publicizes the perception of a problem by some of the citizenry. Reich continued:

> He then encourages and instigates the convening of various forums—in community centers, schools, churches, and workplaces—where citizens are to discuss whether there is a problem and, if so, what it is and what should be done about it. The public manager does not specifically define the problem or set an objective at the start. He merely discloses the complaints. Nor does he take formal control of the discussions or determine who should speak for whom. At this stage he views his job as generating debate, even controversy. He wants to bring into the open the fact that certain members of the community are disgruntled and create possibilities for the public to understand in various ways what is at stake. He wants to make the community conscious of tensions within it, and responsible for dealing with them. In short, he wants the community to use this as an occasion to debate its future.[90]

The citizen administrator engages the citizenry as a fellow citizen who bears obligation to reason with them about the desirable ends for the political community. In doing so the democratic process is not subverted by administrative expertise and discretion, and is instead enhanced by deliberation among citizens, one of whom is encumbered by the citizenry with special responsibility. The citizen administrator is responsible for upholding the sovereignty of the people while also making available to them certain technical skills and knowledge. In order to do this consistently he or she needs to manifest the virtue of being predisposed to reason substantively and to do so collectively with other reasoning citizens.

As Giandomenico Majone has maintained, this "government by discussion" extended to the administrative role does not imply that the administrator should be a neutral group facilitator. Not only is that not truly possible, but there is nothing to be gained by pretending that the practitioner does not have special knowledge to contribute to deliberation among citizens. He or she has both technical knowledge and experience that should be advanced and shared. When this is done within a more fundamental substantive perspective of the administrator it is reasonable and useful that the administrator enter the debate as an advocate for his or her position.

Majone insists that the key to this perspective on the administrative role is that it should eschew the approach to policy analysis based on instrumental rationality, and instead understand the primary task as one of improving the quality of public discourse. This requires a focus on substantive reasoning about the desirability of various alternatives for action. As Majone asserts, "To say anything of importance in public policy requires value judgments, and these must always be explained and justified."[91]

This kind of deliberative engagement of the citizenry based on substantive rationality is highly consistent with Yves Simon's position. It is supportive of his argument for the importance of indirect administration of authority through existing community associations and leaders. It is consistent with his requirement that legitimate authority be understood as "the capacity to issue communications permitting reasoned elaboration in terms of the values, beliefs, and interests of the political community to which they apply," rather than employing force or coercion. This implies that administrators should have the ability to provide such elaboration clearly rooted in "a set of values which the person possessing authority shares with his followers." Only an inclination to reason substantively and to do so *with* the citizenry can produce this capacity.

These three central virtues—public spiritedness, prudence, and substantive rationality—together with the core citizenship virtue of self-interest rightly understood, provide the moral core of the citizen administrator role. Are they the only virtues of public administration? Of course not! Rather, they are the essential attributes for one charged with fiduciary responsibility for the citizenship of others. A fully explicated moral repertoire for such responsibility would involve a number of other virtues that are derived from these four and the nature of the citizen administrator's obligations to his or her fellow citizens. Implicit in public spiritedness is the necessity for honest communication with the citizenry. It further implies the importance of just policies, but rooted in definitions of justice arrived at through reasoned deliberation with the citizenry, not based on the unilateral expert imposition of some theory such as that of John Rawls that has been popular among some scholars of public administration.[92]

Also, prudent judgment requires fairmindedness to resist pressure from those who would much prefer expedient judgment. Substantive rationality calls for courage to examine the principles and values implicit in public action in the face of efforts to conceal and obfuscate such considerations. The development of a detailed normative ethical portrait for the citizen administrator only begins with clarity about the core virtues of the practice, and does not end here. It is an ongoing task for members of the practice and the citizenry that cannot be neatly and succinctly detailed in a volume such as this.

CONCLUSION

The central character trait of the democratic citizen in the American tradition of ethical citizenship is civic virtue. Civic virtue has been defined here as self-interest rightly understood. Self-interest rightly understood reflects a recognition of the individual's interest in serving the common good. The common good has been defined here as the experience of community. Therefore, the central character trait of the democratic citizen in the American tradition of ethical citizenship is the *inclination or predisposition to uphold and contribute to the experience of community.*

The citizen administrator carries out his or her penultimate fiduciary responsibility to the citizenry by providing and producing particular common goods represented by public goods and services. However, the public administrator's ultimate fiduciary responsibility requires the possession of the character trait of civic virtue defined as self-interest rightly understood. He or she should be inclined to provide and produce particular common goods in ways that support and enhance *the* common good—the experience of community. Public administrators should do so by respecting, encouraging, and supporting the communities and their constituent associations that are the matrices of civic virtue defined as self-interest rightly understood. These approaches include the systematic planning of opportunities for common work reflecting the values of the existing communities, and the indirect administration of public policy.

The citizen administrator engages in indirect administration by working through existing communities, their associations, and their authorities. If it is to be credible and evoke a cooperative response, his or her exercise of authority on behalf of government, in relation to other existing communities, must be rooted in the shared values of that community of communities. Ultimately, administrative authority must be understandable as supportive of the common good represented by the experience of community. Otherwise, governmental authority will increasingly be viewed by the citizenry as an alien, hostile, and oppressive force.

Civic virtue, the central character trait necessary for the legitimate practice of public administration in a democratic society, requires support by three other subordinate virtues: public spiritedness, prudence, and substantive rationality. These supplemental but highly important character traits focus the attention of the administrator where it belongs: on the citizenry. They encourage reasoned deliberation with citizens and the integration of techniques, values and ethical principles.

In turn, other third level virtues, values, and principles are to be derived from these three core character attributes. The elaboration of a detailed and specific code of ethics and a fully articulated list of appropriate virtues for public administrators lies beyond the scope of this book and beyond its appropriate purview. Much more is necessary for a thorough and complete ethical prescription including treatments of ethical obligations to colleagues, politicians, and the law. Consistent with the understanding of *practice* presented in this chapter, such specification is more properly the responsibility of communities of practitioners such as professional associations, undertaken with the serious participation of the citizenry.[93] The perspective presented in this book is intended to provide a fundamental orientation for such a dialogue.[94]

In the next chapter we consider the implications of the view of the citizen administrator presented here for our understanding of the public and private realms. If the public administrator is obligated to encourage and support the experience of community how does that affect the definitions of public and private? Communities are generally thought of as private entities and public administrators are usually considered by definition as functioning within the public realm. Are communities then more properly understood as public, or do public administrators have obligations that transcend the public arena?

REFERENCES

1. DENNIS T. THOMPSON, *The Democratic Citizen* (Cambridge: Cambridge University Press, 1970), pp. 43–44.
2. JAMES H. KETTNER, *The Development of American Citizenship, 1606–1870* (Chapel Hill: University of North Carolina Press, 1978), pp. 10, 208.
3. JOHN WISE, "A vindication of the government of New England churches," in *Colonial American Writing*, ed., Roy Harvey Pearce (New York: Rinehart, 1950); Michael Walzer, *Obligations: Essays on Disobedience, War and Citizenship* (Cambridge: Harvard University Press, 1970); Lawrence A. Scaff, "Citizenship in America: Theories of the Founding" in *The NonLockean Roots of American Democratic Thought*, ed., J. Chaudhuri (Tucson: University of Arizona Press, 1977).
4. ROBERT PRANGER, *The Eclipse of Citizenship: Power and Participation in Contemporary Politics* (New York: Holt, Rinehart, and Winston, 1968), p. 92.
5. Walzer, *Obligations*, p. 207.
6. CHARLES EVANS HUGHES, *Condition of Progress in Democratic Government* (New Haven: Yale University Press, 1910), pp. 3–4.
7. Pranger, *The Eclipse*, p. 97.
8. *See* Stanley I. Benn, "Privacy, Freedom, and Respect for Persons" in Roland Pennock and

John W. Chapman, eds., *Privacy* (New York: Atherton Press, 1971), p. 22 for a discussion of this liberal conception of privacy that presents the citizen as a "private" citizen with no official public obligations.

9. DONALD MEIKLEJOHN, *Public and Private Morality in America* (Syracuse, New York: Syracuse University Press, 1965), p. 66.

10. SAMUEL WALKER MCCALL, *The Liberty of Citizenship* (New Haven: Yale University Press, 1915), pp. 9, 12.

11. Walzer, *Obligations*, p. 215. *See also* Mark Moore's argument for understanding the obligation of the citizen to pay taxes as an "office" in "On the Office of Taxpayer and the Social Process of Taxpaying," a paper prepared for the Invitational Conference on Tax Compliance, Reston, Virginia, March 16–19, 1983. While Moore's point is consistent with the thesis developed in this text, the role of taxpayer seems better understood for our purposes as one dimension of citizenship and, therefore, not an office in itself; rather one of the duties of the office of "citizen."

12. Pranger, *The Eclipse*, p. 102.

13. DANIEL YANKELOVICH, *New Rules* (New York: Random House, 1981). The argument is developed throughout the book, but *see* chapter 24 for his summary and conclusions.

14. J.G.A. POCOCK, *Politics, Language, and Time* (New York: Atheneum, 1971), pp. 86–87.

15. ALICE B. STONE, AND DONALD C. STONE, "Appendix: Case Histories of Early Professional Education Programs," in ed., Frederick C. Mosher, *American Public Administration: Past, Present, Future* (University, Alabama: University of Alabama Press, University), pp. 276–277, 281–282.

16. Walzer, *Obligations*, p. 216.

17. HERBERT J. SPIRO, *Responsibility in Government: Theory and Practice* (New York: Van Nostrand, 1969), p. 101.

18. DWIGHT WALDO, "Education for Public Administration in the Seventies" in ed., Frederick C. Mosher, *American Public Administration: Past, Present, Future* (University, Alabama: University of Alabama Press, 1975), p. 216.

19. HENRY C. METCALF AND L. URWICK, eds., *Dynamic Administration: The Collected Papers of Mary Parker Follett* (New York: Harper and Brothers, 1940), pp. 101–106.

20. VINCENT OSTROM, *The Intellectual Crisis in American Public Administration* (University, Alabama: University of Alabama Press), p. 131.

21. WESLEY E. BJUR AND GILBERT B. SIEGEL, "Voluntary Citizen Participation in Local Government: Quality, Cost, and Containment, *Midwest Review of Public Administration*, 2 (1977), 135–149; Richard Rich, "Interaction of the Voluntary and Governmental Sectors: Toward an Understanding of the Coproduction of Municipal Services,' *Administration and Society*, 13 (1981), 59–76; Gordon Whitaker, "Coproduction: Citizen Participation in Service Delivery," *Public Administration Review*, 40 (1980), 240–246; Charles H. Levine, "Citizenship and Service Delivery," *Public Administration Review*, Special issue on "Citizenship and Public Administration" (1984), 178–187.

22. *See* the report by The League of California Cities, *Task Force on Local Governments Grass Roots: Preliminary Recommendations* (1981), for a discussion of some of these.

23. DANIEL J. ELAZAR, "Is Federalism Compatible with Prefectorial Administration?," *Publius* (1976), 3.

24. NORTON LONG, "The Three Citizenships," *Publius* (1976), 21.

25. This concern for the consumer image of the citizenry emerged again in *Publius* (1981). *See* in particular pp. 21, 49, 52–53.

26. DAVID H. ROSENBLOOM, "Constitutionalism and Public Bureaucrats," *The Bureaucrat* (1982), 54.

27. JACK RABIN, "The Profession of Public Administration," *The Bureaucrat* (1981–82), 11.

28. *Webster's New World Dictionary*, Second College Edition, 1970.

29. ALASDAIR MACINTYRE, *After Virtue*, 2nd ed. (Notre Dame: Notre Dame University Press, 1984), pp. 181–225.

30. *Ibid.*, pp. 188–190.

31. With respect to their attraction to external goods, MacIntyre's distinction between practices and organizations is too simplistic. *See* note no. 32.

32. This tendency is true also of organizations specifically established to support and develop practices—professional associations are examples of such organizations. A practice may

be corrupted by the external goods sought by its professional association, and may soon begin to orient itself more toward the pursuit of money, political power, social status, and seek protection from its clients rather than concentrate the whole-hearted development of its practice.

33. *Ibid.,* pp. 193–194.

34. *Ibid.,* pp. 194–196.

35. Philippa Foot, one of the leaders in regenerating philosophical treatment of virtue, argues in *Virtues and Vices and Other Essays in Moral Philosophy* (Berkeley: University of California Press, 1978) that in developing contemporary thinking on the subject it is best to go back to Aristotle. For Aristotle, moral virtues were understood as habits that constituted our "states of character," specifically concerned with choice. They are the inner, although not innate, dispositions that make it possible for people to resist the pleasures that divert conduct from the good ends of human existence and keep them from being intimidated by the pain that may be required for noble acts. They help people to maintain a "mean" in their conduct between extremes and excesses. Virtues drawn from the political community of which one is a member seen by Aristotle as essential for the fulfillment of citizenship. Far from being irrelevant to the rough and tumble world of government, Aristotle indicated in *Nicomachean Ethics,* book II that the cultivation of these habits of conduct was considered one of the central responsibilities of legislators because without them democratic government would be impossible. According to Richard McKeon in *The Basic Works of Aristotle,* it seems clear that *Politics* and *Nicomachean Ethics* "treat a common field" (New York: Random House, 1941). Politics without attention to the cultivation of virtue was simply thought to reflect a defective understanding of the ends and purposes of political activity.

36. For examples of this tradition more directly related to American thought *see:* Adam Smith, *The Theory of Moral Sentiments* eds., D.D. Raphael and A.L. Mackie (Oxford: Clarendon Press, 1976), pp. 216, 231; John R. Howe, *The Changing Political Thought of John Adams* (Princeton: Princeton University Press, 1966), pp. 30–32, 87–88. When we examine more direct contributors to our own American tradition of moral and political philosophy we find a lively interest in virtue and a belief that the concept has great political importance. For two illustrative examples, *see* Adam Smith and John Adams. Adam Smith devoted the entirety of part VI of *The Theory of Moral Sentiments* to a consideration "Of the Character of Virtue," giving extensive attention to the virtues of justice, benevolence, valor, and prudence. For Smith, these virtues were not simply private qualities, but bore social and political consequences. He insisted that "The wise and virtuous man is at all times willing that his own private interest should be sacrificed to the public interest of his own particular order or security. He is at all times willing, too, that the interest of this order or society should be sacrificed to the greatest interest of the state or sovereignty, of which it is only a subordinate part." Smith saw these implications of virtue as absolutely essential for the fulfillment of one's obligations as a citizen. One is not a citizen who does not obey and uphold the laws and "is certainly not a good citizen who does not wish to promote, by every means in his power the welfare of the whole society of his fellow-citizens."

In John Adams we find an expression of the American Puritan tradition of virtue without the theological trappings. Although this included a commitment to particular Puritan virtues such as industry, frugality, and prudence, according to Howe, virtue more often meant "a concern for the welfare of society as a whole as opposed to one's own purely selfish interests." More than a list of inclinations or dispositions, for Adams virtue was a matter of the will to discipline one's selfish passions "and the conscious choosing of social good over immediate personal advantage." Drawing from Montesquieu, Adams maintained that every form of government was suited to a characteristic of its people. Tyranny depends on inciting fear among the people, monarchies require honor, but republican governments must have a virtuous people in order to function and survive. Republics will not work without citizens who are able to exercise power for the public good. Adams believed that public virtue was "the necessary foundation of America's new government.

37. Peter Geach, discussing the resurgence of interest in the ethics of virtue in *The Virtues* (Cambridge: Cambridge University Press, 1977), observed that for some time philoso-

phers had neglected virtue as a subject of serious interest and development, but offered no insight into the reason for this lapse. Foot attributed the neglect of the concept of virtue to the dominance of the analytic school of philosophy, but she indicated also that the situation had begun to change during the ten to fifteen years prior to this.

38. STUART HAMPSHIRE, *Morality and Conflict* (Cambridge: Harvard University Press, 1983); James D. Wallace, *Virtues and Vices* (Ithaca: Cornell University Press, 1978); R.E. Ewin, *Cooperation and Human values: A Study of Moral Reasoning* (New York: St. Martin's Press, 1981); William Frankena, *Ethics* (Englewood Cliffs: Prentice Hall, 1973).

39. Following this line of argument it seems clear that this primary obligation is shared with those who practice politics. The practices of public administration and politics are both primarily obligated to support, protect, and encourage the practice of citizenship, each in its own way.

40. *See also* Robert Jay Lifton, "Protean Man,: *The Religious Situation: 1969,* ed., R. Cutler (Boston: Beacon Press, 1969), pp. 812–828, for another image evoked by the fragmented experience of modern people, that of the quick change artist of vaudeville shows. A similar perspective found in John Orr and Pat Nicholson, *The Radical Suburb: Soundings in Changing American Character* (Philadelphia: Westminster Press), 1970.

41. = RICHARD VETTERLI AND GARY BRYNER, *In Search of the Republic: Public Virtue and the Roots of American Government* (Totowa, New Jersey: Rowman and Littlefield, 1987), p. 4.

42. *Ibid.,* p. 19–20.

43. *Ibid.,* p. 79.

44. *Ibid.,* p. 3.

45. *Ibid.,* pp. 249–259.

46. ALEXIS DE TOCQUEVILLE, *Democracy in America,* v.2 (New York: Alfred A. Knopf), pp. 121–122. *See also* John P. Diggins' discussion of Tocqueville's concept of self-interest rightly understood in *The Lost Soul of American Politics: Virtue, Self-interest, and the Foundations of Liberalism* (Chicago: University of Chicago Press, 1984), pp. 230–252.

47. *Ibid.*

48. *Ibid.,* p. 123.

49. *Ibid.,* pp. 106–110, 115–120.

50. Although Tocqueville looked to voluntary associations as the cultivators of self-interest rightly understood, Lloyd G. Nigro and William D. Richardson also see a role for public administration to play in "Self-Interest Properly Understood: The American Character and Public Adminstration," *Administration & Society,* vol. 19, no. 2, August 1987, pp. 157–177.

51. Vetterli and Bryner, *In Search,* p. 250.

52. Vetterli and Bryner, *In Search,* p. 52. I argue in the next chapter that to refer to all these mediating institutions as "private" implies a far too narrow understanding of the public realm; "government" all too easily becomes synonymous with "public." The suggestion is that many so called "nonprofit" associations are more appropriately termed "public nongovernmentals."

53. ALEXIS DE TOCQUEVILLE, *Democracy in America,* Volume 2 (New York: Alfred A. Knopf, 1945), p. 124.

54. GORDON S. WOOD, *The Creation of the American Republic, 1776–1787* (Chapel Hill: University of North Carolina Press, 1969), p. 68. These quotations are from sermons of several ministers delivered during the revolutionary period.

55. Quoted in Vetterli and Bryner, *In Search,* p. 236.

56. EDWARD SAMPSON, "The Debate on Individualism: Indigenous Psychologies of the Individual and Their role in Personal and Societal Functioning," *American Psychologist,* 43 (1988), 15–22.

57. Although Sampson does not go on to suggest what those might be, it seems reasonable to assume that associational experience from an early age, public education that provides both a supportive conceptual framework and group experience, and serious encouragement from government to participate in governance, are among the crucial factors.

58. GARY R. ORREN, "Beyond Self-Interest" in *The Power of Public Ideas,* ed. Robert Reich (Cambridge: Ballinger Publishing Company, 1988), pp. 13–29.

59. STEVEN KELMAN, "Why Public Ideas Matter" in Reich, *The Power,* pp. 31–53.

60. *Ibid.,* pp. 50–52.

61. *Ibid.,* p. 171.
62. *See* in particular Yves R. Simon, *Philosophy of Democratic Government.* (Chicago: University of Illinois Press, 1951). A fully developed theory of civic virtue built upon communitarian concepts will need to draw upon a much broader array of sources, e.g., William M. Sullivan, *Reconstructing Public Philosophy* (Los Angeles: University of California Press, 1982); Robert N. Bellah and others, *Habits of the Heart: Individualism and Commitment in American Life* (Los Angeles: University of California Press, 1985); Amitai Etzioni, *The Moral Dimension: Toward a New Economics* (New York: The Free Press, 1988).
63. CLARK E. COCHRAN, *Character, Community, and Politics* (University, Alabama: University of Alabama Press, 1982), pp. 3, 7, 13.
64. *Ibid.,* p. 15.
65. *Ibid.,* p. 37. It is important to note that Cochran assumes that in highly mobile modern society communities are not always geographically defined by residential location. Transportation makes nonspatial communities possible among the members of occupational, professional, and affinity groups that are widely dispersed.
66. *Ibid.,* p. 40.
67. *Ibid.,* pp. 18–20.
68. Cochran derives this three-fold conceptualization from Jacques Maritain's *The Person and the Common Good* (New York: Charles Scribner's Sons, 1947). He uses Maritain's formulation to clarify Simon's perspective.
69. CLARK E. COCHRAN, "Yves R. Simon and the Common Good: A Note on the Concept," *Ethics,* 88 (1978) 229–239.
70. *Ibid.,* pp. 233–234.
71. *Ibid.*
72. *Ibid.,* p. 238.
73. *See also* the author's work in "Public Administration in an Age of Scarcity: A Citizenship Role for Public Administrators" in *Politics and Administration: Woodrow Wilson and Contemporary Public Administration,* eds. James Bowman and Jack Rabin (New York: Marcel Dekker, 1984), pp. 297–314.
74. Cochran, *Character,* p. 50.
75. *Ibid.,* pp. 15, 123, 141.
76. *Ibid.,* p. 89.
77. *Ibid.,* p. 144.
78. *Ibid.,* p. 144.
79. *Ibid.,* p. 159.
80. Discussed in *Ibid.,* pp. 83–89.
81. Simon, *The Philosophy,* pp. 36–48.
82. Irving Kristol, "Republican Virtue," *Kettering Review* (Fall 1988) 8–18.
83. *See* Steven Kelman's coinage and use of this term in "Why Public Ideas Matter" in Reich, *The Power,* pp. 31–53. Kelman uses it to refer to behavior that demonstrates concern for others as well as one's self. In this text it is adapted to the functions of the administrator which require him or her to show concern for the "others" or "citizenry," as well as being concerned for professional interests.
84. *See* the discussion of these justifications in Terry L. Cooper, "Citizen Participation" in *Organization Theory and Management,* ed. Thomas D. Lynch (New York: Marcel Dekker, 1983), pp. 13–45.
85. ELIZABETH K. MINNICK, "Some Reflections on Civic Education and the Curriculum," *Kettering Review* (1988) 33–41. Although Minnick does not use the term "prudence," her treatment of judgment is highly consistent with the concept of prudence as practical judgment.
86. CHESTER A. NEWLAND, "Public Executives: Imperium, Sacerdotum, Collegium? Bicentennial Leadership Challenges," *Public Administration Review* 47 (1987) 45–56.
87. Simon, *The Philosophy,* p. 279.
88. ALBERTO GUERREIRO RAMOS, *The New Science of Organization: A Reconceptualization of the Wealth of Nations* (Toronto: University of Toronto Press, 1981). *See* in particular chapters 1–2.
89. ROBERT REICH, "Policy Making in a Democracy" in Reich, *The Power,* pp. 144–145.
90. *Ibid.*

91. GIANDOMENICO MAJONE, "Policy Analysis and Public Deliberation," in Reich, *The Power*, pp. 157–178.
92. This statement is not intended as a rejection of Rawls, but of the notion that public administrators should behave like detached experts in determining the meaning of justice in any instance. The introduction of Rawlsian or other theories of justice may quite likely be helpful in such deliberation.
93. Two serious deficiencies in the code of ethics developed by The American Society for Public Administration are its lack of a coherent fundamental perspective of this kind and the absence of deliberation with the citizenry in its development.
94. For an indication of how such a perspective might be developed in greater detail *see* Terry L. Cooper, "Hierarchy, Virtue, and the Practice of Public Administration: A Perspective for Normative Ethics," *Public Adminstration Review* 47 (1987), 320–328.

6
THE PUBLIC OBLIGATIONS OF THE PUBLIC ADMINISTRATOR: THE PUBLIC-PRIVATE CONTINUUM IN A DEMOCRATIC SOCIETY

The conceptualization of the citizen role, and the view of the public administrative role derived from it that has been developed in previous chapters, requires a clear understanding of the nature of the public realm. It is within this realm that both roles find their relevant functions and within which they act upon their particular ethical norms. It is essential now to elucidate the nature of the public and the private areas of life in American society and to identify the spheres within which the citizen administrator role bears responsibility.

The first step toward such a conceptualization is to forthrightly acknowledge the dichotomous thought patterns that we employ in our ideas about public and private phenomena, and the language that maintains them. Referring to the public and private dimensions of life as though they were *sectors*, even if we use the term more broadly than the economic sense, creates and sustains the illusion that we are dealing with phenomena that can be *bounded*. For a complex web of interdependent relationships that range from feelings and thoughts that are almost purely private to the use of facilities, spaces, and resources that involve masses of people, we substitute a notion of neatly compartmentalized distinctions. Even the uses of *arenas* and *realms*, as has been done in this chapter, are spatial metaphors that may constrain both thought and action.

ORIGINS OF THE DICHOTOMY

The terms *public* and *private* are of Latin derivation, and correspond to older Greek concepts. *Publicus* is the Latin root of *public* which refers to those things that are possessed by "the people corporately," that are "authorized, provided, maintained" by the state and its officials, and includes all acts that affect everyone in the state. It also encompasses those things that are "available to, shared or enjoyed by, all members of the community;" anything that is "common to all" or "universal."[1] A variation on this root word from which we have derived *republic* is *res publica*, or *respublica*. This term means "the common weal, a commonwealth, state, republic."[2] "Common weal, or more typically, *commonweal* is defined as *common well-being*." "*Commonwealth* refers to *public welfare* or general *good*," and secondarily to "*the body politic*," especially when viewed as "*a body in which the whole people have a voice or an interest*," as in a republic.[3]

Thus the etymology of the term *public* indicates a breadth and depth of meaning that transcends government. Its most fundamental denotations are the shared, communal, universally accessible dimensions of collective life, as well as those things that have general impact upon the interests of all; the realm of interdependence. The normative connotations of the word, as found in *res publica*, have to do with the common good or well-being. The state is clearly included in the meaning of *public*, but in a secondary, apparently derivative status.

The less commonly cited Greek equivalents from an earlier era are *koinos* and *demosios*.[4] *Koinos* denotes that which is *common* or *general*. Variations on this root word refer to that which is *shared in common*, the *common weal* and those matters that are *of public or general interest*. *Demosios*, which is also translated *public*, indicates those things *belonging to the people or state*, as well as those that are commonly used.[5] The denotations of shared interests, communal holdings, and general accessibility seem even more pronounced in these Greek words, although the state is once again subsumed under them in derivative status.

When we turn to *private* we find as a root the term *priuatus* with central meanings that include: *Restricted for the use of a particular person or persons*; *Belonging as private property to oneself, one's own*; *One's own property, one's own house or land*; *One's own interest*; *Not holding public office*; *Individual to a person or thing, peculiar, special*.[6] Taken together these definitions suggest those possessions that are removed from general access and common use, as well as those matters that do not affect the interests of others, but are exclusive to the domain of a particular person. This is the realm of independence, autonomy, and inaccessibility to the collective people.

The Greek antecedents of the Latin root once again involve two terms: *idios* and *oikeos*. *Idios* denotes *one's own way, pertaining to oneself, one's own property, separate, distinct*. *Oikeos*, on the other hand, refers more specifically to that which is *in or of the house*; that which is *of persons of the same household, family or kin*; or to *things belonging to one's house or family*. The meanings discovered here overlap with those of the Latin *priuatus* with perhaps a stronger association to household and family.

These ancient terms reflect the early establishment of distinctions between the individual and the collective traditional society. Roelofs explained that the citizen emerged in Athens as "the individual is wrenched free of the multiple attachments of the clan," or *gen*, as the tribal subdivisions of that city-state were called. It was this identification of the individual that made possible the idea of democracy. A confederation of tribes and gens could then be replaced with "a new organic whole" through which individuals were related as citizens.[7] Roelofs emphasized the strong link that existed between the citizen and political community. He maintained that in the Greek tradition the community remained the fundamental reality. Political participation was never appropriately viewed as a means for fulfilling personal ambitions, but rather as an opportunity for contributing to the common life of the city.[8]

Once the distinction between public and private realms was acknowledged conceptually and legally, the relationship was a very unstable one. Roelofs noted that as the glory of the Athenian era began to dim, withdrawal from the public arena began to occur. One manifestation of this waning of interest in public life was the retreat of the philosophers into contemplative academies.[9]

According to Sennett, this same orientation of the individual to the political community could be found in Rome until the fading of the Augustan Age and the emerging fascination with various Near Eastern religions during the first three centuries A.D. The individual Roman citizen still conformed to the rules of public obligation, but without the passion that had been diverted to a mystical transcendence of the formalities of the res publica. The connections between the public and private realms became attenuated as time and emotional fervor focused on the private religious quest.[10]

Bensman and Lilienfield pointed out that this historical emergence of a private sphere for individuals from the collective life of the community is a typical phenomenon. They argued:

> In primitive and ancient societies the distinction between the public and private does not exist. The individual, linguistically and intellectually, is so deeply integrated into an extended family system and into locality-based social relationships—usually defined by tradition—that all of his or her behavior (and that of all others) is subject to mutual surveillance, so much so that the individual cannot conceive of himself as having an identity apart from the family, tribe, or neighborhood. Conceptions of separate private and public "domains" are minimal.[11]

The precise series of mechanisms that over time break the dominance of tradition and allow differentiation of public and private roles, spaces, and activities are not clear. However, two contributing factors do appear to be relatively clear as we approach our own era historically. First, the tenuous notions of privacy as a realm of individual prerogative were given much greater emphasis and intensity with the rise of liberalism in the seventeenth century.[12] The Lockean social compact clearly established in intellectual and political history an assumption that was fundamentally different from those of traditional societies. It was not the tribe, clan, or village that was the natural phenomenon, but rather individuals in possession of the "executive power of the law of nature" through the operation of their own rational faculties.[13] According to this formulation, the private realm of the individual is prior and natural, while the public realm of collective interdependent life is only a derivative, dependent artifact of human judgment.

Concretely and specifically, the social compact theory of Locke challenged the feudal theory dominant in England since the middle ages, and reversed its premises. Under the tradition articulated by Sir Edward Coke in the famous Calvin's Case in 1608 the feudal system with its monarchy was unalterably rooted in natural law. Individuals were viewed by Coke as eternally bound to the king by birth and fixed into an inescapable relationship of allegiance. Locke's doctrine disputed the ultimacy and naturalness of the feudal arrangements, identifying them instead as contingent social constructs that could be altered by individuals under certain conditions.[14]

This primacy of the private was carried further in the philosophy of the utilitarians, especially that of Jeremy Bentham in his denial of the reality of the community.[15] If society most fundamentally consists not of natural communities at all, but only of individuals in search of interests rooted in pleasure and pain, the most private of all realms of experience becomes the most fundamentally natural reality. There is little left to the public dimension of life except mechanisms for protecting these individually based private interests and resolving conflicts among them. Sullivan summarized this state of affairs as follows:

> The liberal conception drew a firm distinction between public and private realms, thereby gaining autonomy for religious and intellectual as well as economic pursuits. But this reduced the public realm to formal institutions in which the conflicts among the "interests" of civil society were umpired and negotiated, draining public life of intrinsic morality and significance.[16]

Once again, as seems to have been true in Rome and Greece, the extrication of the individual from the ties of an integrated traditional society leads to an unstable polarity. Individual and public realms, once distinguished from the matrix of fixed tradition, seem difficult to maintain in any kind of balance. The individual set free from the tribe, or clan, or divinely ordained system of feudalism becomes less interested in the public realm of interdependent life, and preoccupied with private intellectual development, religious pursuits, personal autonomy, development of the self, or private property to the neglect of those things held in common, used by all, and accessible to all.

The liberal tradition is only one of the crucial factors involved in the emergence of a public-private distinction. The second of these is modernization, particularly as manifest in urban industrial society. Modern society of the cities drew people from homogeneous settings governed largely by tradition and characterized by familiarity.[17] Industrial cities of the nineteenth century created agglomerations of heterogeneous individuals who were largely strangers to each other and each other's traditions and cultures. Although, according to Lofland, much of life occurred in public, jointly shared spaces, in preindustrial cities, the opposite is true of the modern city. Confronted by strangers with different values, customs, and beliefs and abetted by modern technology and specialization, many activities once conducted in places accessible to, used by, and visible to all, were moved into spaces set apart and placed under the control of one or a limited number of individuals. Elimination of body wastes, punishments and executions, water collection, garbage and waste disposal, distribution and collection of news, buying and selling, entertainment, individual religious expression, education of the young, and socializing are among those functions that have been privatized but were once conducted largely in public.[18]

Flaherty described the beginnings of this transition in colonial New England. Cohesive homogeneous Puritan communities of the seventeenth century minimized privacy and encouraged collaboration in the public work of creating "a City Set upon a Hill" in New England towns and cities. "A pervasive moralism, the concept of watchfulness, the encouragement of mutual surveillance, and the suppression of self to community goals" bound individuals to the priorities of the community.[19] As the Puritan tradition waned in the late seventeenth century a desire for privacy emerged as a typical precursor to industrial society in the eighteenth century.[20]

Sam Bass Warner, Jr. similarly traced this evolution in greater detail with respect to Philadelphia. Although eighteenth century Philadelphia was described as a unified community with an active public sphere, by the late nineteenth century it had become a city dominated by privatism. Democratic government, oriented toward the well-being of the whole city, waned as informal street life diminished. Social life and communal concerns retreated into private organizations such as parish churches, lodges, benefit associations, social and athletic clubs, political clubs, volunteer fire companies, and gangs.[21] (This historical account of one city is generally consistent with Wolin's broader analysis.)[22]

Warner viewed these developments in Philadelphia as both a microcosm of American society and of other modern cultures. By the late eighteenth century, American urban society was dominated by the priority of the private arena. He asserted that under these conditions "the first purpose of the citizen is the private search for wealth; the goal of a city is to be a community of private money makers." The shared interdependent dimensions of life beyond those involved in the acquisition of private resources fell at least into second place. The role of the political community was viewed as essentially one of providing a stable, peaceful, and open economic environment for the pursuit of private interests.[23]

Sennett argued that this preoccupation with the acquisition of personal wealth intensified during the rapid industrialization that took place during the nineteenth century and, in turn, encouraged the identification of the family as a place of escape both from the hurly-burly struggle of the business world, and the chaotic urban environment. The dominant assumption, in Sennett's view, was that "the public was a human creation; the private was the human condition."[24]

In this context the family became "a shield," an orderly stable world of its own; a natural phenomenon in contrast to the conventional world of culture outside the home. One ventured out into the public realm to advance one's personal economic interests in the competitive struggle for profit, and then retreated to the privacy of the home where respectability and virtue could be maintained.

The association of "natural" with "private" and "culture" with "public," which had begun a century earlier, was hardened by "the traumas of nineteenth century capitalism." The result, according to Sennett, was the gradual erosion of the will to control and shape the public order "as people put more emphasis on protecting themselves from it."[25] Again we see the ascendance of the fundamentality of the private realm set apart from the communal.

This opposition of the public and the private with its assumptions about the priority of individual interests, has evolved over time into a more focused way of thinking that simplistically associates "private" with "business" and "public" with "government." Meiklejohn maintained that "our discourse follows the economic model, in which the private interest literally is a man's profit and the public interest appears as reduction of that profit by taxes and other social restraints." He concluded: "To private gain, public advantage appears alien and hostile."[26] Thus, when we address the question of public-private relationships, our thinking and our language tend to be cast in economic categories such as public *sector* and private *sector*.[27] In this way, the institutions associated with making money, on the one hand, and taxing and regulating enterprise, on the other, move into center stage and preoccupy us with their adversarial relationship.

We remind ourselves from time to time, that the play is truly more complex; there are other actors associated with both the public and private dimensions of life. However, they do not compel our serious attention as frequently, nor is our thinking about them as well developed.

A PUBLIC-PRIVATE CONTINUUM

Having outlined the origins of our dichotomous thinking about public and private activities, the next step in developing a more adequate conceptualization of these different spheres of life logically follows from the first. It is to begin treating public-private relationships as though they existed on a continuum with numerous gradations in between.[28] Bensman and Lilienfield offered the minimal conceptual ingredients for such a continuum. In order to break out of dichotomous thinking, they described three realms: *the private, the quasi-public,* and *the public.*[29] The insertion of the *quasi-public* realm was intended to provide for those conditions and relationships that fall between those that are entirely, or largely under the control of an individual and those that are entirely under, or largely controlled by, collectively determined rules, norms, and sanctions. It recognized that there are vast areas of informal activity and information exchange that can be controlled by those affected only to a limited extent.

Implicit in this insertion of the *quasi-public* realm were some assumed attributes of *public* and *private.*[30] Before proceeding further, it might be useful to make these explicit. Both the etymology of public and private and their treatment in the literature included in the references for this chapter suggest the following characteristics of ideal types of the two phenomena in their pure and, therefore, never fully actualized forms:

Public	*Private*
Open to surveillance by all	Closed to surveillance by others
Accessible by all	Inaccessible by others
Available for use by all	Unavailable for use by others
Owned collectively by all	Owned by an individual
Significant, extensive and lasting direct or indirect consequences for all	No consequences for others
Oriented toward common good	Oriented toward personal interests of an individual
Interdependence	Independence

It should be noted that the use of negatives in the private attributes reflects the historical emergence of privacy and individualism from communally oriented traditional societies. The establishment and maintenance of private aspects of life involve *depriving* the public of certain dimensions of an individual's existence. Therefore, the defining of the private occurred historically through negation. The positive content of the private realm must be defined through individual autonomous decisions and actions.[31]

Having presented these two lists of characteristics of the ideal types of the public and private, it is necessary to indicate, once again, that they should not be viewed as dichotomous alternatives. Rather, they represent the extreme poles of a continuum on which human existence is played out. As Palmer argued: "Properly understood, public and private interact, shape one another; depend on each other for their very existence."[32]

Although there is interdependence between the ends of the continuum and among the various phenomena representing gradations in between, there is also clearly a tension involved in moving toward either end. For example, movement toward the public end requires giving up the autonomy of independence and freedom from surveillance, and accepting the obligations of interdependence and openness to the scrutiny of others; movement toward the private end entails giving up the experience of relatedness to a larger community of persons and accepting the restrictions of solitude and intimacy with a few persons.

The continuum is represented by Figure One, with its eight gradations of relationships. Although detailed elaboration of each of these relationships lies beyond the scope of this chapter, a brief summary of each will suggest a sense of the continuum:

1. Personal   This category of experience concerns one's own thought and feeling processes that remain isolated from all other persons; one's innermost fantasies, speculations, abstractions, suspicions; one's unexpressed feelings of pain, pleasure, guilt, jealousy, pride, hope, etc.; one's knowledge of one's own acts that remain concealed from others. In terms of the two lists of attributes above, these intrapersonal experiences resulting from the relationships one has with oneself, are clearly the most private. They are the property solely of an individual, they are beyond access, surveillance, and use by others, and unless they lead to conduct that moves one toward the public end of the continuum they are without consequences for others. They may also be entirely oriented toward the interests of the self and independent of influence by others.

Even our personal thoughts and feelings are not often purely private in these respects since any socialized person's thoughts are likely to reflect the interests and influence of others. Thus it seems that even one's relationship with oneself is not often purely private; this would be impossible unless it were possible to conceive of a completely unsocialized individual in something like a Lockean state of nature.

2. Intimate   We move to those relationships and the spaces where they occur, that involve one or a very few persons in the sharing of profound and highly personal experience or information. These relationships are one step away from the intrapersonal relationships discussed above. The individual gives up control of thoughts and feelings by communicating them to a few trusted others. Secrecy and confidentiality are either assumed or explicitly requested to be maintained by the participants, who would usually include

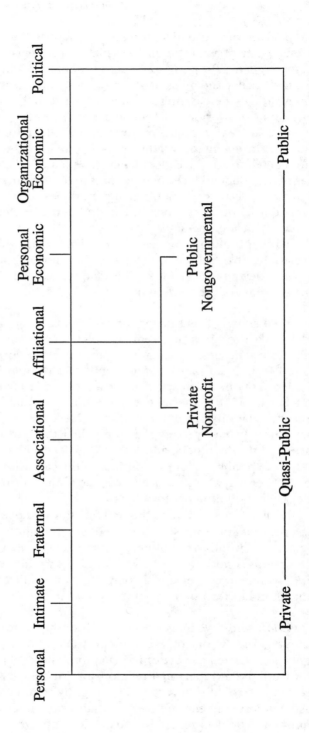

FIGURE 1
Public-Private Continuum

persons such as spouses, lovers, close family members, and best friends. Access, surveillance, and partial ownership of these personal experiences is opened to a limited circle of others thereby creating some degree of interdependence, acknowledging some mutuality of interests and giving rise to some consequences for those others. The larger the number of others included in this intentionally discreet relationship, the less private and the more public it becomes. Also, the less trustworthy and indiscreet the others are, the more public the relationship becomes unintentionally.

3. Fraternal   This category includes a broader range of relationships and their locations that are characterized by sociality, friendliness, and ongoing, or regular, communication and contact. Participants include one's circle of acquaintances, friends, and neighbors, as well as other persons encountered frequently. These relationships are less oriented toward maintaining confidentiality about highly personal thoughts and feelings and more toward the friendly, gregarious, and casual exchange of ideas, opinions and observations. These are companionable and convivial, rather than intimate, relationships. They include relationships at work, friends of the family, and those who share a leisure interest such as tennis or golf.

It is generally assumed that information shared with these others will be available for use by third parties, open to their surveillance by others through eavesdropping, and reflect a larger network of interdependence and interests, unless they are transformed into intimate relationships by explicitly entering into communication conditioned on confidentiality. These fraternal communications may well have consequences for others, even beyond those toward whom the information is intentionally directed, as in the case of gossip.

4. Associational   Included here are the relatively brief and discontinuous contacts one has with a multitude of strangers in the course of daily life in modern urban society. These range from extended one time conversations on airline flights, or debates in a public forum, to brief social exchanges over a cup of coffee in a crowded restaurant, or over a drink in a bar, to purely instrumental, functional relationships with largely anonymous people such as supermarket clerks, bus drivers, waiters, telephone operators, flight attendants, cab drivers, secretaries, office clerks, librarians, parking lot attendants, and mail carriers.

These relationships do not generally involve a choice to engage in personal interaction with particular persons, but are based rather on circumstance, such as happening to find oneself sitting next to some unchosen individual on an airplane, or based on need, such as having to deal with some unchosen person who happens to be the bank teller when one finds it necessary to withdraw funds. These associational relationships are open to surveillance by anyone who happens to be in the vicinity, or anyone who chooses to be there particularly to observe one's actions, although, typically, access to personal information is limited. These relationships are available for use by anyone with the necessary resources; that is, one wanting to exploit such a relationship could by plan arrange to be the bank teller or the airline seat neighbor, or could make use of the information gained after the fact.

Particular interactions in this category may affect large numbers of people, but certainly not everyone, nor generally speaking, even large portions of the population. Words uttered in an informal debate in a supermarket check line may be persuasive enough to influence those overhearing; a conversation on an extended flight may lead to a business deal; a bus driver's attitude may start her passengers off on the right, or the wrong, foot on the way to work.

In these relationships, personal information that is to be controlled only by oneself, or one's intimates, is guarded, although personal communication may occur if one believes the very fact of anonymity will protect one from any consequential use of the information. The assumption in these instances, such as baring one's soul to a bartender, is that releasing the information does not jeopardize one's personal independence, nor is it likely to produce serious, extensive, and undesirable consequences when detached from one's biography.

5. Affiliational   At this point, we have a category of relationship where both private and public attributes are significantly present. Here we are dealing with relationships involving organizational affiliations that are somewhat regular and consistent. These would include organizations such as social clubs, service clubs, neighborhood organizations, recreation groups, labor unions, political clubs, environmental associations, religious organizations, professional associations, civil rights organizations, student associations, youth groups, and single issue advocacy groups.

In sum, these are the voluntary nonprofit, so-called *third sector* organizations. Membership in these organizations is generally a matter of individual choice, or initiative. They are owned, controlled, and supported collectively—not by all, but by their members that vary considerably in number. Also, they expose one to surveillance by others significantly more than is the case with the preceding three categories; the potential exposure varies according to the size of the membership, the openness of the organization's internal environment, and its openness to the external environment.

These organizations may vary considerably between characteristics that are more private and those that are more public. For example, professional associations may be accessible only to those who have achieved certain professional standards, religious organizations may require a commitment to a particular doctrine, or neighborhood organizations may be open only to those who reside within a specified area. On the other hand, social clubs, recreational clubs, and youth groups may be open to anyone who wishes to join.

Similarly, these organizations may exhibit significant differences in the orientation of their goals. Labor unions, professional associations and single-issue advocacy groups may be primarily focused on the specific interests of their members, while others such as service clubs, environmental associations, humanitarian groups, civil liberties organizations, and, in some cases, religious organizations may have a broader orientation toward what they perceive to be the common good.

These organizations may engage in actions that generally have few, if any, significant consequences for others, such as the typical activities of recreation groups, youth groups, social clubs, and some religious organizations, although they may on occasion undertake projects that have impact beyond their membership. The conduct of other organizations such as labor unions, political clubs, civil rights associations and single-issue advocacy groups tend to have very serious, extensive, and lasting consequences for large masses of people, if not all people.

Although the organizations that fall into this affiliational category are generally lumped together under the label *private nonprofit*, it might be more appropriate to think in terms of at least two subsets. Those toward the left end of this part of the continuum might be better referred to as *private nonprofit* while those falling more to the right might more accurately be termed *public nongovernmental*. The former manifest more of those attributes associated with privateness, but do not seek financial profit, while the latter evidence more public characteristics, but are not organs of government.

6. Personal Economic   At this point, it is more difficult to clearly distinguish the boundaries of a category of relationship. Here we deal with the transactional relationships involved in one's decisions about employment, disposition of earnings, savings, and personal expenditures for shelter, food, clothing, transportation, and entertainment that, as the position on the continuum indicates, are definitely less private than the three previous categories, but, nevertheless, include significant degrees of individual choice. Much larger numbers of people are involved in these relationships and transactions; there is far less control, either over the range of options, or the consequences of one's actions, by any given individual. Typically these transactions occur in places to which many other people have access, that they may observe and may use, if they have the required resources.

The individual is exposed to a greater degree of surveillance by others in these economic relationships, although generally not of a direct "face-to-face" nature. Governmental agencies such as the Social Security Administration, the Internal Revenue Service, state motor vehicle departments, local building and safety departments, and local fire departments gain access to personal information as a result of employment, earnings, and ownership of property. Business firms acquire personal information about individuals through such sources as credit applications, credit card purchasing patterns, employment applications, subscription mailing lists, motor vehicle records, and insurance applications.

Thus, although there is still considerable independence in choosing which transactional relationships one will enter into, and with whom, once chosen these relationships are significantly more public than the previous categories. They are subject to much more surveillance, access, and use by others, most of whom are neither intimates, nor friends, nor passing acquaintances, nor members of organizations to which we belong. They are largely anonymous individuals over whom we have little control. Generally, not only do we not know who gains access to these relationships and acquires partial ownership of them, but neither do we know what they are doing with the information they gain or when they are using it. Consequently, our independence is considerably reduced by these relationships and we become much more interdependent with the local, national and international economic systems. These personal economic decisions and the relationships they entail have far more consequences that are potentially significant, extensive, and long lasting than any in the previous categories. For example, our purchase of aerosol sprays may contribute to the destruction of the ozone layer; our decisions about home purchases may shape the future of our children as a result of the quality of the school system and the socio-economic status of the community; and our investments in the stock market may influence the future of major corporations.

It seems clear, then, that what we generally refer to as our private financial affairs are, in fact, to a great extent public in nature. Especially in modern societies, when we enter the marketplace, we are moving into a web of relationships that manifest the attributes of publicness to a significant degree. While we may act as though these are private relationships in our pursuit of individual self-interest, we do so in neglect of their actual public nature.

7. Organizational Economic   These are the large scale structural relationships that compose the economy of a society. They include all the business relationships of the society, but are practically determined by large corporate organizations and governmental activity. These organizations are generally owned by large numbers of shareholders, but controlled routinely by a few, including top level executive managers and boards of directors. A body of law, including corporate law, equal opportunity regulations, labor relations statutes, environmental legislation, securities and exchange laws and tax laws provide some governmentally imposed collective controls that reflect the publicness of the so-called "private" corporation. These organizations exhibit both public and private attributes. The internal affairs of these organizations are typically inaccessible to all but government agencies responsible for administering the laws related to their conduct, and, as organizations, are not available for use by all, except as consumers of the goods and services they produce. Their goals are not primarily oriented toward the common good, but to a limited collective good—that of the shareholders, board, and management of the corporation.

The consequences of corporate activities are generally significant, extensive, and long-lasting. Corporate decisions about plant location may produce heavy positive or negative impacts on local economies; the competence, or lack of competence, of the management and personnel of key major corporations may advance or retard national interests in competition with other nations for technological dominance; and the lack of ethical sensitivity of corporate leadership may lead to the production and sale of goods that are detrimental to human well-being with disastrous results for large numbers of people.

These corporations are inescapably involved in highly interdependent national and international relationships with each other, as well as with government, labor unions, academic institutions, and the citizenry, on the one hand, while, on the other hand, they strive for independence. That is, corporations generally resist acting in a manner that is consistent with the public nature of their relationships to their social and economic environments. They tend to seek organizational autonomy in order to maneuver for corporate interests in spite of their interlocking relationships with government through contracts, regulatory law, and subsidy; without acknowledgment of their interrelationships with local economies; and apart from their ultimate dependence upon a viable natural environment. It seems clear then, that this category of relationships on the public-private continuum is one of the most confused and problematic, and therefore, may require more discussion than the other categories in the continuum.

We have highly public phenomena that strive to act like private phenomena, and are often thought of as appropriately private entities in the popular mind. However, it has not always been so. Even a cursory examination of the origins of corporations both in the United States and Great Britain reveals that corporations were created as public instruments, and have come to be viewed as private, strictly profit oriented organizations, only rather recently. For example, Paul J. McNulty asserted that "Among forms of business enterprise, the corporation was traditionally regarded as more public in character than proprietorships and partnerships." He continued with a quotation from Oscar and Mary Handlin, suggesting that in early Massachusetts the corporation was "conceived as an agency of government, endowed with public attributes, exclusive privileges, and political power, and designed to serve a social function for the state. Turnpikes, not trade, banks, not land speculation, were its province because the community, not the enterprising capitalists, marked out its sphere of activity."[33]

McNulty maintained that conceiving of the corporation as a quasi-public institution with social responsibility beyond the making of profit "is neither a new nor a radical idea; it is, rather, a return to a traditional American ideal which, if not always fully honored in the past, is today too little known or appreciated." He concluded that, in fact, corporations have become even more public in nature in recent decades as they have become more intertwined with modern society, and more involved in partnerships with government.

Supportive of this general perspective of the corporation as a public entity, though not a part of government, is substantial historical research that supports the Handlins' contention that the privileges of incorporation were originally granted only for the purpose of serving some clear and specific public need, or accomplishing some identifiable public goal. Seavoy, for example, made it quite clear that incorporation was bestowed originally only on associations that established their intent to perform "vital public services such as religious and secular education, or undertook the construction on internal improvement projects."[34] These were "private" corporations only in the sense that their officers held no public office by virtue of their corporate titles.[35] Although these corporations might be either profit-making or nonprofit-making, competitive businesses were almost never granted incorporation until the middle 1850s or later. Prior to that time the only justification government had for allowing the status of incorporation, with such unusual legal provisions as limited liability, was determined by the public service performed.[36]

Similarly, James Willard Hurst observed that from the start in the 1780s the corporation in America was viewed as "a distinct social and political as well as economic factor in the general life." He indicated that almost all corporations in the United States in these years were for some community interest such as supplying transport, water, insurance, or banking services which implied that incorporation was "inherently of such public concern that the public authority must confer it."[37] In fact, well into the middle of the nineteenth century the most frequent and visible use of incorporation was for public utilities.[38] It was not until the late nineteenth and early twentieth centuries that a shift occurred from emphasis on the public responsibility of the corporation to its usefulness for profitable enterprise and economic development.[39]

One final but significant factor that contributes to the publicness of the corporation is its impact on the political efficacy of the citizenry. Carole Pateman, after reviewing the research literature on participation, concluded that since corporations are, in fact, political systems they influence significantly the political attitudes and behavior of those who work within them.[40] Participatory democracy is heavily dependent upon the kind of socialization for citizenship that occurs in the workplace. To the extent that citizens have real opportunities for real participation in governing their work environments they are more likely to be active participants in the political arena. Thus, in this additional way it is clear that corporations and the organizational economic relationships through which they function are heavily endowed with public attributes, particularly in their consequences and interdependence with the larger society.

The implication is that business bears public obligation by virtue of its location in the continuum. To the extent that businesses and corporations engage in activities that manifest interdependence with other parts of the society and produce social impacts that are significant, extensive, and long lasting, they are public entities, with a kind of corporate citizenship responsibility.[41] As such, they incur obligations to demonstrate civic virtue, not an exclusive commitment to profit maximization and organizational power. The social responsibility of corporations should be rooted neither in philanthropy, nor in public relations; but in the responsibilities inherent in the public role, in the very nature of their relationships with society.

This public obligation of the business community does not necessarily imply public ownership, although that is one possible option. It does clearly suggest that in order to carry out its public role a business must cultivate an ethic of civic virtue or be subjected to regulations in the public interest. This is one of the costs of liberty as one moves toward the public end of the continuum. Freedom of action must be constrained either through self-control, or through the sanctions of the political community, *to the extent* that activities exhibiting interdependent relationships and social consequences that are potentially significant, extensive, and long lasting are involved. Corporations must either orient themselves in a serious manner to the common good or be required to do so through the instruments of the political community: governmental policies, rules, regulations, and procedures. One or the other must be done in order to preserve the continuum of public-private relationships that are necessary for a democratic society.

8. Political   Here, we are concerned with those relationships that constitute the democratic political community, including governmental structures. Membership in this community is open to all citizens. Also, the government and its various organizations that the political community establishes as its fiduciary agent is obligated to be generally open to surveillance by all, available for use by all, owned collectively by all, and oriented toward the common good.

The legal and administrative activities of the government generally have consequences that are significant, extensive, and lasting. Policies adopted and implemented by government affect very large numbers of people, often over long time periods in a variety of ways, including their economic status, family life, social relationships, residential patterns, health, and physical environment. Both the democratic political community and its governmental structures involve high degrees of interdependence. Thus, the political aspects of life and society manifest public attributes more clearly than any to the left of the continuum.

It is for this reason that the introduction of private attributes into the activities of government evokes such strong reactions; such conduct is viewed as corrupt or, at the very least, inappropriate. Secrecy, inaccessibility, control by only a few individuals, the serving of particular interests, and the severance of accountability to the people all represent violations of the public nature of political relationships in a democratic society. They are recognized as inconsistent with the inherent "publicness" of government. All these attributes fit more appropriately as one moves toward the left end of the continuum.

If we return now to Bensman and Lilienfield's three realms of *private*, *quasi-public*, and *public*, it would appear that the *quasi-public* emerges with *intimate* relationships and logically includes all of the categories through and including *economic organizational*. These scholars did not develop the *quasi-public* realm in this way, but merely indicate that it begins with *intimate relationships*. It does so because this class of relationships necessarily involves social expression, even if only with one person. Social expression then is more or less beyond the control and ownership of the individual, more or less susceptible to surveillance and use by others, and therefore, the first step into a relationship with a degree of publicness, although still far more private than public.[42]

IMPLICATIONS AND CONCLUSIONS: THE CITIZEN ADMINISTRATOR AND THE PUBLIC-PRIVATE CONTINUUM

Although much further development of this public-private continuum is both possible and desirable, it must suffice, for the purposes of this chapter, as a representation of the kind of thinking needed to fully elaborate the citizen administrator role. Let us conclude then with a brief discussion of six crucial points concerning the citizen administrator and this continuum.

1. Political community is essential for democratic government. Government is to be understood as the primary instrument of the political community for the general ordering of the social context.[43] Political community is structured around certain myths about the meaning of the past and certain ideals about its future that are shared by the citizenry. These are expressed in a more or less well articulated system of traditions and regime values. Unless there is a set of shared traditions and regime values around which citizens can focus their expectations for each other and their collective existence, there can be no horizontal authority capable of directing the government. To the extent that the horizontal authority of a democratic political community is lacking, the government is in its own hands, or the hands of a few. Under these circumstances, government becomes an alien instrument, an insubordinate agent without democratic authority and without moral legitimacy or credibility.

The government's continued existence without authority from the political community is a threat to the viability of the community, since its renegade conduct tends to subordinate the community to the ends of government. In these circumstances, government increasingly presents itself and its activities as *the* public realm and denies, or ignores, the political community and its component elements. It was Etzioni's opinion that:

> The sharp rise in government in the last decades may have been caused by the decline of mutuality and involvement in shared concerns, with government stepping in as a kind of substitute-mutuality and community-of-last-resort. Or, the expansion of government may have undermined mutuality and community, feeding into a retreat from community already under way for other historical reasons. Most likely both processes took place, with the government stepping in to help replace what the community was neglecting, to fill a vacuum, and at the same time overstepping, pushing back, further undermining the community.[44]

In order to maintain and enhance democratic government, these mutually reenforcing processes that contribute to the atrophication of community and expansion of the administrative state must be reversed. This can be done, in part, through appreciation of the essential nature of political community by public administrators and through their support and encouragement of it.

2. The democratic political community is characterized by complex interdependence that includes the full public-private continuum.   Its most fundamental unit is the individual whose private personal experience is symbiotically related to his or her, intimate, fraternal, associational, affiliational, personal economic, organizational-economic, and political relationships. The individual self is a product of these relationships and in turn, gives form to them.

It is true that some degree of personal private experience is essential for community; the inner self needs to be protected from over socialization if creativity, innovation, and critical reflection are to inform the various collective relationships.[45] However, Sennett was correct in arguing that preoccupation with the personal and intimate diminishes the development of civil relationships and impedes the development of civil community where relative strangers interact to form the res publica, or common weal.[46]

Palmer also appropriately maintained that our exaggerated emphasis on individual autonomy and our reluctance to engage strangers erodes those public dimensions of life that are *prepolitical* in nature. He insists that a healthy political process depends on the preexistence of healthy public relationships through which strangers come to know that they share a common life. He concluded:

> Without a public which knows that it shares a common life, which is capable of feeling, debating, and deciding, politics becomes a theatre of illusion, with

everyone watching the drama on stage, hoping to play some part, while the real action goes on backstage in the form of raw and unrestrained power. . . . Public life creates the community which both establishes legitimate government and holds it accountable to what the people want.[47]

Similarly, Jurgen Habermas insisted that the "public sphere," is a "realm of our social life in which something approaching public opinion can be formed,"beginning with "every conversation" in which individuals assemble and associate freely to "express and publish their opinions—about matters of general interest."[48] In this most mundane sense the public sphere is prior to the exercise of governmental authority and serves to mediate between society and the state. Thus, the full range of relationships identified on the continuum are essential for the formation of a political community able to function as a public.

Warner cautioned us not to assume that a healthy affiliational network of voluntary associations alone is sufficient for public life. He pointed out that Philadelphia had an abundance of small-scale ties in the 1830-1860 period represented by a plethora of clubs, lodges, and parishes; but they were "closed social cells" unconcerned with the common life of the city. The street life of the city where identification among strangers is created and a public sphere in Habermas'sense emerges had withered away.[49] The full range of interdependent public and private elements is required for the full realization of effective democratic political community.

3. The associational and affiliational relationships are the key linkages in the interdependent continuum.   Sullivan maintained that the greatest danger to democratic society today lay in "the declining effectiveness of just those intervening structures, the civic associations of all sorts that serve to mediate between individual and state."[50] These organizations may become the "closed social cells" that Warner worried about in nineteenth century Philadelphia unless the individuals who compose them have a vivid identification with their fellow citizens who are strangers. This commonality comes only through impersonal association in public places. It grows in the conversation and debate amongst those who are strangers, or relative strangers—in coffee shops, parks, barber shops, public forums, beauty parlors, taxis, laundromats; on buses, trains, airplanes; or in bars, at community meetings, in supermarket checkout lines, and; medical waiting rooms. These exchanges reveal the interdependencies of the public-private continuum. Therefore, affiliational relationships move toward the common good to the extent that they are informed by vital associational relationships.

This kind of associational experience builds a sense of reality and appreciation for the public dimensions of life. Palmer asserted that, "As our public experience dwindles, we come to regard the 'public' either as an empty abstraction or as a sinister, anonymous crowd whose potential for violence fills us with fear."[51] This has been borne out repeatedly by the reactions of students from sheltered middle- and upper-class environments who have had little experience with strangers and street life. As they describe the public places of the city, and people who are unknown, and assumed to be different, a fearful, hostile image emerges.

This problem can be understood as *inadequate and inaccurate typifications of unknown others*.[52] The less face-to-face interaction one has with others the less accurately one is able to develop complex symbolic constructs for understanding how these strangers fit into a system of human types with much in common, and also with many subtle and interesting differences. The stranger becomes a caricature, a pseudotype, that over time becomes a stereotype; that is, a typification that is static, fixed, and resistant to change. The more the types we employ to order and interpret reality are divorced from direct human experience the less one recognizes oneself in them; the less one is able to recognize our common humanity and shared interests. The stranger becomes an "alien other" with whom community is perceived to be impossible.

Affiliational relationships informed by this broader association with strangers are essential to the maintenance of the interdependencies of democratic society. They link the individual in an ongoing fashion to broader concerns than those of personal, intimate, and fraternal relationships. They connect the largely private relationships to the largely public. They are the training ground for conflict resolution, consensus building, and acting on collective concerns.[53]

Affiliational relationships that occur in voluntary nonprofit organizations provide a buffer between the individual and the large economic and governmental structures of society. They provide support for autonomous action, a basis for assertiveness in large-scale modern society and a lever for change. They are nodes of power that make it more difficult for the government to turn upon its citizens and usurp their authority.[54]

4. Civic virtue, orientation toward the common good, becomes more necessary as one moves toward the public end of the continuum.   The public ideal of civic virtue emerged in response to the growth of private autonomy in western society. As individual privacy was recognized as legitimate, it became necessary to encourage these atomistic individuals to consider the common good in order to maintain social cohesion and political community.[55] The concept of civic virtue replaces, in functional terms, the role of tradition and shared culture of the premodern tribe, clan, and village.

Civic virtue becomes more important as a norm for relationships toward the right end of the continuum because the acceptance of public roles "entails the repression, channelizing, and deflection of 'private' or personal attention, motives, and demands upon the self in order to address oneself to the expectation of others."[56] That is, they require citizens who conduct themselves in accordance with the principle of self-interest rightly understood, citizens who recognize their own self-interest in serving the common good, that has been defined in the previous chapter as the experience of community. This applies to all citizens, since citizenship properly conceived is the public office of the individual in a democratic society, and to the public administrator as fiduciary citizen.

It should be noted that the cultivation of civic virtue is not properly the sole responsibility of the government. There is too great a risk that such an effort would become self-serving and coercive. As both Palmer and Sullivan suggest, this kind of civic education is best accomplished by the affiliational and associational relationships and experiences.[57]

5. The citizen administrator bears responsibility for acknowledging, respecting and supporting the existence of a community of communities that includes the affiliational, organizational economic, and political portions of the continuum.   For example, administrators considering entering into public-private partnerships are obligated to include more than just business and government in these arrangements. In structural terms, organizations representing the affiliational portion of the continuum are essential for any partnership that seeks the common good through a collaborative effort of the public and private dimensions of society. As has been argued in the previous section, these organizations are the key links between those aspects of life that are largely private and those that are largely public. Including these organizations in public-private partnerships provides mechanisms for channeling a range of private values, preferences, and needs into collective activities, as well as infusing private life with public obligation and experience, on the other.

Partnerships that seek to redevelop parts of a city, provide sanitation, develop recreational facilities, provide transportation, deliver health services, build housing, or engage in economic development need the perspectives of corporate, private nonprofit, and public nongovernmental organizations if what is produced is to be sensitive to, and supportive of, appropriately private dimensions of democratic society. Similarly, both corporations and voluntary associations need to be confronted with their responsibilities for the common weal, consistent with their public obligations by virtue of their location on the public-private continuum. Otherwise they may become *closed social cells* with destructive effects on the chain of relationships essential to a democratic society. Both dynamics are essential for the integrity of the public-private continuum that, in turn, is one of the requisites of democratic society. Government, as the trustee of the interests of the democratic political community, is ultimately obligated to acknowledge and uphold the continuum of relationships that make democracy possible.

6. Citizen administrators as representatives of the most public end of the continuum need an understanding of efficiency appropriate to that role if they are to manifest civic virtue. Care must be taken to avoid pushing government into suboptimization. Efficient governments should not be understood simply as those that maximize the output of particular public services for given inputs. Their penultimate efficiency may be understood in those terms; however, an ultimately efficient government should be viewed as one that maximizes the full range of public-private relationships for any given inputs. The viability of personal privacy, as well as intimate, fraternal, associational, affiliational, personal economic, organizational economic, and political relationships are the outputs that must be assessed in some fashion.

Government should provide inputs into each part of this continuum only when necessary to preserve or enhance the full range of public-private relationships, toward supporting and enhancing the experience of community, and should do so in an efficient manner. It should intervene in ways that are designed to achieve the greatest positive impact on the experience of community for the resources available. It should adopt policies that produce positive effects with the least control.

In the case of public-private partnerships, this means that government should always be looking beyond the efficiency of a particular project to its impact on other areas along the continuum, toward creating and enhancing the experience of community. Partnerships that represent the most efficient contributions to this common good should be preferred to those that only serve the ends of business, or the goals of some special interest group, or the limited organizational interests of government agencies.

Consequently, the efficient citizen administrator is not one who focuses only on the limited efficiency of particular projects, tasks, and activities. He or she is more fundamentally concerned with the efficiency by which each of these helps or hinders the long term delicate process of building a sense of democratic political community in which self-interest rightly understood can be cultivated and maintained.

REFERENCES

1. *Oxford Latin Dictionary* (Oxford: The Clarendon Press, 1968).
2. *Harper's Latin Dictionary*, E.A. Andrews, ed. (New York: American Book Co., 1907).
3. *The Shorter Oxford English Dictionary*, 3rd ed., (Oxford: The Clarendon Press, 1973).
4. Greek terms used here have been transliterated for typographical convenience.
5. These Greek terms and those to follow are cited in S.C. Woodhouse, *English-Greek Dictionary* (London: Routledge and Kegan Paul, 1959), and in Henry George Liddell and Robert Scott, *A Greek-English Lexicon* (Oxford: The Clarendon Press, 1925).
6. *Oxford Latin Dictionary.*
7. MARK ROELOFS, *The Tension of Citizenship, Private Man, and Public Duty* (New York: Rinehart and Co., 1957), pp. 39–40.
8. *Ibid.*, p. 46.
9. *Ibid.*, pp. 44–45.
10. RICHARD SENNETT, *The Fall of Public Man: On the Psychology of Capitalism* (New York: Vintage Books, 1974), p. 3.

11. JOSEPH BENSMAN and ROBERT LILIENFIELD, *Between Public and Private: The lost Boundaries of the Self* (New York: The Free Press, 1979), p. 172.

12. STANLEY I. BENN, "Privacy, Freedom, and Respect for Persons" in Roland Pennock and John W. Chapman, eds., *Privacy* (New York: Atherton Press, 1971), p. 22.

13. JOHN LOCKE, *Two Treatises of Government*, Peter Laslett, ed. (Cambridge: Cambridge University Press, 1960), pp. 95–96.

14. This is discussed in greater detail in chapter one. *See also* Roger Howell, "The Privileges and Immunities of State Citizenship," *Johns Hopkins Studies in Historical and Political Sciences.* Series xxxvi, no. 3 (Baltimore: The Johns Hopkins Press, 1918), p. 559.

15. RICHARD J. BISHIRJIAN, *A Public Philosophy Reader* (New Rochelle: Arlington House, 1978), pp. 20–21. *See also* Andrew Levine, *Liberal Democracy: A Critique of the Theory* (New York: Columbia University Press, 1981), pp. 105–120.

16. WILLIAM M. SULLIVAN, *Reconstructing Public Philosophy* (Los Angeles; University of California Press, 1982), p. 13.

17. LYN H. LOFLAND, *A World of Strangers: Order and Action in Public Places* (New York: Basic Books, 1973), pp. 3–9.

18. *Ibid.,* pp. 29–55.

19. DAVID H. FLAHERTY, *Privacy in Colonial New England,* Charlottesville: University Press of Virginia, 1972, p. 15.

20. *Ibid.,* p. 18.

21. SAM BASS WARNER, JR., *The Private City* (Philadelphia: University of Pennsylvania Press, 1968), pp. 11, 59–62.

22. SHELDON WOLIN, "The Age of Organization and the Sublimation of Politics" in *Politics and Vision: Continuity and Innovation in Western Political Thought* (New York: Little, Brown and Co., 1960).

23. Warner, *The Private,* pp. x, 3–4.

24. Sennett, *The Fall,* p. 98.

25. *Ibid.,* pp. 19–20, 90.

26. DONALD MEIKLEJOHN, *Public and Private Morality in America* (Syracuse, New York: Syracuse University Press, 1965), p. 3.

27. I have been unable to identify the origins of "sector" as a tern for describing divisions between public and private. However, it seems to have originated in some type of economic parlance.

28. W.T. Jones in "Public Roles, Private, and Differential Moral Assessments of Role Performance," *Ethics* 94 (1984), 603–620, begins with a similar argument, in this case concerning the need to consider social roles as falling along a spectrum ranging from private to public.

29. Bensman and Lilienfield, *Between Public and Private,* p. 172.

30. A difference between the approach to dealing with public-privatye distinctions utilized here and those adopted by others is that they have tended to begin with organizations and a list of organizational attributes that are more private or public. The attempt in this text is to address the distinction at a more fundamental level by establishing the general characteristics of public and private relationships in society and then locating organizations as one type of relationship along a spectrum of these attributes. In the former approaches there tends not to be a normative assessment of the extent to which organizations of different types are, in fact, conducting themselves consistently with their inherent characteristics, while this is attempted here. For examples of the other approach, *see* Hal G. Rainey, Robert W. Backoff, and Charles H. Levine, "Comparing Public and Private Organizations," *Public Administration Review,* 36 (1976), pp. 233–244; and Barry Bozerman, *All Organizations are Public: Bridging Public and Private Organizational Theories.* San Francisco: Jossey-Bass, 1987.

31. HERBERT SPIRO, "Privacy in Comparative Perspective," in Pennock and Chapman, *Privacy,* p. 130.

32. PARKER J. PALMER, *The Company of Strangers* (New York: Crossroad, 1981), p. 72.

33. PAUL J. MCNULTY, "The Public Side of Private Enterprise: A Historical Perspective on American Business and Government," *Columbia Journal of World Business,* 13 (1978), 122–130. McNulty quoted Oscar Handlin and Mary F. Handlin, "Origins of the American Business Corporation," *Journal of Economic History,* 5 (1945), p. 22.

34. RONALD E. SEAVOY, *The Origins of the American Business Corporation, 1784–1855: Broadening the Concept of Public Service During Industrialization* (Westport, Connecticut: Greenwood Press, 1982), p. 255. *See also* by the same author: "The Public Service Origins of the American Business Corporation," *The Business History Review,* 52 (1978), 30–60.
35. *Ibid.,* p. 48.
36. *Ibid.,* p. 257.
37. JAMES WILLARD HURST, *The Legitimacy of the Business Corporation in the Law of the United States, 1780–1970* (Charlottsville: University Press of Virginia, 1970), pp. 11, 15.
38. *Ibid.,* p. 17.
39. *Ibid.,* pp. 62–73.
40. CAROLE PATEMAN, *Participation and Democratic Theory* (Cambridge: Cambridge University Press, 1970), *See* in particular chapters 3 and 4.
41. *See* John Dewey, *The Public and Its Problems* (Chicago: Swallow Press, 1927), for a discussion of these attributes of public phenomena.
42. Bensman and Lilienfield, *Between Public and Private,* p. 175.
43. Roelofs, *The Tension,* pp. 39–40.
44. AMITAI ETZIONI, *An Immodest Agenda: Rebuilding America Before the Twenty-First Century* (New York: McGraw-Hill, 1983), p. 49.
45. DAVID H. FLAHERTY, *Privacy,* pp. 3–4. *See also:* Roelofs, *The Tension,* pp. 4, 22, 39; Bensmann and Lilienfield, *Between Public and Private,* p. 174.
46. Sennett, *The Fall,* pp. 3–12, 264.
47. Palmer, *The Company,* p. 23.
48. JURGEN HABERMAS, "The Public Sphere: An Encyclopedia Article (1964)," *New German Critique,* 3 (1974), 49–55.
49. Warner, *The Private,* pp. 61–62, 156.
50. Sullivan, *Reconstructing,* pp. 222–223.
51. Palmer, *The Company,* p. 21.
52. ALFRED SCHUTZ, *The Phenomenology of the Social World* (Evanston, Indiana: Northwestern University Press, 1967), provides a theoretical framework for understanding this problem.
53. Palmer, *The Company,* p. 40.
54. For elaboration of this point *see* Peter L. Berger and Richard John Neuhaus, *To Empower People: The role of Mediating Structures in Public Policy* (Washington, D.C.: American Enterprise Institute, 1977).
55. Bensman and Lilienfield, *Between Public and Private,* p. 172.
56. *Ibid.,* p. 174.
57. Sullivan, *Reconstructing,* p. 153; Palmer, *The Company,* pp. 40–45.

7
CONCLUSION: THE RESTORATION OF CITIZENSHIP IN THE PRACTICE OF PUBLIC ADMINISTRATION

Having offered a normative ethical proposal for the practice of public administration characterized as that of the citizen administrator, I must say something about how to move toward its realization. It is my intention to avoid the dual temptations to leave the reader without any suggestions for implementation, or to trivialize an enormous collective task with pat answers and all too neat prescriptions. The realization of an ethical ideal is not to be accomplished through an annual conference theme, a special issue of a professional journal, or even a triennial plan. This is the work of a generation that must involve many people of diverse opinions, including both scholars and practitioners, as was the case for the Progressive movement in establishing the character attributes, values, and principles that are central to public administration today.

The restoration of citizenship norms, values, and perspectives in the practice of public administration is an educational task broadly defined. It includes experiential learning in the workplace and the development of a new professional identity, as well as more theoretically oriented classroom instruction. Professional education of this fundamental sort must address both the cognitive and the affective dimensions of the learning process. It seems clear that the three main arenas that must be engaged in an adequate professional education of citizen administrators are university programs in public administration (both degree oriented and in-service), professional associations, and the organizations within which administrators work. The approximate realization of the citizen administrator ideal requires initiatives from each of these influences on the norms for the administrative role.

I will discuss each arena briefly, offering some general observations about what needs to be done. In each case it is essential that we maintain a clear distinction between the world as it is and the world as we would like it to be. Normative proposals as descriptions of the latter are usually at odds with the former; change from the status quo is involved. Change almost always entails resistance, conflict, and confusion. We should expect to encounter all these in realizing the orientation for public administration advocated. The questions the reader should be asking him or herself are: Do I agree with the normative proposals advanced, and if so, how can I deal with the admittedly thorny problems of achieving fundamental change?

UNIVERSITY EDUCATION IN PUBLIC ADMINISTRATION

As the literature on civic education in the public schools has suggested, adequately dealing with the education of people for citizenship requires regular attention from an early age and throughout the entire first twelve years of schooling.[1] Although I believe in the validity of such a claim, this focus will be much more limited in scope, confined to the role of university courses and training programs oriented to the practice of public administration. The justification for such a delimitation is based not only on the practical necessity of maintaining a well-bounded topic in order to finish a book, but also on a realistic strategic assessment of the problem.

Sometimes the argument is advanced that citizenship values in public administration cannot be cultivated until we develop a greater sense of citizenship among the American people, and this requires careful and consistent teaching during those most formative years leading to adulthood. My assumption is that however important such attention to childhood and youth may be, fundamental change never occurs in a neat sequential linear fashion. It is necessary to consider the various leverage points in society that might contribute to bringing about the desired change. Approached in this way, the formal professional education and training programs are *one* potential lever for change in a larger array of more or less powerful instruments.

Although these instruments of change may not be as effectively employed in the absence of large numbers of young adults emerging from the public schools imbued with citizenship concepts, skills, and commitments, they may still produce positive effects that may enhance and encourage general citizenship education, and that also may reinforce the professional education of citizen administrators. A cyclical feedback process may be set in motion that will produce more self-conscious and competent citizens, and public administrators who view themselves fundamentally as fiduciary citizens.

When we consider university based programs in public administration education, it seems important that they confront students, whether entry level or midcareer, at the outset with the necessity for reflection about the core values of American public administration. This might be done during the admissions and orientation processes, perhaps through required essays as part of the application package, in the course of selection interviews, or during orientation lectures and discussions. However this is accomplished, students applying for acceptance into public administration professional education programs should be made aware that they are seeking entry into a field that is rooted in democratic values and finds its ethical identity in the complex traditions of American citizenship. University programs should specify that the cultivation of such an identity is to be the centerpiece of professional preparation, with the very necessary technical knowledge and skills required for administrative practice placed in the service of the citizenry.

What is suggested is emphatically not a process of indoctrination accompanied by detailed dogma or an officially sanctioned credo, but rather the projection of a serious expectation of a commitment to study, examine, and critically understand the tradition of democratic citizenship in the United States, and to find one's place within its broad and varied streams. The intention is that students should see the development of their professional identity emerging from this tradition—in some kind of continuity with it. If, for whatever reason, students do not find it possible to commit themselves to shaping a career around the core values of the American regime, they should then seriously consider whether a career in the administration of the people is right for them. No one else should make that decision for them through a test of loyalty to a prescribed doctrine or adherence to so-called "correct thinking," but anyone preparing to enter public service should understand that "service" is to be rendered to more than themselves or the director of some government organization. They should know that public administration is service to the citizens of the United States and the democratic values on which their citizenship office is established. The requisite nature of that knowledge should require reflection and an overt decision by those assuming the fiduciary office of public administrator.

Confrontation with this decision and the cultivation of a professional ethic rooted in citizenship might be accomplished in a variety of ways. One of the first core courses in a public administration program ought to be a required administrative ethics course either substantially or wholly devoted to the ethical tradition of American citizenship as the foundation for the practice of public administration.[2] Such a course is more essential than one emphasizing the techniques of ethical decision making; that is also important, but secondary. This course might well be paired with a second core course on politics and administration. In that course the political implications of a citizenship ethic for the relationships among the citizenry, elected officials, and public administrators in a democratic society could be considered, both descriptively and normatively. The roles of voluntary associations in public action would be a key element of this course. Throughout the curriculum courses on topics such as public policy, personnel, budgeting, leadership, organization development, and management these basic ethical and political orientations should be reintroduced for further reflection, development, and integration with the technically oriented aspects of practice.

Running concurrently with these two courses there might be an experiential component called an *internship* for preservice students and a *practicum* for those already employed in public administrative practice. The internship would be for a more substantial amount of time than the practicum, but both would involve participation in some organization other than a government agency. The requirement would be for ongoing active involvement in some citizens' organization falling into the *public nongovernmental* category discussed in chapter six. The student would be placed in some voluntary association that is providing services, seeking political change, or both, for a part-time participation experience as a citizen. The point of these experiences would be to gain experience as a citizen and to learn how citizens' organizations function, both of which should contribute to the cultivation of public spiritedness. They would also provide experiential "grist" for other courses toward the development of prudence in acting administratively on behalf of one's fellow citizens.

The intention in such a set of arrangements would be to cultivate a basic perspective with a set of values and attitudes that would then provide an orienting point of reference for the more technical and applied courses in the curriculum. The hope would be to make these "nuts and bolts" courses subservient to a professional ethic grounded from the beginning in the citizenship traditions.

PROFESSIONAL ASSOCIATIONS

One useful and appropriate role that public administration professional associations such as *The American Society for Public Administration* (ASPA), *The International City Management Association* (ICMA), and *The National Association of Schools of Public Affairs and Administration* (NASPAA) could perform would be that of offering advice concerning professional education.

For example, ASPA sponsored a study by an ad hoc Working Group on Ethics Education on "Ethics Education in Public Administration and Affairs" that offered recommendations concerning the necessity of the treatment of ethics in the public administration curriculum. The Working Group noted that of the seventy-four course outlines it received from instructors of ethics courses, only nine emphasized democratic regime values.[3]

The first of the Working Group's five recommendations was that NASPAA clarify one of its curricular standards (3.21) by explaining in as much detail as possible the meaning of its requirement that public administration curricula enhance students' "values, knowledge, and skills to act ethically." It also called upon NASPAA to provide "guidelines for implementation and accountability mechanisms to assure compliance with the standard."[4] As the substantive content of such an elaborated guideline for ethics courses, the Working Group endorsed educating students in "(1) the democratic regime values (liberty, equality, etc.) implicit and explicit in United States Constitutional history; (2) the role of government in dealing with conflicting social values; and (3) the ethical and philosophical underpinnings of public policy debates."[5]

Through studies and recommendations of this kind, professional associations provide a vantage point for viewing the educational needs of the practice as a whole that may not be as easy to achieve by any particular university program. In this way, faculty members in universities offering public administration programs may be helped to see beyond their own peculiar circumstances, faculty interests, backgrounds, and organizational pressures. A follow-up study focusing specifically on the teaching of democratic citizenship values would be a useful next step.

Beyond providing a broader perspective on university education, professional associations might play an important role in encouraging citizenship values through recognition of those who exemplify these values. For example, a group of exemplary citizen administrators, a model university program, and outstanding citizen oriented government agencies from around the nation might receive awards at the annual conference. A book profiling the accomplishments of each might be published. Granting such awards and preparing such a book could provide an opportunity each year for members of the association to think again about what is meant by citizenship values, and how they are appropriately embodied in the practice of public administration and public administration education. Over time these books would provide a cumulative collection of exemplary role models for those entering the profession. The association might choose to constitute these exemplary persons and organizational representatives as a citizenship advisory body to spend the ensuing year reviewing the association's progress in incorporating citizenship values into its practice.

Special conferences focusing upon citizenship and public administration might be sponsored by professional associations periodically. ASPA, the National Academy of Public Administration, and the Charles F. Kettering Foundation cosponsored the first national conference on citizenship and public administration in 1983.[6] Although this initial assembly consisted almost entirely of scholars, additional sessions sponsored by these or other associations held periodically, including practitioners and citizen group representatives, could be useful in creating an ongoing exploration of the relationship between public administrators and citizens. The papers delivered at these sessions could be published in special issues of professional journals such as the March 1984 special issue of *Public Administration Review* that included the presentations of the 1983 conference.[7]

A further step that could be undertaken by professional associations might be the inclusion of one or more citizen group representatives in their governing bodies, such as the ASPA National Council. Selected with an eye to more than token participation, these citizen leaders could provide a regular check on the tendency of a professional group to become preoccupied with its own members and their well-being. An annual written commentary on the state of the association's support for citizenship values by these citizen representatives might be effective in creating an opportunity for periodic reflection on this concern.

THE WORKPLACE

The first consideration in utilizing the influence of the workplace of public administrators might be the active recruitment of people for employment with active citizenship backgrounds. In addition to attempting to acquaint uninitiated administrators with citizenship perspectives after hiring, why not attempt to employ citizens who have been active participants in their communities, citizens' associations, and in the political process? In evaluating applicants for positions, merit points might be assigned for their history of citizenship activities, along with points for educational achievement, previous work experience, references, and performance on examinations. Just as previous political experience is typically evaluated for candidates for elective office, prior citizenship experience might be considered in hiring those who will be "citizens in lieu of the rest of us."

Similarly, under the assumption that once hired active citizenship should not be abandoned, the performance of the practicing administrator might be evaluated in terms of ongoing participation in citizens' organizations and community affairs. One check on the tendency of bureaucratic organizations to displace other values and perspectives, focusing attention and priorities inward, is the maintenance of other roles with their different sets of obligation and interest. The citizen role, according to the argument developed in this book, is a key social role from which the administrative role should be derived and given ethical content. Consequently, its preservation by practicing administrators should be viewed as an employment related task.

In order to provide active citizenship experience where little or none exists, government agencies might also consider granting leaves to public administrators to work in citizens' associations.[8] Some major corporations in the business community have been doing this for some time. In government, one similar program that provided a precedent was the provision of the *Intergovernmental Personnel Act of 1970*, permitting employees at one level of government to take leave to work at a different level. The justification was similar to the proposal advanced by this text, in that both assume the need to expand one's knowledge and experience in a related role. For example, before becoming an urban redevelopment project manager, a year or six months working with some community organization might be helpful preparation.

Another approach might be to arrange for inservice training on community perspectives, issues, organization types, leadership styles, and change strategies. These might be conducted by citizens' associations or jointly provided by them and universities. In most urban areas there are nonprofit organizations that work with a broad range of community associations to assist with funding and technical assistance which could provide such training. These include organizations such as United Way, the Urban League, and municipal reform groups such as municipal leagues. The joint planning for this kind of training as well as its execution could provide a valuable exchange of ideas and perspectives.

A final consideration might be building the support of citizenship values into the routine review of a government agency's projects. During planning, initial implementation and throughout the life of a project, the extent to which the project is demonstrating respect for the role of the citizenry and upholding the values of citizen involvement might be reviewed. This concern might be examined regularly along with more typical concerns such as environmental impact, cost containment, schedules, personnel allocations, and the supply of necessary materials.

STANDING IN ONE WORLD AND REACHING FOR ANOTHER

These suggestions for the cultivation of citizen administrators and citizen administration are only the more obvious ones which are suggestive of various methods for moving from an ideal role description to the actual practice of public administration. The point of sketching out such proposals is not intended to provide an easy "how to" guide for creating citizen administrators, but rather to anticipate the reticence I sometimes encounter in the face of fundamental normative proposals. The too frequent response is that such propositions "are not the way things are in the real world," which, of course, is always true. However, change never comes from merely staring at the world as it is.

Certainly Saul Alinsky was right when he said to his community organizer trainees that the most important thing to understand is the difference between the world as it is and the world as they would like it to be.[9] The most common pitfall for agents of change, according to Alinsky, was to confuse these two—either to have their vision confined to the way things are, transfixed by harsh reality, and believe that the world must be ever thus; or to allow their gaze to wander off into dreams of a better world and become hypnotized into believing that world had arrived. Not maintaining a clear distinction between the world as it is and the world as they would like it to be, according to Alinsky, would only lead to frustration, confusion, ineffective action, and ultimately paralysis.

Change occurs as we face the reality of our world squarely, but with visions of how we would like it to be. The proposed actions offered here are intended only to overcome the conviction that ideals are unapproachable and to stimulate more imaginative ideas for achieving a more democratic administrative state—to provide "myths" that we can "live by and live for."[10]

REFERENCES

1. For examples of these debates *see* William Bennett and Robert Bellah, "Citizenship and Character Revisited," *New Perspectives Quarterly*, 3 (1986), 26–31; Robert K. Fullwinder, "Civic Education and Traditional Values," *Report From the Center for Philosophy and Public Policy*, 6 (1986), 5–8; Jack L. Nelson, "The Uncomfortable Relationship Between Moral Education and Citizenship Instruction: in Richard W. Wilson and Gordon J. Schochet, eds. *Moral Development and Politics* (New York: Praeger, 1980), pp. 256–285; Christina Hoff Sommers, "Ethics Without Virtue: Moral Education in America," *The American Scholar*, 53 (1984), 381–389.

2. A study of ethics education in public administration programs by April Hejka-Ekins found that only 16 percent of the 139 schools responding viewed the democratic ethos as now prevalent in the field of public administration and only 4 percent of those offering ethics courses emphasized the democratic ethos. *See* "Teaching Ethics in Public Administration," *Public Administration Review*, 48 (1988), 885–891.

3. BAYARD L. CATRON and KATHRYN G. DENHARDT, "Ethics Education in Public Administration and Affairs, Research Report and Recommendations," Washington, D.C.: American Society for Public Administration, October 1989, p. 10. The findings and recommendations in this report were presented to the annual NASPAA meeting in October 1988 and were favorably received.

4. *Ibid.*, p. 3.

5. *Ibid.*, p, 4.

6. This was the "National Conference on Citizenship and Public Service" held April 14–16, 1983 in New York city. The key organizer of this pioneering conference was H. George Frederickson.

7. *Public Administration Review*, Special Issue, "Citizenship and Public Administration," eds. H. George Frederickson and Ralph Clark Chandler (March 1984).

8. Enabling legislation would probably be necessary in most jurisdictions.

9. Two examples of Alinsky's use of this principle are found in Saul D. Alinsky, *Rules for Radicals: A Pragmatic Primer for Realistic Change* (New York: Vintage Books, 1971), pp. xix, 12–15.

10. See this full quotation from Dennis Thompson at the beginning of chapter 5 on p. 241.

INDEX